ria
i.

al

Gallery, the old

THE HUNGARIAN NATIONAL GALLERY
The Old Collections

THE HUNGARIAN NATIONAL GALLERY
The Old Collections

CORVINA KIADÓ

Title of the original:
A Magyar Nemzeti Galéria régi gyűjteményei. Corvina Kiadó, Budapest, 1984
Translation by ELIZABETH HOCH
Translation revised by ELIZABETH WEST
Prefaced and edited by
MIKLÓS MOJZER

The authors:
ENIKŐ BUZÁSI
Nos. 125–126, 131–133, 137–143, 163–166, 183, 188–191, 193, 195–196, 203–204, 207, 210–211
ANNA JÁVOR
Nos. 134, 136, 146–150, 152–153, 156–158, 160–161, 167–170, 172–175, 179–181, 185–186, 194, 199, 202
MIKLÓS MOJZER
Nos. 127, 129–130, 135, 144–145, 151, 154–155, 159, 162, 171, 176–178, 182, 184, 187, 192, 197–198, 200–201, 205–206, 208–209
GYÖNGYI TÖRÖK
Nos. 1–35, 37–46, 48–59, 61–64, 66–69, 72–73, 77, 87, 119
JÁNOS VÉGH
Nos. 36, 47, 60, 65, 70–71, 74–76, 78–86, 88–118, 120–124, 128

Black-and-white photographs by
ÉVA AJTÓS and ISTVÁN PETRÁS
Colour plates by
LÁSZLÓ GYARMATI and ALFRÉD SCHILLER
Design and drawings by
FERENC BARABÁS

ISBN 963 13 1652 1

PREFACE The Hungarian National Museum, founded in 1802, acquired the collection made by Miklós Jankovich (1773–1846), the first expert to make a systematic collection of early Hungarian art. His collection was the basis of the earliest works now housed in museums throughout the country.

From around 1850 to the end of the First World War, the collection of Hungarian works in the National Museum was continuously enriched either by official acquisition or by donation. From 1878 on, the Budapest Museum of Applied Arts—formed partly from certain collections transferred from the National Museum—also acquired some valuable examples of Hungarian art, especially from the medieval period; and from around 1900 the Museum of Fine Arts, founded at the time of the millennial celebrations in Hungary in 1896, made similar efforts to collect old Hungarian paintings and sculpture. From 1910–1920 all three museums made special efforts to secure and display new acquisitions. It was then that Elek Petrovics, Director General of the Museum of Fine Arts, decided to bring together the works exhibited in these three places, thus creating a single collection. He completed the arrangements for putting his plan into effect before his retirement. The works transferred from the National Museum and the Museum of Applied Arts between 1934 and the outbreak of the Second World War, formed the nucleus of the Old Hungarian Collection in the Museum of Fine Arts. When it became necessary to take these works to a place of greater security during the war, many of them were stored in unsuitable conditions and were badly damaged. In 1952 the collection—already separately administered—was recognized as a department of the Museum. At the beginning of the 1950s this department absorbed also the small collection of baroque pictures which had been acquired by and housed in the former Budapest Gallery founded in 1933. The Old Hungarian Collection continued to form a department of the Museum of Fine Arts until 1973 when it was transferred to the Hungarian National Gallery established in 1957 to collect pieces of eleventh to twentieth century Hungarian art. Heads of the Old Hungarian Collection department were Jolán Balogh (until

1949), István Genthon (1949–52), Dénes Radocsay (1952–70) and Mrs. L. Gerevich (1970–77).

In Buda Castle, where the newly established National Gallery came to be housed, the collection is now exhibited in more favourable conditions than at any previous time. Before 1974 it was never possible to exhibit more than a selection of the works, and then usually for only a short time. Here it is possible to have a permanent exhibition, and the necessary restoration of damaged pictures is also ensured. At present, and for a long time to come, the fate of the collection will depend upon the skill of the art restorers now working at the Gallery and employing the most up-to-date methods. Most of the damaged works were in poor condition when originally acquired by the various museums; some of them were touched up or superficially restored —often merely to prevent total decay. This applies particularly to the medieval works, very few of which had been in collections where it was possible for them to be adequately looked after. The restoration and preservation of these works therefore now involves much laborious work.

The present collection—the works on view and those in reserve—are grouped according to the form of the art as well as the period. The medieval and Renaissance stone carvings (eleventh to sixteenth centuries) taken over together with a few fragments of frescoes from the Hungarian National Museum and the Museum of Fine Arts constitute the earliest remains in the Museum. At present the majority of the exhibits, and also the most valuable, are the medieval pictures and sculpture dating from the fourteenth to the mid-sixteenth century. Late Renaissance and baroque art from the second half of the sixteenth to the end of the eighteenth century is not so extensively represented. In terms of history, therefore, the range of what is now known as the Old Hungarian Collection extends from the foundation of the Hungarian State to the years around 1800.

Since 1974 all early Hungarian works of graphic art, drawings, engravings and various minor forms of art have been housed in the Department of Prints and Drawings in the National Gallery, all examples of the applied and decorative arts remaining in the appropriate departments of the Hungarian National Museum and the Budapest Museum of Applied Arts.

In the case of the Old Hungarian Collection, we should make clear that by "Hungarian" we wish to convey "from the territory of Hungary," meaning "historic Hungary," for the country has been the home not only of Hungarians, but also of many other nationalities. In former times, in Hungary as in other countries, artistic and cultural life was not sealed off from outside influence: Hungarian art has always absorbed the contributions made by visiting artists and the impact of works from other countries. The Carpathian Basin is one of the important areas of early European and in particular Central European art, which has its own special atmosphere. The purpose of the Old Hungarian Collection is to convey this particular historic identity. In this sense, the Old Collection in the Hungarian National Gallery is the local, cultural and intangible heritage of the Hungarians as well as of the neighbouring peoples; when viewed in this historic perspective, the collection conveys the very essence of the unity and character of early Hungarian art.

Remains of stone carvings provide evidence of the architectural beauty of the first Hungarian cathedrals. Fragments of pillars, capitals, bases and brackets, sections of reliefs and statues, mutilated as they are, bear witness to the early existence of some architectural and sculptural creations. The carvings from Pécs, Székesfehérvár and Kalocsa are of special interest. Remains of royal and monastic buildings from the times of the Árpád dynasty (1000–1301) provide splendid examples of the Roman carvings that once adorned buildings in Hungary. There are fewer remains of Gothic ornamental and figural carvings but early Renaissance examples are somewhat more common. There are eloquent remains from the Court of Matthias Corvinus (1458–1490) bearing witness to the northward radiation of the Italian Renaissance in Europe and in particular to its influence on Hungarian architecture. Hungary was the first and most important area to absorb the influence of the Italian Renaissance: an influence demonstrated by a number of reliefs, fragments from sepulchres and brackets now in the collection.

The earliest remains of Hungarian wood-carvings date from the mid-fourteenth century, the age of the Hungarian Anjous. About half a dozen of these precious works serve to introduce a series of winged altars and panel paintings from the succeeding period. The National Gallery has an impressive collection of altarpieces, chief ornaments of the late Gothic churches from the first third of the fifteenth century to the beginning of the sixteenth century. These vary in size, numbering about twenty in all, a pitiful number when we think of the original wealth of the Carpathian Basin, but representing a rich heritage in relation to similar treasures in other museums. The winged altars surviving in their entirety date from the turn of the fifteenth–sixteenth centuries and the decades that followed under the rule of the Jagiellon dynasty (1490–1526). They originate from small towns and villages of what was formerly known as Upper Hungary and Transylvania. Here they had a better chance of survival than in other parts of the country where under the Turkish occupation and later in the course of baroque reconstructions, the old furnishings of the churches were destroyed. Secular objects of art were unfortunately even more often exposed to destruction than the religious ones. True, their role was at first less significant that that of the objects created for devotional purposes, but gradually they assumed a more widespread and important role. With the development of secular forms of European art the peoples of the Carpathian Basin soon became aware of new possibilities, from the masters themselves and from their works. However, the decay of cultural values in Hungarian castles and monasteries, the lack of a royal court within the borders of the country as well as the lack of cultural expectations by the populace, made such art a rarity. It is for this reason that seventeenth century art is not fully represented in Old Hungarian Collection. There are also few secular works from the late Renaissance and baroque periods, and hardly any Hungarian cabinet pictures. Some of the gaps, however, are filled by the works of Hungarian masters who lived and worked abroad. As to religious works, the group of baroque altarpieces splendidly illustrates the contemporary and later styles which followed the Gothic winged

8

altars. Apart from contemporary frescoes, it is on the altars that we find the most impressive paintings in Central Europe. This form of art was intended to influence people in every walk of life. The policy of the Gallery is to collect not only examples of this type of picture but also to acquire and exhibit the colourful sketches made for baroque oil paintings, the so-called *bozzettos*.

Most of the statues were also once integral parts of altars. Some of them can be classed among the finest in Europe; others rank among the best to have been found in Hungary. Not only the collection of monumental baroque works but also that of baroque statuettes is sadly incomplete. Portraits and cabinet pictures from the period of the Enlightenment are prominently displayed, as well as the Hungarian remains of late baroque historical paintings, which developed from the altarpieces and were the forerunners of nineteenth century historical paintings of Hungarian national subjects.

Every gallery, exhibition or museum collection exemplifies a particular aspect of art and the exhibits have been selected for this particular purpose. History cannot be reconstructed in full in any museum or exhibition. However wide-ranging their interests, those responsible for selecting the exhibits must necessarily exercise a disciplined restraint. Examples of folk art, for instance, have been acquired for the Old Collection in Buda Castle only in exceptional cases, to demonstrate the development of this type of art. The collection of this new, fascinating and important branch of art rests with the Ethnographical Museum and other learned institutions. Icons and liturgical paintings and statues from the Eastern Churches similarly lie outside the sphere of the National Gallery. This specific form of art concerns the Budapest Museum of Applied Arts and other specialized collections. Neither is it incumbent upon the National Gallery to trace or preserve historic relics, that is to say, to attempt to illustrate the course of Hungarian history by means of paintings or other forms of representational art, such as portraits of outstanding personalities; this responsibility lies with the Gallery's sister-institution, the Historical Department of the Hungarian National Museum. Under the title "Old Art" the

Gallery endeavours to preserve and present—with certain concessions—works illustrating the development of a "grand art" in Hungary; the collection therefore corresponds in character with that of the modern, nineteenth and twentieth century collections. It is extremely important that the Old Collection should be closely connected with the later works, thus ensuring the impression of historical continuity. The Hungarian National Gallery grew out of the traditional nineteenth century concept of gallery-museum and, as a sort of historical museum of fine arts, it is akin to those in other countries, near or distant, its aim being to create a flavour that is both national and historic.

In the galleries, in the catalogues and in the inventories the names of artists are indicated as printed in the special literature. The names of Hungarian-born artists who emigrated but retained some contact with their native country, also those of foreign artists who settled in Hungary, are indicated in the Hungarian way. By following this principle we are complying with the respective Hungarian traditions.

The inventory of the Old Collection lists at present about a thousand items. The inventory number given to each exhibit when still housed in the Museum of Fine Arts is still valid. This volume includes a number of works temporarily on loan from provincial museums and collections. These are mainly of the baroque period, borrowed in order to partially fill the gaps in our still incomplete collection of works from that period. We are indebted to their owners—provincial museums, Church collections and private individuals who have generously lent them for exhibition for a specified period, and we extend to them herewith our grateful thanks for their courtesy.

Miklós Mojzer

SELECTED BIBLIOGRAPHY AND ABBREVIATIONS IN TEXT

AÉ – *Archaeologiai Értesítő*

Aggházy 1959 – Aggházy, Mária: *Barokk szobrászat Magyarországon* [Baroque sculpture in Hungary]. Budapest, 1959

Aggházy 1967 – Aggházy, M.: "Steierische Beziehungen der ungarländischen Barockkunst." AHA XIII (1967), 313

AHA – *Acta Historiae Artium Academiae Scientiarum Hungaricae*

Balogh 1957 – Balogh, Jolán: "L'origine du style des sculptures en bois de la Hongrie médiévale." AHA IV (1957), 251–253

Balogh 1966 – Balogh, Jolán: *A művészet Mátyás király udvarában* [Art at the court of King Matthias]. I–II. Budapest, 1966

Balogh 1975 – Balogh, Jolán: *Die Anfänge der Renaissance in Ungarn*. Graz, 1975

BMH – *Bulletin du Musée National Hongrois des Beaux-Arts*

Clasen 1974 – Clasen, Carl Heinz: *Der Meister der Schönen Madonnen. Herkunft, Entfaltung und Umkreis*. Berlin–New York, 1974

Dercsényi 1972 – Dercsényi, Dezső: *Románkori építészet Magyarországon* [Romanesque Architecture in Hungary]. Budapest, 1972

Dercsényi 1975 – Dercsényi, Dezső: *Romanische Baukunst in Ungarn*. Budapest, 1975

Dercsényi 1975 – Dercsényi, Dezső: *Romanesque Architecture in Hungary*. Budapest, 1975

Entz 1966 – Entz, Géza: "Les pierres sculptées de la cathédrale de Kalocsa." BMH 28 (1966), 31–56

Feuer-Tóth 1981 – Feuer-Tóth, Rózsa: *Renaissance Architecture in Hungary*. Budapest, 1981

Galavics 1971 – Galavics, Géza: "Program és műalkotás a XVIII. század végén" [Late 18th-century art and its content]. *Művészettörténeti Füzetek 2*

Galavics 1973 – Galavics, Géza: "A barokk művészet kezdetei Győrben" [Beginnings of Baroque art at Győr]. *Ars Hungarica* (1973)

Galavics 1980 – Galavics, Géza: "A Rákóczi-szabadságharc és az egykorú képzőművészet" [The Rákóczi struggle for freedom and the fine arts of the time]. *Rákóczi-tanulmányok* [Rákóczi studies]. Ed. by Béla Köpeczi, Lajos Hopp, Ágnes R. Várkonyi. Budapest, 1980

11

Garas 1941 – Garas, Klára: *Kracker János Lukács 1717–1779*. Budapest, 1941 (in Hungarian)

Garas 1955 – Garas, Klára: *Magyarországi festészet a XVIII. században* [Painting of the 18th century in Hungary]. Budapest, 1955

Garas 1960 – Garas, Klára: *Franz Anton Maulbertsch 1724–1796*. Budapest, 1960

Garas 1974 – Garas, Klára: *Maulbertsch és kora. A Szépművészeti Múzeum kiállítása* [Maulbertsch and his age. Exhibition at the Budapest Museum of Fine Arts]. Budapest, 1974

Gerevich, L. 1971 – Gerevich, László: *The Art of Buda and Pest in the Middle Ages*. Budapest, 1971

Gerevich, L. 1973 – Gerevich, László: *Budapest története* [The history of Budapest]. I. Budapest, 1973

Gerevich, T. 1938 – Gerevich, Tibor: *Magyarország románkori emlékei* [Romanesque remains in Hungary]. *Magyarország művészeti emlékei* [Artistic remains in Hungary]. I. Budapest, 1938

Glatz 1975 – Glatz, Anton C.: *"Doplnky k spišskej tabul'ovej mal'be z obdobia 1440–1540 I." Zbornik Slovenskej Národnej Galérie* [About the problems of panel painting of the Szepes region between 1440–1540. I. Collection of the Slovak National Gallery]. Galéria 3 Staré Uménie, Bratislava, 1975

Homolka 1972 – Homolka, Jaromir: *Gotická plastika na Slovensku* [Gothic sculpture in Slovakia]. Bratislava, 1972

Jávor 1979 – Jávor, Anna: *Kracker János Lukács 1717–1779. A Magyar Nemzeti Galéria kiállítása* [János Lukács Kracker 1717–1779. Exhibition at the Hungarian National Gallery]. Budapest, 1979

Lázár 1933 – Lázár, Béla: *Mányoki Ádám (1673–1757) élete és művészete* [Life and art of Ádám Mányoki (1673–1757)].

Lehrs – Lehrs, Max: *Geschichte und kritischer Katalog des deutschen, niederländischen und französischen Kupferstichs im 15. Jahrhundert*. Wien, I–IX (1908–1934). I (1908), II (1910), III (1915), IV (1921), V (1925), VI (1927), VII (1930), VIII (1932), IX (1934)

Mányoki Catalogue 1957 – *Mányoki Ádám emlék-kiállítás.* [Ádám Mányoki memorial exhibition]. Szépművészeti Múzeum 1957. Budapest, 1957

Marosi 1984 – Marosi, Ernő: Die Anfänge der Gotik in Ungarn. Esztergom in der Kunst des 12–13. Jahrhunderts. Budapest, 1984.

Marosi, E.–Tóth, M. 1978 – *Árpád-kori kőfaragványok* [Stone-carvings from the Age of the Árpáds]. Ed. by Melinda Tóth and Ernő Marosi. Catalogue. István király Múzeum, Székesfehérvár, May–August, 1978

Mojzer MÉ 1981 – Mojzer, Miklós: "Késő reneszánsz és barokk művészet. A Magyar Nemzeti Galéria állandó kiállítása" [Late Renaissance and Baroque art. Permanent exhibition of the Hungarian National Gallery]. MÉ XXX, (1981), No. I

MM – *Magyar Művészet*

MMMÉ – *A Magyar Művészettörténeti Munkaközösség Évkönyve.* Budapest, 1951–1954

M – *Művészet*

MÉ – *Művészettörténeti Értesítő*

Művészet Magyarországon 1780–1830. – *Művészet Magyarországon 1780–1830* [Art in Hungary, 1780–1830]. Exhibition at the Hungarian National Gallery. Budapest, 1980

OSZMÉ – *Az Országos Szépművészeti Múzeum Évkönyvei*

Pigler 1929 – Pigler, A.: *G. R. Donner.* Leipzig–Vienna, 1929

Pigler 1941 – Pigler, Andor: *Bogdány Jakab* [Jakab Bogdány]. Budapest, 1941

Polak-Trajdos 1970 – Polak-Trajdos, Ewa: *"Więzy artystyczne Polski ze Spiszem i Słowacją, od połowy XV. do początków XVI. wieku"* [Artistic connections between Poland and the Szepes region in Slovakia from the middle of the 15th to the beginning of the 16th century]. *Rzeźba i malarstwo.* Wrocław–Warszawa–Kraków, 1970

Radocsay 1955 – Radocsay, Dénes: *A középkori Magyarország táblaképei* [Panel paintings in medieval Hungary]. Budapest, 1955. (Corpus, with complete bibliography)

Radocsay 1963 – Radocsay, Dénes: *Gótikus festmények Magyarországon*. Budapest, 1963; idem: *Gothic Panel Painting in Hungary*. Budapest, 1963; idem: *Gotische Tafelmalerei in Ungarn*. Budapest, 1963

Radocsay 1964 – Radocsay, Dénes: *Les Primitifs de Hongrie*. Budapest, 1964

Radocsay 1967 – Radocsay, Dénes: *A középkori Magyarország faszobrai* [Wood-carving in medieval Hungary]. Budapest, 1967. (Corpus, with complete bibliography)

Radocsay 1969 – Radocsay, Dénes: "Die Schönen Madonnen und die Plastik in Ungarn." *Zeitschrift des deutschen Vereins für Kunstwissenschaft* XIII (1969), 49–60

Rózsa 1973 – Rózsa, György: *Magyar történetábrázolás a XVII. században* [Representation of Hungarian history in the 17th century]. Budapest, 1973

Schallaburg – *Matthias Corvinus und die Renaissance in Ungarn 1458–1541*. Catalogue. Schallaburg, 1982, Mai–November

Stange 1961 – Stange, Alfred: *Deutsche Malerei der Gotik. Österreich und der ostdeutsche Siedlungsraum von Danzig bis Siebenbürgen in der Zeit von 1400 bis 1500*. München–Berlin, 1961

Török 1973 – Török, Gyöngyi: "Die Ikonographie des letzten Gebetes Mariä." AHA XIX (1973), 151–205

Török 1978 – Török, Gyöngyi: "Táblaképfestészetünk korai szakasza és európai kapcsolatai" [Early panel painting in Hungary and its relations in Europe]. *Ars Hungarica* VI (1978), No. 1, 7–27

Török 1980 – Török, Gyöngyi: "A Mateóci Mester művészetének problémái" [Problems posed by the art of the Master of Mateóc]. MÉ XXIX (1980), 49–80

Török 1981 – Török, Gyöngyi: "Einige unbeachtete Plastiken des Weichen Stils in Ungarn und ihre Beziehungen zu dem Skulpturenfund in der Burg von Buda." AHA XXVII (1981), 209–224

Török–Osgyányi 1981 – Török, Gyöngyi–Osgyányi, Vilmos: "Reneszánsz kőfaragványokról. I. A pesti Belvárosi plébániatemplom egykori reneszánsz főoltára. II. Néhány reneszánsz faragvány a Magyar Nemzeti Galéria és a Budapesti Történeti Múzeum gyűjteményében" [On Renaissance stone-carvings. I. The former Renaissance high altar of the Inner

City Parish Church in Pest. II. Some Renaissance carvings in the collections of the Hungarian National Gallery and the Budapest Historical Museum]. MÉ XXX (1981), 95–113

Voit 1969 – *Magyarország műemléki topográfiája. Heves Megye Műemlékei* [Topography of Hungary's monuments. The monuments of Heves County]. I. Ed. by Pál Voit. Budapest, 1969

Zlinszkyné Sternegg, M. – Zlinszkyné Sternegg, Mária: *"A szentgotthárdi volt cisztercita apátság története és művészetének emlékei." Történeti, művelődéstörténeti, helyismereti tanulmányok* [Szentgotthárd: The history and artistic remains of the former Cistercian monastery]. Ed. by Lajos Kuntár and László Szabó. Szombathely, 1981

Arnótfalva	— Arnutovce (Czechoslovakia)
Bács	— Bač (Yugoslavia)
Bakabánya	— Pukanec (Czechoslovakia)
Barka	— Bôrka (Czechoslovakia)
Bártfa	— Bardejov (Czechoslovakia)
Bazin	— Pezinok (Czechoslovakia)
Berki	— Rokycany (Czechoslovakia)
Berzenke	— Bzinov (Czechoslovakia)
Besztercebánya	— Banská Bystrica (Czechoslovakia)
Brünn	— Brno (Czechoslovakia)
Cseklész	— Bernolákovo (Czechoslovakia)
Cserény	— Cĕrin (Czechoslovakia)
Csíkmenaság	— Armăşeni (Rumania)
Csíksomlyó	— Şumuleu (Rumania)
Csíkszentlélek	— Leliceni (Rumania)
Dénesfalva	— Danišovce (Czechoslovakia)
Dubravica	— Dúbravica (Czechoslovakia)
Eperjes	— Prešov (Czechoslovakia)
Frics	— Fričovce (Czechoslovakia)
Garamszentbenedek	— Hronský Beňadik (Czechoslovakia)
Gógánváralja	— Gogan (Rumania)
Gyulafehérvár	— Alba Iulia (Rumania)
Hervartó	— Hervartov (Czechoslovakia)
Héthárs	— Lipany (Czechoslovakia)
Igló	— Spišská Nová Ves (Czechoslovakia)
Jakabfalva	— see Szentjakabfalva
Jánosfalva	— Janovce (Czechoslovakia)
Jánosrét	— Lučky pri Kremnici (Czechoslovakia)
Káposztafalva	— Hrabušice (Czechoslovakia)
Kassa	— Košice (Czechoslovakia)
Kislomnic	— Lomnička (Czechoslovakia)

16

Kismarton	— Eisenstadt (Austria)
Kisszeben	— Sabinov (Czechoslovakia)
Körmöcbánya	— Kremnica (Czechoslovakia)
Krig	— Vojňany (Czechoslovakia)
Leibic	— L'ubica (Czechoslovakia)
Lippa	— Lipova (Rumania)
Liptónádasd	— Trstené (Czechoslovakia)
Liptószentandrás	— Liptovský Ondrej nad Váhom (Czechoslovakia)
Liptószentmária	— Liptovská Mara (Czechoslovakia)
Lőcse	— Levoča (Czechoslovakia)
Maldur	— Maldur (Czechoslovakia)
Máriatölgyes	— Dubnica nad Váhom (Czechoslovakia)
Máriavölgy	— Marianka (Czechoslovakia)
Marosvásárhely	— Tirgu Mureş (Rumania)
Mateóc	— Matejovce (Czechoslovakia)
Medgyes	— Mediaş (Rumania)
Monyhád	— Chimňany (Czechoslovakia)
Mosóc	— Mošovce (Czechoslovakia)
Nagykároly	— Careii Mari (Rumania)
Nagyszalók	— Vel'ký Slavkov (Czechoslovakia)
Nagyszombat	— Trnava (Czechoslovakia)
Nagytótlak	— Selo (Yugoslavia)
Nagyvárad	— Oradea (Rumania)
Necpál	— Necpaly (Czechoslovakia)
Nedec	— Niedzica (Poland)
Németlipcse	— Partizánská L'upča (Czechoslovakia)
Németújvár	— Güssing (Austria)
Nyitra	— Nitra (Czechoslovakia)
Okolicsnó	— Okoličné (Czechoslovakia)
Ószandec	— Stary Sącz (Poland)
Podolin	— Podolinec (Czechoslovakia)
Pozsony	— Bratislava (Czechoslovakia)
Pöstyén	— Piešt'any (Czechoslovakia)
Privigye	— Prievidza (Czechoslovakia)
Ruszkin	— Ruskinovce (Czechoslovakia)
Selmecbánya	— Banská Štiavnica (Czechoslovakia)
Stomfa	— Stupava (Czechoslovakia)

Svedlér	— Švedlár (Czechoslovakia)
Szászsebes	— Sebeş (Rumania)
Szentbenedek	— Mănăstirea (Rumania)
Szentjakabfalva	— Jakub (Czechoslovakia)
Szepesbéla	— Spišská Belá (Czechoslovakia)
Szepesdaróc	— Spišské Dravce (Czechoslovakia)
Szepeshely	— Spišská Kapitula (Czechoslovakia)
Szepesszombat	— Spišská Sobota – Poprad (Czechoslovakia)
Szepesváralja	— Spišské Podhradie (Czechoslovakia)
Szlatvin	— Slatvina (Czechoslovakia)
Szmrecsány	— Smrečany (Czechoslovakia)
Tájó	— Tajov (Czechoslovakia)
Toporc	— Toporec (Czechoslovakia)
Trencsén	— Trenčin (Czechoslovakia)
Turdossin	— Tvrdošin (Czechoslovakia)
Újszandec	— Nowy Sącz (Poland)
Varannó	— Vranov (Czechoslovakia)
Zboró	— Zborov (Czechoslovakia)
Zólyom	— Zvolen (Czechoslovakia)
Zólyomszászfalva	— Sásová (Czechoslovakia)

Plates

The upper part of the cornice is decorated with bunches of palmettes. The narrower leaves rising vertically from the base of the frieze are looped over the ribbons fastening the palmettes together. The fragment is from the earliest group of stone carvings characterized by the palmette motif —one of the most popular and widespread motifs in Byzantine art. The Gallery has three fragments of stone carvings of this type. The other two are from Veszprém and Sződ. Similar fragments may be seen in Tihany and Szekszárd (Tihany Museum and Béri Balogh Ádám Museum in Szekszárd). The importance of these carvings is enhanced by the fact that they are generally remains of ruined eleventh century buildings. The binding of the palmettes seen on the Hungarian carvings is a solution not to be found on any foreign architectural remains known to us today.

Dömös was the favourite residence of Prince Álmos, brother of Coloman Beauclerc. There, around 1105–1108, he established a provostry. A number of small capitals unearthed during excavation of the crypt of the church are now in the Gallery. Béla II, son of Álmos, completed the foundation and defined its rights in a document dated 1138. It is thought that this huge capital—one of the finest examples with figural decoration from the twelfth century—originates from the church rebuilt at that time. The carving depicts animals fighting each other, a subject generally interpreted as symbolizing the struggle between good and evil.

The diagonal corners show the joint head of a lion and bear respectively, each animal holding a paw on a human head; an eagle is seen holding a captured rabbit. The mounted figure behind the lion evokes the atmosphere of a hunting scene and certain details, for instance the horse-trappings, point to a demand for realistic representation. A striking feature of the carving is the roundish modelling of the animals, not previously seen in Hungarian sculpture. It suggests the influence of Lombard art, which can be seen also on capitals of the Cathedral in Esztergom, rebuilt in the second half of the twelfth century.

Fragment of a cornice from Pilisszentkereszt

Mid-eleventh century

Fresh-water limestone,
29 × 68 × 50 cm
Inv. No. 55.1570
Transferred in 1939
from the National Museum
to the Museum of Fine Arts
Bibliography:
Gerevich, T. 1938: 12;
Entz, Géza: Deux pierres sculptées à décor de palmettes de Sződ.
BMH 15 (1959), 27–33;
Török, László: XI. századi palmettás faragványaink és a szekszárdi vállkő. A szekszárdi Béri Balogh Ádám Múzeum Évkönyve.
I (1970), 107, 109, 123, 124;
Marosi, E.–Tóth, M. 1978: 32, 82, 211

Capital from Dömös

First third
of twelfth century

Amphibolite andesite.
Height 64 cm,
abacus 109x109 cm,
lower diam. 94 cm
Inv. No. 55.1599
Transferred in 1939
from the National Museum
to the Museum of Fine Arts
Bibliography:
Gerevich, T. 1938: 141;
Gerevich, László:
A koragótika kezdetei Magyarországon. A Magyar Tudományos Akadémia II. Társadalmi-Történettudományi Osztályának Közleményei XXIII (1974), 156–157;
Marosi, E.–Tóth, M. 1978: 19, 38, 102;
Marosi 1984: 22, Plate 64

This carving found its way to the museum from the archbishop's collection in Kalocsa. It is probable, however, that it originates from Óbuda, rather than from the town of Kalocsa. This possibility is supported by the fact that in the eighteenth century large numbers of carved stones were taken from Buda to Kalocsa for the construction of the episcopal buildings there; fragments similar in style can also be found in Buda. In the frame of the scene, the interlace is inhabited by animals. Similar motifs may be seen among the carvings in St. Peter's Church in Óbuda. The style bears witness to the influence of Lombard and Emilian carvings which also incorporate some French elements. Combined French and Italian elements appeared in Buda simultaneously with the sculptural style of Pécs.

The subject of the relief has given rise to even more conjecture than its origin. At one time the figural composition was believed to represent the Apostle Peter together with an angel; later it was thought to represent Christ with the Apostle Thomas; more recently, however, it has been regarded as a fragment of "Abraham's encounter with the Holy Trinity in the shape of three angels". As to its function, this has been variously defined as the side slab of a sarcophagus, or part of a parapet, or a gatepost; now it is believed to have been part of a rood-screen and that the carving represents the story of the three angels bringing news of Isaac's birth, which could be interpreted as an Old Testament prefiguration of the Annunciation.

Fragment of a rood-screen with figures from the scene of Abraham and three angels
Mid-twelfth century

Fresh-water limestone,
79 × 91 × 26 cm
Inv. No. 55.1600
Transferred in 1939
from the
Hungarian National Museum
to the Museum of Fine Arts.
Now on loan
to the Hungarian
National Museum
Bibliography: Radocsay,
Dénes:
Le fragment
du sarcophage de Kalocsa.
BMH 11 (1957), 17–27;
Dercsényi 1975: p. 194,
Plate 43; Levárdy, Ferenc:
Abraham
et les trois anges.
L'iconographie du relief
de Kalocsa.
BMH 32–33 (1969), 21–43;
Gerevich, L. 1971: 18;
Marosi, E,–Tóth, M. 1978:
22, 38–39, 129, 132;
Marosi 1984: 20, Plate 62

Ladislas I founded a Benedictine abbey in honour of St. Giles at Somogyvár, in 1901. Work on the monastery church, a basilica with three aisles and three apses, continued well into the twelfth century. This carving, also some fragments now in the Rippl-Rónai Museum in Kaposvár, may have been part of the rood-screen. The abbey with its Gothic cloister may have been built in the second decade of the thirteenth century. It is thought that the double capital—also housed in the Gallery—was once part of the decorative stone-work in the cloister. Until the fifteenth century the abbey was occupied by French Benedictine monks.

The frieze is covered with a relief pattern of interlace and fan-like semi-palmettes through which birds are seen taking cover. The motif of doves pecking at leaves is a symbol of the Eucharist and comes from Early Christian art. Stone carvings found in Óbuda, among them a fragment of a rood-screen (Plate 3) and a frieze with a hunting scene, are similarly decorated with animals enmeshed in interlace and palmettes.

Frieze from Somogyvár
Mid-twelfth century

Marble, 27 × 52 × 10 cm
Inv. No. 53.582
Transferred in 1939
from the Hungarian
National Museum
to the Museum of Fine Arts.
On temporary loan
to the Hungarian National
Museum
Bibliography:
Gerevich, T. 1938: 161;
Gerevich, L. 1971: 19;
Marosi, E.–Tóth, M. 1978:
39, 134;
Marosi 1984: 21

The second Gothic cathedral of the Kalocsa episcopacy with its axis deviating from that of the former eleventh century church, the three-aisled basilica with transept and ambulatory with radiating chapels opening into each other was the only Hungarian church which reflects a markedly French influence with regard to both the style of its carvings and its ground-plan. There is a close relationship between the excavated fragments from Kalocsa and those surviving from Esztergom and Pilisszentkereszt, and it is now thought that the building was started under Primate Bertold (1205–1219), brother of Queen Gertrudis, member of the princely family of Andechs-Meran.

The stone-carving illustrated here is believed to have formed the capital of a pillar in one of the side-aisles. The pronounced forward movement of the bud is characteristic of a number of capitals from the period. The sharply cut, well defined leaves bear witness to the great skill of the stone carver.

Capital of pillar from Kalocsa
1200–1225

Fresh-water limestone,
29 × 72 × 50 cm
Inv. No. 55.1588
Transferred in 1939
from the Hungarian
National Museum
to the Museum of Fine Arts
Bibliography: Entz 1966: 36;
Marosi, E.–Tóth, M.1978:
218–219;
Marosi 1984: 103, 122, Plate
249

4

5

The original purpose of this marble slab is still undecided. The Latin inscription on the round-arched niche (NULLUS MIRETUR UT HUIC CUR BENEDICTIO DETUR) alludes to the text of Isaac's blessing. The horizontal frame above and below bears the names of JACOB and ESAU, sons of Isaac, respectively. Clearly only one of these can refer to the standing figure clad in ecclesiastical vestments, his hands lifted in prayer in the pose known from Early Christian art. The carving may have adorned a portal with a series of figures placed above each other illustrating the story of Isaac's blessing. The portal is thought to have formed part of the rich twelfth century sculptural decoration of St. Peter's Cathedral built in Pécs after 1064. Originally, the lines engraved in the marble were probably filled with some other material of a different colour. Although this is the only known encrusted figural fragment among the many carvings surviving from Pécs, the folds of the garment show a certain stylistic affinity with the representation of the apocalyptic figures of the elders which once ornamented the cathedral (cf. Plate 7).

Detail of a doorway (?) from Pécs
Third quarter
of twelfth century

Yellowish-white marble,
83 × 51 cm
Inv. No. 55.975
Transferred in 1939
from the Hungarian
National Museum
to the Museum of Fine Arts
Bibliography: Szőnyi, Ottó:
A pécsi
püspöki múzeum kőtára
[The Department
of Stonework.
Remains of the Episcopal
Museum in Pécs].
Pécs, 1906. 3.;
Gerevich, T. 1938:
169, 179–180;
Dercsényi 1975:
193, Plate 36;
Marosi 1984: 67, 228

This standing figure, stocky and bearded, with a musical instrument in his right hand, is one of the twenty-four elders described in the Revelations of St. John. His attire shows certain elements of Byzantine court fashion, much favoured by noblemen in Western Europe at that time. Over a full-length robe he wears a tunic with a rich floral pattern, and a decorative border round the neck and hem with rows of beads. The cloak hanging from his shoulders is embellished with a pattern of circles and is fastened with braid. He wears a crown on his head. The statue was part of the twelfth century rood-screen of the Cathedral in Pécs, from which fragments of the figures of other elders and standing angels have also survived, one of the latter owned by the Gallery. It also reflects the French trend of European sculpture, more distantly the Burgundian art of the age, and is the earliest example of Hungarian sculpture executed in such a style.

Apocalyptic elder from Pécs
Third quarter
of twelfth century

Limestone, 74 cm
Inv. No. 55.977
Transferred in 1939
from the Hungarian
National Museum
to the Museum of Fine Arts.
On temporary loan
to the Hungarian
National Museum
Bibliography:
Dercsényi 1975:
192–193, Plate 41;
Marosi, E.–Tóth, M. 1978:
137–138, 148–149
(With detailed bibliography);
Marosi 1984: 228

6

7

This head of a king was most probably part of one of the figures decorating the doorway of the Cathedral in Kalocsa. Fragments of the portal, of the same red marble, were unearthed during excavations in the last century. Constructed of alternating stone and red marble, the Kalocsa portal may have been similar to the western portal of the former St. Adalbert's in Esztergom, built before 1196.

The head, formed in a summary manner, is one of the finest examples of Romanesque stone-carving in Hungary. It is elaborated also at the back and is crowned with a hoop-like headdress decorated with three Greek crosses. In shape the crown resembles the death-crown found in the grave of Béla III. The simplicity of the form, the elaboration of the beard, moustache and hair in parallel straight lines and the strongly outlined wide-open eyes are responsible for the monumental character of the head. Formerly it was thought to be the head of King St. Stephen, founder of the Cathedral, but it may rather be that of one of the biblical kings adorning the portal.

Head of a king from Kalocsa
First quarter
of thirteenth century

Massive red limestone
from Piszke,
Hungary, 17 cm
Inv. No. 53.364
Transferred in 1936
from the Hungarian
National Museum
to the Museum of Fine Arts.
On loan
to the Hungarian
National Museum
Bibliography:
Gerevich, T. 1938:
102, 178, 183;
Entz 1966: 48;
Dercsényi 1975:
198–199. Plate 81;
Marosi 1984: 129, Plates
312–313

All we know of the medieval church in Szentkirály, Vas County, is that the portal was once decorated with the relief illustrated here. It shows the two donors, between them Christ enthroned. His right hand raised in blessing and in His left hand a Bible. The Byzantine character of the enthroned Saviour and the archaized fluted folds of his robe are typical features of thirteenth century Christ in Majesty representations.The two donors kneel on either side, gazing reverently at Christ. They may have been members of a distinguished landowning family in Vas County. The man holds the model of a church; the woman holds the lower part of the shaft of a column. The headdress of the woman, bound under the chin, is in the contemporary French fashion. The bodies of the kneeling donors, represented in the same size as Christ, completely fill the semicircular composition, the size being also of iconographic significance. The stone-carver was undoubtedly acquainted with North Italian-Lombard sculpture. This is demonstrated in the firmly rounded modelling of the kneeling figures.

Tympanum from Szentkirály
Third quarter
of thirteenth century

Marble, 66 × 119 × 20 cm
Inv. No. 55.976
Acquired from the Museum
in Szombathely.
On loan to the Hungarian
National Museum
Bibliography: Balogh, Jolán:
1. Sur les statues
de l'époque Arpadienne.
2. La lunette
de Szentkirály.
BMH VIII (1956), 20–32;
Dercsényi 1975: 205
Plate 142; Marosi, E.–
Tóth, M. 1978: 21, 59;
Marosi 1984: 133

8

9

The Johannine church in Pöstyén, built with twin chancels and presenting a very unusual ground-plan analogous only to the Franciscan church in Zboró, already lay in ruins in the early years of the nineteenth century when, however, it was still being referred to as a church adorned with twenty-three ornamental carvings. Of these, a few capitals with foliage decoration and the fragment of architectural detail and carving illustrated here are now in the Gallery.

The arch of what was presumably a niche lies within a rectangular frame and is overlaid on either side with succulent trifoliate leaves sprouting from tendrils. The capitals now in the Gallery are similarly decorated. The upper horizontal edge of the frame is smoothly levelled to form a base for the surmounting relief carvings. In the middle of this platform a bearded male figure is seated between kneeling angels. The angel on the left holds a triangular shield with the Hungarian coat of arms showing the apostolic cross; the one on the right holds a badly damaged helmet with an ostrich head, as worn by the Anjous. The seated figure turning slightly to the right gives an impression of solemnity. The heraldic badges indicate that he may have been one of the kings of the Anjou dynasty. At one time the figure was thought to represent Charles Robert. However, the style of the carving and the bearded face are characteristic of the 1370s, and the head is now believed to represent Louis the Great of Hungary. Softly modelled figures executed in a similar style can be seen in the relief of the Death of the Virgin, adorning the southern portal of the Buda Castle Church of Our Lady, built in the 1370s.

Crown of a niche from Pöstyén
1370–1380

Sandstone, 98 × 88 × 26 cm
Inv. No. 55.1604
Transferred in 1939
from the Hungarian
National Museum
to the Museum of Fine Arts.
On loan
to the Hungarian
National Museum

Bibliography:
Éber, László:
Pöstyéni dombormű
a Nemzeti Múzeumban
[A relief from Pöstyén
in the National Museum].
AÉ 29 (1909), 289–293;
Csemegi, József:
A budavári főtemplom
középkori építéstörténete
[Medieval architecture
of Budavár Cathedral].
Budapest, 1955: 93, 100;
Mencl, Václav:
Šariš v Dejinách
gotickej architektúry [The
Sáros region in the history
of the Gothic architecture].
Vlastivedný časopis XVI
(1967), 14

There were countless varieties of standing Virgin and Child figures in French art around 1300. Although the Virgin illustrated here cannot be directly related to any one of them, it may have been inspired by the French stone Madonna in the Abbey of Fontenay, dating from around 1300, but adapted to the local Austrian taste. The statue in the Salesian monastery in Vienna, dating from 1320–1330, is closely related to the Madonna with Child in the Hungarian National Gallery. It was traditionally believed by the nuns to have originated in Hungary, a belief corroborating the supposition that the Viennese figure served as model for the Toporc Virgin.

The Master of the First Toporc Virgin developed an individual style which greatly influenced the sculpture in the Szepes region and the neighbouring Little Poland. This is evident, not only in the Ruszkin and the third Újszandec Virgins, but in a whole series of more remotely linked carvings. In all of them we find the main characteristics of the Madonna with Child now in Budapest—the serene facial expression, the slightly curving S-line of the figure emphasized by the fact that the left leg supports the main weight of the body, the folds of the garment following the curve of the right leg and the slight inclination of the head to the right. The most remarkable feature of the carving is, however, the drapery of the robe which is thrown over the right arm and hangs in deep horizontal folds across the body. This is in striking contrast with the lightness of the frilled veil falling over the Virgin's shoulders. The vertical line of the cloak hanging from her right shoulder gives the figure a block-like, closed form. Although this is not characteristic of the French models, it is to be seen on the Madonna with Child from the Salesian monastery in Vienna. The stocky appearance is enhanced by the size of the Child, which is much too large in proportion to that of the Virgin. The stiff, rigidly upright posture of the Child is broken only by the crossed legs; the arms, formerly providing some animation, are now missing. The posture, however, is characteristic of the many statues of this type created at that time. The Child is shown wearing a long tunic as traditionally represented in the previous century.

The First Virgin and Child from Toporc
1340–1350

Lime-wood,
with traces of paint.
115.5 cm
Inv. No. 55.900
Transferred in 1939
from the Hungarian
National Museum
to the Museum of Fine Arts

Bibliography:
Radocsay 1967:
26–27, 220-221;
Dutkiewicz, J. E.:
Małopolska rzeźba
średniowieczna 1300–1450
La sculpture du Moyen Age
en Petit Pologne:
Cracow, 1949;
36, 53, 54, 56, 93, 132, 134,
136, 162, 165, 259;
Balogh 1957: 231;
Zykan, M.:
Zwei gotische
Madonnenstatuen
und ihre Restaurierung.
Österreichische Zeitschrift
für Kunst und
Denkmalpflege XXII
(1968), 171–184

In this slender, ethereal carving, the Virgin is shown supporting the Child high on her right arm. The long folds of her robe hang vertically from her right hand thus emphasizing the slenderness of her figure. Her close-fitting silvery wrap is richly fluted, the folds forming drop-shaped hollows in the middle. The disproportionately elongated, supple but seemingly unstable figure and the modelling of the drapery are reminiscent of the Silesian Virgins with lions.

The Silesian Virgins constitute a special iconographic type, besides establishing a characteristic style which in the second half of the fourteenth century greatly influenced the sculpture of the neighbouring Bohemian territories and the Szepes region. This influence is clearly reflected not only in the Virgin illustrated here but also in the statues of the apostles adorning the pinnacles of the high altar in Lőcse. The French origin is beyond doubt. Although the pose of the Child held aloft and the slight S-bend of the Virgin's body are also characteristic of the Toporc Virgin (cf. Plate 11), closer comparison shows that there is a difference between the two both in style and date. The surface carving of the Szlatvin Virgin is shallow; it is modelled more like a relief. This, together with the disproportionately elongated lower part of the body and especially the characteristic so-called thumb-mark folds, point to Silesian influence. However, the carver imparted an individual charm to this figure which distinguishes it from the Virgins of neighbouring areas. The face of the Virgin is framed by a headdress carved to represent lace falling softly over her shoulders. She wears a silver cloak which is rather rare; from under the worn surface of this the red bole grounding is apparent. This statue, incomplete as it is—the once rich trimming of the crown and the two hands being now missing—exemplifies the high standard of fourteenth century wood-carving.

Virgin and Child from Szlatvin

1370–1380

Painted lime-wood, 111 cm
Inv. No. 53.371
Transferred in 1936
from the Hungarian
National Museum
to the Museum of Fine Arts
Bibliography: Radocsay
1967: 28–29, 218–219;
Kampis, A.:
La Vierge de Szlatvin.
BMH 23
(1963), 13–20

The three virgin martyrs were often represented in the Middle Ages, and these figures may have decorated the inner side of the wing of an altar-piece. Broad horizontal wings with sufficient space for three figures side by side, were particularly popular in Silesia, and here both the type of the face and the style of the carving reflect a Silesian influence. Few fourteenth century altarpieces with wood-carving have survived anywhere in Europe; from medieval Hungary only the shutters of the altar from Szepes (Plate 14) and the two from Krig are known. They are embellished with reliefs of saints standing in a row below baldachines composed of architectural motifs. It is possible that the background of the relief from Maldur was similarly decorated.

The round faces and archaized schematic smiles of the three female saints are reminiscent of the Silesian Virgins with lions. There is a very strong resemblance between the facial expression of the most famous Virgin with lion (from Skarbimierz), now in the Wrocław Śląskie Museum, and that of St. Agnes (?) from Maldur. In the relief illustrated here it is only in the gaily undulating folds of the saints' robes, and the arrangement of the drapery, that the artist has been able to vary the figures. St. Catherine gathers up her robe with her left hand, St. Agnes (?) with her right. From under their arms the folds hang in tortuous lines. The so-called attributes—objects associated with their martyrdom and legends—help us to recognize the saints. The cog-wheel and dragon relate unequivocally to St. Catherine and St. Margaret, respectively. The palm-branch in the hand of the third saint is characteristic of all martyrs, and the book held in her right hand gives us reason to suppose that the figure is that of St. Agnes. Originally the heads of the three saints were adorned with crowns, from which only the lower part, the rims, now remain.

St. Catherine, St. Margaret and St. Agnes (?) from Maldur
1370–1380

Lime-wood with traces of paint,
104, 104 and 106 cm respectively
Inv. No. 55.892.1–3
Transferred in 1939 from the Hungarian National Museum to the Museum of Fine Arts
Bibliography:
Radocsay 1967: 32–33, 196–197

The small wings illustrated here are of considerable importance from the point of view of the development of winged altars. The outer sides are decorated with paintings, the inner sides by fourteenth century reliefs representing the Annunciation. Gabriel is shown holding in his left hand a banderole with the inscription "Ave Maria gratia". His right hand, which pointed to the Virgin, is missing. Nor has the central shrine of the altar survived. This probably contained a carving of the Virgin and a relic, and almost certainly terminated in a point, since the wings also form an acute angle when closed. The upper part of the inside wings contain small reliquaries with banderoles referring to the now missing relics. This feature illustrates a period of development in the fourteenth century, when altars began to serve the function of the earlier reliquaries finely executed in metal-work.

The form of the Gothic niches containing the figures shows an architectural influence, apparent also in the steeply pointed upper terminations and the brackets below the figures. These are widely used motifs in fourteenth century sculpture and painting alike. Similar niches enframe, for instance, the reliefs of the female saints on the wings of the altar from Krig dating from the end of the fourteenth century. The parallel folds of the Virgin's drapery starting from high and the wide sleeves of the angel's garments falling into deep large pleats, follow the Italianate trend which crystallized, becoming more coordinated and showing more rounded forms, particularly in painting, in the 1360s.

**Two wings
of a small altar
for private devotion
with relief carving
of the Annunciation.
Provenance unknown;
presumably
from the Szepes region**
c. 1360

Lime-wood,
layer of paint damaged.
The figures
of the angels
and the Virgin 16 cm,
the wings 39 × 10 cm
Inv. No. 55.878. 1–2
Transferred in 1939
from the Hungarian
National Museum
to the Museum of Fine Arts
Bibliography:
Radocsay 1967: 47, 171

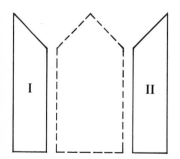

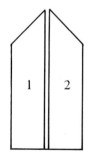

*I Angel
from the Annunciation
II The Virgin
from the Annunciation
1 A Bishop Saint
2 St. Wenceslas*

14

The carving of St. Dorothy may justly be called the finest example of the International Soft Style to have been created in Hungary. The slender figure of the saint is unique among related carvings from the neighbouring areas. It is even more slender than the Beautiful Virgins, while the tubular folds of the robe gathered to one side, together with her attribute, the flower basket, closely follow the outline of the body. Although the folds of the robe draped over her arms remind us of the "classical" order, the robe itself is not given an independent form but follows faithfully the soft S-line of the figure. Neither has her serious, absorbed expression the suavity seen in the faces of German and Bohemian statues of the period. It also differs from its Hungarian contemporaries, e.g. the Virgin from Kislomnic, St. Magdalen from Dénesfalva, and its counterpart, St. Catherine from Barka, in the delicacy of the carving, the serene facial expression, the balanced arrangement of the folds and the unusual proportions of the figure. In the Hungarian sculpture the statue is of exceptional significance.

St. Dorothy from Barka
1410–1420

Lime-wood, with traces of paint.
169.5 cm
Inv. No. 52.653
Acquired in 1947 by the Museum of Fine Arts from the József Pécsi Collection on an exchange basis.
Bibliography:
Radocsay 1967: 44–45, 150;
Radocsay 1969: 60.
Radocsay, Dénes: A barkai Szent Dorottya [The statue of St. Dorothy from Barka.]
Művészet, (1969) 26–27;
Török 1981: 215.

In the late fourteenth and early fifteenth centuries there emerged in Central Europe a new style of sculpture and painting which, because of its characteristic mellow forms, was referred to as the Soft Style. This carving of St. Paul, also three others in the collection (cf. Plates 15, 17 and 18), belong to its second, more mature phase though in this figure the most typical features of the art of around 1400 are retained. This work exemplifies the style in a number of ways—the undulating borders of the robe draped over the arms of the figure, folds not yet arranged in the later tubular forms separated from the trunk, also the acute angles formed where the drapery touches the ground and the two sharp, so-called hairpin folds in the centre. Originally the Apostle held a sword in his left hand and a book in his right hand. His head, slightly tilted to the right, was recarved at a later date, but even so it retains a hint of this particular type of sculpture. Another work with the same type of head is a contemporary carving of St. Jacob the Apostle which came from Pernegg and is now in the Innsbruck Museum.

The Apostle St. Paul (?) from Szentjakabfalva
1410–1420

Lime-wood, the painting damaged.
120 cm
Inv. No. 7055
Permanent deposit by the Association of Friends of the Art Museums in the Museum of Fine Arts before 1936
Bibliography:
Radocsay 1967: 45, 213;
Radocsay 1969: 60;
Török 1981: 215

15   16

The figure of the Man of Sorrows, standing and showing his wounds became—like the Pietà—a subject for representation in its own right, quite apart from the story of the Passion; it was also a subject frequently chosen by individuals for private worship. The best-known carvings of the Man of Sorrows, the so-called *Imago pietatis*, are outstanding examples of the Soft Style. Here, as in Silesian and Austrian relics of the period, Christ's shroud falls in elaborate folds from his shoulders both in front and at the back. The curves of the shroud as it reaches the ground between his feet are reminiscent of those seen in statues by the Austrian Master of Großlobming and his circle. Stylistic analogues to this statue were copiously recovered in Buda Castle in 1974 which bear signs of the influence of the Master of Großlobming. The arrangement of the central hairpin folds is akin to that seen on the apostle from Jakabfalva or St. Dorothy's carving from Barka, although the folds of the drapery at the sides differ from the former in that they do not follow the outlines of the body, having been carved independently, similarly to the No. 13 torso of the stone finds of 1974. Some characteristics, especially the self-contained aspect of the work, are close to the iconography of the Man of Sorrows, in which Christ is pointing to the wound in his side with one or both hands. The Man of Sorrows is a unique piece in the early fifteenth century Hungarian sculpture, not only because of its special iconographic interest but because it is so powerful an expression of Christ's suffering; also on account of the classical arrangement of the folds of the drapery. On the back of the statue, the shroud has a huge fold in the manner of the Beautiful Virgins, which makes it analogous to the Nos. 6 and 16 bishop figures of the statues found up on Castle Hill. This fold is complemented by smaller so-called thumb-print folds which play a more prominent role here than on the carvings from Barka and Jakabfalva, and are thus closer in style to the St. Dorothy carving of the Gallery (Inv. No. 7596) and torso No. 1 of the Castle Hill find and torso No. 9 of the 1974 find. These similarities prove that stone and wood-carving were closely related in early fifteenth century Buda, with priority enjoyed by stone sculpture.

Man of Sorrows from the Transdanubian region
1410–1420

Painted lime-wood, 99 cm
On loan from the Museum of Veszprém Diocese
Bibliography: Egyházi gyűjtemények kincsei. Budapest, Iparművészeti Múzeum [Treasures of Ecclesiastical Art. Budapest, Museum of Applied Arts]. October, 1979–January, 1980. Catalogue No. 1.–cf. Török 1981: 209–224

17

The Second Virgin and Child from Toporc is a characteristic example of the Beautiful Virgins in Hungary. The statues of Beautiful Virgins first appeared in stone in Central European art around 1400. These representations of a standing Virgin playing gently with the Child were the direct predecessors of the altar carvings and the most beautiful products of the Soft Style. It was not, however, among art historians that the term "beautiful" was first used: theological writings of around 1400 emphasized the physical and spiritual beauty of the Virgin. The apple also has an important theological meaning in these representations of Beautiful Virgins: it is not the orb, which is usually represented with a cross, but the fruit itself, the apple that caused the Fall of man. It is an expression of the Virgin's role in the redemption when, a second Eve, she offers the apple, the symbol of sin, to Christ, the second Adam. In this particular carving both the Virgin and the Child are holding an apple, but this is quite exceptional.

The Second Virgin of Toporc differs in many respects from the southern Bohemian and Austrian type of Beautiful Virgins. The abstracted, peacefully smiling Madonna betrays no close connection with the Child. This is very different from the classical Beautiful Virgins where the Madonna plays with a lively Child. Here the Virgin's characteristic features are a calm bearing, a slight tilt of the head and a more closed form. Her beauty is enhanced by an unusual crown surmounted by ornamental vine-leaves and by the one time perhaps gilded, now white colour of the robe lined with blue.

The work is related to relics of stone sculpture originating from Buda workshops around 1400. The sandstone female saints and Madonna torsos, also a console with the head of a young girl, which can be seen in the Budapest Historical Museum, indicate that, as a type, the Beautiful Virgin was well known to Buda sculptors. It is very likely that Buda was the centre from which the type spread to more distant, chiefly northern regions of the country. The superb stone statues recently excavated in the Castle provide additional proof of the importance of the sculptors' workshops of that period in Buda.

The Second Virgin and Child from Toporc
c. 1420

Painted lime-wood, 139.5 cm
Inv. No. 57.15 M
Transferred in 1939 from the Hungarian National Museum to the Museum of Fine Arts
Bibliography: Radocsay 1967: 45, 221; Radocsay 1969: 60; Clasen 1974: 149, 202–203

St. Catherine of Alexandria was the scholar saint of early Christianity. She is shown here with the attributes of her martyrdom: the cog-wheel and the sword. The work only partially resembles that of the earlier Soft Style statues. Although the saint's robe hangs from her arms just as softly as that of the second Virgin from Toporc (Plate 18), the folds across the front are very ample compared with the hairpin folds of the second Virgin's robe. The difference is even more evident if we compare the carving to that of St. Dorothy from Barka or to the somewhat earlier Apostle from Szentjakabfalva (Plates 15, 16). Such a comparison reveals that the structure of St. Catherine's figure is more tectonic, the S-curve having almost disappeared; the face is rounder and resembles that of the contemporary Madonna with Child in the Minorite church at Lőcse. It is thought that the two carvings were made by the same master. The statue of St. Catherine from Podolin demonstrates a departure from the Beautiful Virgin type around 1420–1430; it is clearly representative of the last stages of the period characterized by the Soft Style.

St. Catherine from Podolin
1420–1430

Painted lime-wood, 150 cm
Inv. No. 5231
Purchased by the Museum of Fine Arts in 1918
Bibliography:
Radocsay 1967: 45–46, 206;
Radocsay 1969: 60

This scene, part of an originally horizontal panel now broken off on the left side, represents a scene from "the doubts of Joseph" and may have formed part of a large altarpiece of the Virgin. The missing left side depicted the figure of St. Joseph and an angel—as we realize when we inspect the lower left corner of this work where fragmentary remains of a wing, a halo, some red drapery, the attributes of St. Joseph, a brown straw hat with a stick through it and a small water-barrel, are still discernible. The meaning may be found in the so-called apocryphal texts well known in the Middle Ages. Their representation was revived in the art of the early fifteenth century, popularized by a new emphasis on the human traits of the Virgin and Christ. The theme of the panel illustrated here can be traced back to the Greek apocryphal text of the *Proto-Evangelium Jacobi*, dating from the second century. Joseph, returning home and finding Mary pregnant, is seized by doubts which are dispersed by a dream in which an angel appears to him. The spinning wheel is a narrative element borrowed from traditional representation of the Annunciation and also found in the *Apocrypha*. The flowers in the foreground, also the wash-basin, cauldron of water and towel on the left, are symbols of the Virgin; the latter are motifs frequently adopted in German and Austrian painting under the influence of Netherlandish art. These, and the requisites for spinning—the reel on the right, the spindle held by the Virgin, the thread and the distaff—are so accurately depicted by the artist that this work is regarded as one of the first attempts to represent the utensils of the age in a realistic manner. The Virgin is not concentrating on her work but, with her head bent a little sideways, gazes dreamily ahead. The undulating folds of her robe, which suggest her pregnancy, are characteristic of the Soft Style close in style to the paintings from the neighbouring Vienna of Austria. The master of the painting is a worthy follower of the so-called International Gothic style developed around 1400, and also adopted by Thomas de Coloswar, creator of the Calvary altar from Garamszentbenedek—an outstanding example of Hungarian painting.

The Virgin at the Spinning-wheel from Németújvár

1420–1430

Tempera on larch-wood, 89 × 78 cm
Inv. No. 52.656
Acquired by the Museum of Fine Arts from the Batthyány Collection

Bibliography:
Radocsay 1955: 49, 410–411; Radocsay 1963: 15, 45–46; Urbach, Zsuzsa: Dominus Possedit me . . . (Prov. 8, 22). Beitrag zur Ikonographie des Josephzweifels. AHA XX (1974), 199–266: Török 1978: 16–17

20

An early photograph of this statue shows a crown on the saint's head and an orb in his left hand. On account of the battle-axe—originally held in the right hand—the saint was identified as St. Ladislas when first mentioned in the literature. The facial type is in keeping with the traditional representation of the royal knights in medieval Hungary. From the downward cast of the eyes turned slightly to the right, the thickset figure and the frontal view emphasized by the flowing robes, it would seem that the carving must have stood on the left side of a central shrine of an altarpiece. From the point of view of fashion and style of carving, it corresponds almost entirely with the figure of St. Sigismund on the shrine of the winged altar dating from 1430–1440 in San Sigismondo, a parish church in southern Tyrol, but there are also numerous analogous Hungarian stone statues among those unearthed in Buda Castle in 1974. The wide belt worn below the waist, the armour, the slantwise-laced jacket, also the stockings and split leather shoes, can be seen, for example, on a large mounted figure and on a herald with a helmet in his hand. There is also a very close relationship between the face of St. Ladislas and a male head similarly found at Buda Castle: the hair, beard and moustache, and especially the wrinkles on the brow and the crow's feet in the corners under the eyes scratched into the ground-colour, are in both works represented in the same realistic manner. The narrow face and serious expression are typical features of representation of royal figures of a period when masters were endeavouring to replace ideal faces by more realistic likenesses. The difference between the drapery softly flowing from the arms and the harder lines of the jacket also demonstrates the transition between the two styles; the structure of the whole square-built figure and the proportions are early indications of the new sculptural approach of the 1440s.

**St. Ladislas.
Of unknown
provenance**
1430–1440

Lime-wood, painted
but damaged, 98 cm
Inv. No. 7597
Purchased by the Ministry
of Culture
from the Lajos Ernst
Collection
for the Museum
of Fine Arts
in 1939
Bibliography:
Radocsay 1967:
48, 171.
Török 1981: 217–221

This type of representation of the Holy Trinity —the Man of Sorrows held by God the Father with the Holy Ghost in the likeness of a dove—was widely adopted in European art around 1400 when it was customary to show particular reverence for the dead Saviour. Though of unknown provenance, it is thought that the panel comes from the western border region of Hungary, and is the only known Hungarian example of this iconographic type in painting. The earliest similar representation known to us is an example of French Burgundian art from around 1380. Pictures with half-length figures developed under the powerful influence of representations of the Pietà in which the Man of Sorrows is held by one or more angels. In respect to half-length figures, this work is similar to the Münster panel by the Master of St. Veronica (1395–1415). In the type of head adopted for the figure of God the Father there is a certain relationship with the Sankt-Lambrecht votive panel (around 1430), now in Vienna, and with the Holy Trinity in the Hungarian National Gallery. The finely tooled haloes and border adornments were very popular in Viennese painting at the beginning of the fifteenth century. They can also be seen on other panels more Austrian in style. In the Budapest collection they may be seen on The Virgin at the Spinning-wheel (Plate 20) from Németújvár. In this the dove representing the Holy Ghost also shows kindred traits. The folds of the draperies, especially of those enveloping St. Peter and St. Paul on the one-time reverse of the panel, show that the picture of the Holy Trinity with Man of Sorrows must have been painted at a somewhat later date than the mentioned analogues. It is believed that this painting was once on the obverse of the right wing of a small triptych or diptych.

The Holy Trinity with Man of Sorrows. Of unknown provenance
c. 1440

Tempera
on pine-wood panel,
64.5 × 51.5 cm
Inv. No. 52.658
Transferred
from the Szombathely Museum
to the Museum
of Fine Arts
Bibliography:
Radocsay 1955:
329; Török 1978: 18–19

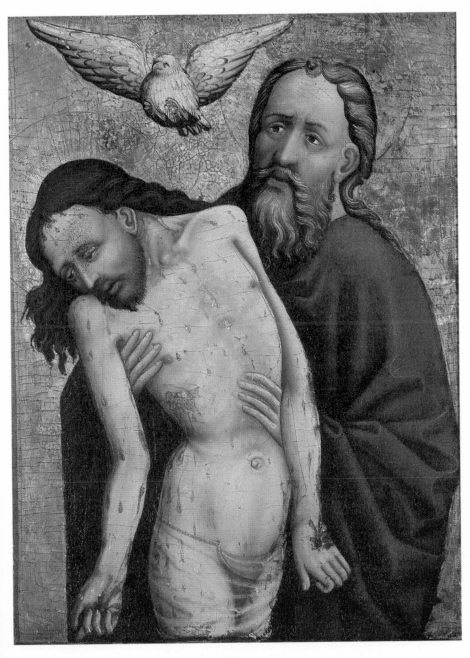

Although the frame of this small portable altar for private devotion—from the Piarist monastery in Trencsén—was renovated during the baroque period, it is still a good example of the type of combined reliquary and altar widely used in the fourteenth century and still popular in the first half of the fifteenth. In the fourteenth century the middle part of the altar consisted of a shrine surrounded by recesses containing the relics. This was usually adorned with goldsmith's work or sculptural scenes. The Byzantine half-length figure of the Madonna was particularly popular among painters of around 1400, as it was well suited for the generally smaller central picture of a triptych. Full-length figures of saints, especially those of the two martyr virgins, were frequently painted on the shutters of winged altars and also, in fifteenth century Bohemian art, on the frames surrounding the Madonna with Child pictures. In contrast to the figure of the Virgin, the two female saints represent the ideal type closely related to the Soft Style of Bohemia prevalent at the beginning of the fifteenth century—as, for example, the reliquary panel of Roudnice, produced after 1430, which is flanked by similar saints. The small altar from Trencsén constitutes an interesting transition in the development of altarpieces from the reliquary type to the painted triptych.

House altar for private devotion from Trencsén
1440–1450

Centre panel:
tempera on lime-wood,
19 × 11 cm
The wings:
tempera on lime-wood,
40.5 × 11 cm each
Inv. No. 53.579.1–3
Transferred in 1939
from the Hungarian National Museum to the Museum of Fine Arts
Bibliography:
Radocsay 1955: 45–46, 456–457;
Radocsay 1963: 12, 44;
Urbach, Zsuzsa:
A németalföldi
és magyarországi művészet
kapcsolata
a XIV–XV. században
[The relationship between Netherlandish
and Hungarian art
in the 14th–15th centuries].
Ars Hungarica 1975:
326–327

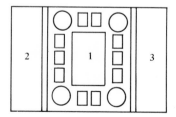
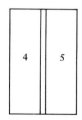

1 *The Madonna and the Child*
2 *St. Catherine*
3 *St. Barbara*
4 *St. Ursula*
5 *St. Dorothy*

23

The Madonna and Child in the central panel of the triptych from Trencsén belongs to a very popular type of devotional representation, Byzantine in origin but recomposed around 1400. The half-length portrait expresses the intimate relationship between the Virgin and Child. The latter is often shown touching his mother's face or garment or trying to snatch at her veil, or, less frequently, but as seen in this picture, reaching out for the ornamental clasp which fastens her cloak. The Virgin's crown is thrown into relief to imitate encrusted gems—a technique that bears witness to the influence of Bohemian art around 1400, while the twisted kerchief around her head and her downcast eyes point to the impact of more contemporary endeavours characteristic of Netherlandish painting. The sharp folds of the cloak indicate an origin not earlier than the middle of the fifteenth century. The finely traced long fingers of the Virgin, also the careful miniature-like elaboration of the picture, provide evidence that the panel is the excellent work of a master of fifteenth century Hungarian painting.

**The central panel
of the house altar
from Trencsén:
Madonna and Child**
1440–1450

Tempera on lime-wood,
19 × 11 cm
For bibliography
see Plate 23

24

This carving is one of the few Gothic carvings originating from the Transdanubian Region (Western Hungary). It is also rare on account of the subject. Legend has it that, in the third century, St. Anthony the Hermit retired to a mountain in Egypt where he lived in a rock-hewn grave for twenty years. Beseeched by his followers, he then founded a monastery. This is suggested in the carving by rocks and a church on the peak of a mountain. St. Anthony is shown wearing a broad-brimmed pilgrim's hat; a pilgrim's bag can be seen on his left. His head rests on the hand with which he grasps his staff. The same saint is depicted similarly seated against rocks in fifteenth century south German sculpture, for instance in a carving from Machtolsheim and another from the Ulm school of art. The only difference between these and the carving from Zalaszentgrót is that in the latter St. Anthony is not surrounded by the rocks but, leaning forward, seems to carry them on his back. Thus the carving gives the effect of a bracket figure. The sharply cut shapes forming the mass of the rocks are in contrast to the soft folds of the robe gathered over the lap of the saint, and the same dissimilarity exists in the carving of these details in the south German statues mentioned above. The detailed representation of the garment buttoned on the right shoulder and worn with a belt, is characteristic of the age and shows an interest in costume.

St. Anthony the Hermit from Zalaszentgrót
1440–1450

Lime-wood,
originally painted
79.5 cm
Inv. No. 6815
Purchased by the Museum of Fine Arts
from the Ludwig Behr Collection, 1934
Bibliography: Radocsay 1967: 87–88, 224;
cf. Baum, J.:
Deutsche Bildwerke des 10. bis 18. Jahrhunderts.
Katalog der Königlichen Altertümersammlung in Stuttgart.
III. Stuttgart–Berlin, 1917, 91

The scenes on the inside wings of the altarpiece are the work of one master, those on the triangular paintings above and on the outside wings are the work of another—an associate of the Master of Mateóc, the most prominent painter in the Polish-Hungarian border region in the fifteenth century.

The inside wings also reflect a northern influence and a knowledge of the style of the altar of St. Barbara in Wrocław which dates from 1447. The master must have modelled his work on this significant Silesian altarpiece in respect of narrative, types of face and manner of representing the vegetation. By setting the scene of the Refusal of Joachim's Sacrifice within an architectural frame as was the custom at that time, the painter succeeded in suggesting the interior of a church. In the other pictures too he endeavoured to place the figures and architectural elements with some degree of realism in the landscape. From this point of view the most successful scene is that of the grieving Joachim where he is shown outside a multi-towered city at the foot of a hill with grazing sheep, a winding road and rich vegetation. The vivid light colours and the naïve atmosphere of a fable serve to minimize the weakness of the drawing. In his manner of suggesting landscape and space, he is representative of a new trend in legend painting, in a style different from that which characterized the work of his predecessors. (See Fig. at Plate 27.)

The inside wing-paintings of an altarpiece from Berzenke
c. 1450

The wings: tempera on pine-wood panel. Each scene measuring 76 × 56 cm
Inv. No. 55.833.1–2, 5–6, 9–10
Transferred in 1939 from the Hungarian National Museum to the Museum of Fine Arts
Bibliography: Radocsay 1955: 72, 96–97, 280–281; Radocsay 1963: 16, 46

The works of the Master of Mateóc illustrate the close connection between Hungary and Poland in the mid-fifteenth century. The painter of this altarpiece probably worked in the workshop of the Master of Mateóc, for he seems to have been acquainted with his work as well as with the panel paintings originating in Little Poland, an area south of Cracow bordering Upper Hungary. In the two scenes depicting the Agony in the Garden and the Virgin of Sorrows the iconographic content is closely related to that seen in the Nedec and Mateóc altars painted by the Master of Mateóc, while the scenes of Christ Carrying the Cross and Christ before Pilate show a knowledge of the altar in Ptaszkowa in Little Poland, painted about 1445–1450. In the style of painting, and the elongated figure of the Virgin, the panels are also related to the Virgin in Czchow. The head of Christ and the representation of the group of soldiers are evocative of the paintings in Ptaszkowa but simpler in form, the architectural elements in the latter being replaced in the panels from Berzenke by a dark wine-coloured background. However, two triangular paintings in the gables of the St. Andrew altar in St. Giles's church at Bártfa show an even closer relationship with the Ptaszkowa altar; in the less significant community of Berzenke the same style is to be seen but in a more provincial form. The outside pictures of this altar illustrate the fact that, historically and geographically, the Master of Mateóc and his workshop were closely connected with Poland.

ASSOCIATE OF THE MASTER OF MATEÓC

The outside wing-paintings of an altarpiece from Berzenke
c. 1450

The wings:
tempera on pine-wood panel.
Size of each scene:
75.5 × 55.5 cm
Inv. No. 55.833.3–4, 7–8
Transferred in 1939
from the Hungarian
National Museum
to the Museum of Fine Arts
Bibliography: Radocsay
1955: 72, 280–281;
Radocsay 1963: 16, 46;
Török 1980: 55–57

1 *The Refusal of Joachim's Sacrifice*
2 *Joachim Grieving*
3 *The Acceptance of Joachim's Sacrifice*
4 *Anne and Joachim at the Golden Gate*
5 *King David*
6 *Prophet Eliseus*
7 *The Agony in the Garden*
8 *Christ Carrying the Cross*
9 *Christ before Pilate*
10 *The Virgin of Sorrows*

27

In his representation of the Nativity for the Németlipcse high altar the painter adopted a type of iconography widely executed in the fifteenth century. Like Master PN (Plate 31), he depicted the Virgin kneeling in worship before her Child. The lantern held by St. Joseph—a more realistic source of light than the candle mentioned in the revelations of St. Bridget—simbolizes the divine radiance of the Holy Child, supreme and eternal. Later the significance of the lantern in St. Joseph's hand was forgotten and it was regarded only as an indication that the scene took place at night. The Child is hailed by a chorus of angels, while the shepherds on the top of the hill realize the glad tidings when they see a star in the sky and an angel appears to them. The painter made no effort to arrange the figures to give a spatial effect, merely filling in the background with the archaic gilding. The large doll-like head of the Virgin is also a convention much employed in the first half of the fifteenth century. All this lends the scene a gentle, naïve atmosphere. The sharp breaks in the folds of the drapery and the violence of the Passion scenes on the altar tell us at first glance that the Németlipcse high altar was created during the years of changing styles that marked the onset of a new age. The ensuing duality in art is manifest both in Polish and Hungarian painting in the mid-fifteenth century. Members of the workshop—presumably large—who painted the multi-panelled high altar and painters in the neighbouring area of Little Poland must have influenced each other, although the link was certainly not as close as that seen in the work of the Master of Mateóc, the most important artist of the mid-century.

The Nativity from the Németlipcse high altar

c. 1450

Tempera on pine-wood panel,
85.5 × 59 cm
Inv. No. 6506
Permanent deposit by the Association of Friends of the Art Museum with the Museum of Fine Arts, 1931
Bibliography:
Radocsay 1955: 73–74, 409–410

In the Middle Ages the church and monastery in Szepesdaróc belonged to the Antonite Order; thus the frescoes of the church represent scenes from the life of St. Anthony, as did the high altar, fragments of which are now in the Gallery. The legend of St. Anthony the Hermit, who so resolutely resisted every temptation proposed by the Devil, was often represented on Hungarian winged altars, for instance the high altar in Zólyomszászfalva, St. Anthony's altar in Szepesszombat and a series of panels from the Szepesbéla altar (Plate 96), which are now in the Gallery.

The bearded, aged hermit is wearing a black cloak on which the T-cross of the Antonites is visible. He carries a staff, as is customary in pictures of this type. In the collection of legends entitled *Legenda aurea,* well known in the Middle Ages, we are told that on one occasion the devil appeared to St. Anthony in the shape of a child who prostrated himself before the saint. But St. Anthony recognized and defeated him by the force of his faith. The painter evidently found it difficult to cope with the then unusual task of painting a prostrate child; he was more successful in depicting the flowers, the bird perched on the rock and the figures of the hermit and Elijah. Although the style of the picture is not directly related to that of the Master of Mateóc, the type of face given to the prophet indicates that the artist must have seen paintings from the Master's workshop. This supposition is corroborated by the fact that, under the influence of the Mateóc high altar, the triangular picture in the gable became a regular feature of the type of altar generally adopted in the Szepes region in the fifteenth century.

The Temptation of St. Anthony the Hermit; in the gable the Prophet Elijah from the Szepesdaróc high altar
1450–1460

Tempera on panel, 80 × 47, and 42 × 40.5 cm, respectively
Inv. No. 55.899
Purchased by the Museum of Fine Arts from Dr. Elemér Kőszeghy in 1944
Bibliography:
Radocsay 1955: 73, 435

The Gallery now owns twelve panels from the high altar of Liptószentmária illustrating the life of the Virgin and the story of the Passion (Plates 31 and 32). Each of the huge wings of the altar was adorned with four scenes. In each triangular painting of the gable is a prophet. The initials PN, believed to be the painter's mark, can be seen both in the Seizure of Christ and on the flag in the Crucifixion.

As in the paintings of the great Netherlandish masters of the fifteenth century here too the setting for the Annunciation is an interior. The representation of the pillared architrave, chequered floor, wooden beams and Gothic windows, all help to give an illusion of space. The spatial effect of Gabriel's figure and the spontaneity of his arrival is well suggested by the mantle fluttering around him in sweeping curves. The Virgin, startled at her prayers by the unexpected arrival of the angel, turns from her reading-stand. This type of representation was particularly popular in Netherlandish painting, one famous example, now in the Louvre, being Rogier van der Weyden's *Annunciation* (*c.* 1435).

MASTER PN

Annunciation from the former high altar in Liptószentmária
1450–1460

Tempera, transferred to a new panel, 95 × 78 cm
Inv. No. 55.890.3
Transferred in 1939 from the Hungarian National Museum to the Museum of Fine Arts
Bibliography:
Radocsay 1955: 73–75, 368–369;
Radocsay 1963: 18, 47

11 / 12 / 13 \ / 17		18 \ / 14 \/ 15 \/ 16			
3	4		7	8	19
	1		2		
5	6		9	10	20

1 St. Barbara
2 St. Catherine
3 The Annunciation
4 The Visitation
5 The Seizure of Christ
6 Christ before Pilate
7 The Nativity

8 The Adoration of the Magi
9 Christ Carrying the Cross
10 The Crucifixion
11 Prophet Samuel
12 Prophet Habakkuk
13 Prophet David

14 Prophet Amos (?)
15 Prophet Jonah
16 Prophet Daniel
17 Prophet Jeremiah
18 Prophet Moses
19 Three Apostles
20 Three Apostles

The iconographic type of the Nativity illustrated here is the Adoration of the Child rather than the Nativity. The theme gained ground under the influence of fourteenth century mysticism as expressed in literature, especially descriptions of the visions of St. Bridget, Queen of Sweden from 1344. According to one account, the Virgin, when her time came, leaned against a pillar and gave birth to her son miraculously without pain. The background of this panel painting is dominated by the two marble pillars of the half ruined roofless building. Such archaic architectural elements in paintings of the Nativity always symbolized Bethlehem. The moment the Child was born the Virgin prayed to Him. Lying in his basket raised like an altar, the Infant turns to his Mother with a gesture of blessing. The yellow ears of wheat in the manger and the Virgin's fair hair hanging below her waist, are some of the notable pictorial details of this panel. The figure of Mary is idealized in the manner of Master PN's Virgins, but other features of the picture indicate that the altarpiece was painted after the middle of the fifteenth century. (See Fig. at Plate 30)

MASTER PN

The Nativity from the former high altar in Liptószentmária
1450–1460

Tempera on pine-wood panel, 96 × 79 cm
Inv. No. 55.890.7
Transferred in 1939 from the Hungarian National Museum to the Museum of Fine Arts
For bibliography see Plate 30

The balance of composition and the rhythmic undulation of the figures against a silver background are especially striking in Master PN's multifigural Christ before Pilate and The Seizure of Christ. In Christ Carrying the Cross the composition is dominated by the figures of Christ and Simon of Cyrene, thus indicating the survival of a type of iconography developed around 1400 and adopted also by Thomas de Coloswar. Although the high altar in Liptószentmária was probably made after the middle of the fifteenth century, the elongated lyric and idealized figures demonstrate that the artistic endeavours of the first half of the century continued to assert themselves alongside the more realistic trends then emerging. In The Crucifixion the distinguished appearance of the soldiers and the fashionable clothing and arms of the fur-capped courtier and his companions provide authentic cultural details of the period. The supposed initials of Master PN can be seen on the flag of the soldier standing at the back. (See Fig. at Plate 30)

MASTER PN

Christ on the Cross from the former high altar in Liptószentmária
1450–1460

Tempera, transferred to a new panel, 91.5 × 77 cm
Inv. No. 55.890.10
Transferred in 1939 from the Hungarian National Museum to the Museum of Fine Arts
For bibliography see Plate 30

On the centre panel of the triptych we see the Virgin and Child with two female saints, a bishop on the obverse of each wing and, on the reverse the Virgin of Sorrows and Man of Sorrows. The whole is so closely related to the high altar of the Virgin Mary from Nagyőr—and this also applies to the elongated figures—that the two altarpieces must be thought of as originating from the same workshop. The iconography and the type of figures also reveal a close link with a whole group of Polish panel paintings. The wings of an altarpiece of Jurków are very closely related to the altarpiece of Liptószentmária, while one from Przydonica comes closest to that from Nagyőr. The white cloak worn by the Liptószentmária Madonna with Child resembles those worn by the Virgin on the altarpiece of the Virgin Mary in Nagyőr and the Polish altars from Cerekiew and Ószandec in that it is characterized by an impressed pattern giving a silvery effect. The silver background is also common in Polish panel paintings. Although the tall slender saints seen here are strongly reminiscent of Master PN's paintings (Plates 30, 31 and 32), they differ in style from the Master's graceful figures. The artist was however associated with the workshop which in the mid-fifteenth century helped to forge an artistic link between Poland and Hungary.

Altarpiece of the Virgin Mary from Liptószentmária
1450–1460

Centre panel:
tempera on lime-wood panel,
85 × 61.5 cm
The inside wings:
Tempera on lime-wood panel,
83 × 25 cm
and 85.5 × 25.5 cm
Inv. No. 55.889.1–3
Transferred in 1939
from the Hungarian
National Museum
to the Museum of Fine Arts
Bibliography: Radocsay
1955: 72–73, 369–370;
Radocsay 1963:
16–18; Török 1980: 78

33

There is a wealth of iconographic detail in this work—originally the central panel of a triptych —representing as it does, in one scene, many characters from the story of the Passion. On the right, the three Marys with jars of ointment, though, according to the Bible it was to the sepulchre that they went on the morning of Easter Sunday; on the left, Joseph of Arimathia and Nicodemus, who took Christ's body from the cross on Friday, the day of the Crucifixion. Together they form a semicircle round the Virgin, grieving as she supports the dead body of her Son in her lap. The Pietà constitutes the central motif in the composition. The elongated figure of Christ, diagonally placed in the composition, reminds us of the Pietà of Avignon. Grief is conveyed in the naïve simplicity of the style. The figures are related in type to those in Polish panels, especially the figure of John the Evangelist who rests his head on one hand, for the same gesture can be seen in the Lamentations from Czarny Potok and Żywiec, and in the figure of a girl mourning the death of St. Emeric on the altar from Mateóc. In the middle of the fifteenth century Polish painting drew its inspiration from the works of the outstanding Master of Lamentation, so named after his painting from Chomranice, which in turn shows the direct influence of a famous Flemish painter, the Master of Flémalle. Although the painter of the Pietà from Turdossin must have seen examples of Polish art—as shown, for example, by the silver background in his pictures—it is apparent from the centrally focussed composition as well as the style that he was by no means dominated by them. The characteristic features of his painting are the delicate tracing of the faces, eyebrows and the outlines of the body of Christ, also the sharp folds of the drapery and the rhythmic alternation of violet, green and red.

The Lamentation from Turdossin
1450–1460

Tempera on poplar panel, 107 × 81.5 cm
Inv. No. 55.918
Transferred in 1939 from the Hungarian National Museum to the Museum of Fine Arts
Bibliography:
Radocsay 1955: 102, 457;
Radocsay 1963: 19, 48

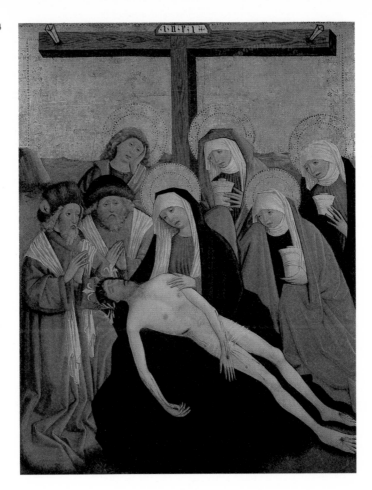

34

This carving is thought to have originated in the former Pauline monastery in Tüskevár, and is the most characteristic example of Transdanubian (Western Hungarian) wood-carving—and indeed of mid-fifteenth century Hungarian wood sculpture in general, of which but little is known. The work is characterized by a combination of Soft Style and the Severe Style of the 1440s, as seen also in the carvings of Jacob of Kassa. The Virgin's veil over her head and her cloak falls in the middle in curving lines which still retain the traditions of the Soft Style, while the drapery gathered up and held in position by her right arm is arranged in sharp folds to form flat surfaces in front and down the sides. This gives the carving a block-like effect. The squat form is relieved only by the round shape of the head and especially by the way the hair is arranged in massive locks, which again is reminiscent of Jacob of Kassa's style. In this carving we see an early indication of the new Severe Style which was to dominate and finally replace the Soft Style characterized by the rhythmic lines seen in the carving of the Beautiful Virgins. This trend is confirmed also by Jacob of Kassa's Virgin for the Freising high altar consecrated in 1443. Here the new style is evident in the lively and naturalistic representation of the Child. The small chubby figure of Jesus reaching out for the hem of the Madonna's robe, also the Madonna's gesture and the folds of her garments, are features which link the work to Hans Multscher's Virgin and Child made for the Sterzing altar (1456–1459). There are in fact many features which link the style of Jacob of Kassa with that of Multscher. Yet the sculptor of the Tüskevár carving did not model his work directly on the art of these masters; he was influenced only by the new style confirmed in their work. His Virgin exemplifies the infiltration of the Severe Style in Hungary in the mid-fifteenth century.

The First Virgin and Child from Tüskevár (?)
1450–1460

Lime-wood,
the original painting worn off.
122 cm
Inv. No. 58.27 M
Donated in 1958
to the Museum of Fine Arts
Bibliography:
Radocsay 1967:
55, 223; Balogh 1957:
233–234

35

There are surprisingly few examples of medieval sculpture from Pozsony, though it was once the gateway to western Europe and, after Buda and Pest, the most important city in the country. As it was the capital of the Hungarian kingdom and the site of the Diet during the Turkish occupation, the churches in Pozsony were constantly modernized, winged altars being considered obsolete and regularly replaced by new ones. The carvings of the Virgin and St. John the Evangelist, originally in the church of the Clarist Order, are the only surviving examples of wood-carving dating from before the end of the fifteenth century. In style they are related to Swabian art of which Hans Multscher's was especially influential, and particularly to the late Sterzing phase, although the soft folds and straightly closed outlines are still characteristic of an earlier style. There is, for example, a striking resemblance between Multscher's motifs and the representation of the Virgin's veil which covers her head and shades her face so that she seems to be looking out of a niche; the introduction of a veil pulled forward over the face is particularly characteristic of the Swabian master's style. In the carving of St. John, the hair, which covers the head like a helmet, and the neck, left naked, serve to emphasize—like the veil in the carving of the Virgin—the plasticity of the head. This same device, namely the breaking up of the mass of the sculpture and the conscious and successful utilization of the sunken "negatives" beside the protruding "positives", is manifest also in the art of Nikolaus Gerhaert van Leyden, a contemporary of Multscher, though younger than he. Towards the end of his life, at the time the Pozsony statues were created, Gerhaert van Leyden was active in Wiener Neustadt at the invitation of Emperor Frederick; his work must therefore have been instrumental in widening the sphere of Multscher's influence. It is noteworthy, for instance, that on the red marble effigy of Provost György Schomberg (Schönberg) on his tomb in the Pozsony collegiate church the Provost's head is covered by a cowl so that he too seems to be looking out of a niche. As he died in 1470, the tomb, made shortly afterwards, must surely have influenced the sculptural style of the local artists.

The Virgin and St. John the Evangelist from Pozsony
1460–1470

Lime-wood panel, re-painted, 67.5 and 67 cm
Inv. No. 53.365–53.366
Transferred in 1939 from the Hungarian National Museum to the Museum of Fine Arts

Bibliography:
Radocsay 1967: 73, 206–207;
Homolka 1972: 16–17

36

The Virgin from Bártfa was not part of a winged altar but an independent picture which may have been hung to serve for private devotion. Originally the frame was decorated, as was the custom for devotional pictures at that time with reliquaries or precious stones, traces of which can still be seen. Fifteenth century painters who represented the Virgin with the Infant Jesus in her lap were able to draw on an inexhaustible mine of iconographic prototypes. The Infant turning over the pages of a book is actually a motif originating in Netherlandish art and was first employed by Rogier van der Weyden. Half-length Virgins represented against a gilded background on panels set in ornamental frames, similar to this picture from Bártfa, were equally popular among painters in Upper Hungary and Poland in the late fifteenth century. In addition to the Virgins from Liptónádasd and Kassa, which are also in the Gallery (Plate 79), similar paintings from Tum, Cracow and Wrocław are to be mentioned. In style the painting illustrated here is closely related to Polish painting, especially the representations of female saints which are decorating the altar of the Holy Trinity (1467) in the Cathedral of Cracow. On the basis of the scenes represented on the reverse of the shutters, Polish art historians have named the artist as "the Master of Choirs"; however, some experts have identified him as Jacob, Master of Szandec, whose authenticated works can be seen in Cracow, Szandec and Bártfa. Although the identity of this artist may still be in doubt, it is certain that from the middle of the fifteenth century, there developed a fertile and lively interaction between the painting of the Szepes region and Sáros, and that of neighbouring Little Poland and Cracow—as seen also in the works of the Master of Mateóc. This artistic connection is splendidly exemplified in the Virgin from Bártfa.

The Virgin and Child from Bártfa

1465–1470

Tempera on lime-wood,
59 × 44 cm,
including original frame
Inv. No. 55.908
Transferred in 1939
from the Hungarian
National Museum
to the Museum of Fine Arts
Bibliography: Radocsay
1955: 98, 164–165, 265;
Radocsay 1963: 20, 48–49
Polak–Trajdos 1970:
121, Plates 114–115;
Spätmittelalter und
beginnende Neuzeit.
Ed. by J. Białostocki.
Berlin, 1972.
206–207. Plate 83

37

On the edge of the bottom step of the throne we can see the sign G 1471 H, indicating the master's initials and the date of origin. On either side of the steps is the coat of arms of the patron, János Ernuszt, citizen of Buda. Ernuszt was Treasurer to King Matthias and in 1470 was appointed Lord Lieutenant of Turóc County.

It can be assumed that since his patron was a member of the aristocracy, Master GH was in touch with artists in Buda, the seat of the Court, and that the altar therefore reflects the art of panel painting in Buda, of which no examples have survived.

In this picture, now in the Gallery, the Holy Trinity as the Throne of Mercy represents a special iconographic type. God the Father is depicted enthroned and holding his crucified Son before him, while the third member of the Trinity hovers above the head of Christ in the shape of a dove. The throne is covered by a "heavenly tabernacle" with curtains held apart by angels. Although this type of Holy Trinity picture had been known since the twelfth century, it was revived by the cult of venerating the body of Christ in the late fourteenth and early fifteenth centuries. The tabernacle, with curtains drawn aside to dramatize the subject, is first seen in Netherlandish painting towards the end of the 1430s in a painting by the Master of Flémalle, now in Leningrad. Thus the picture by Master GH bears witness to the widespread influence of this famous master. The impact of Netherlandish art on Master GH's work is, however, also evident for instance in the elongated type of face given to the angels reminiscent of those in Dirk Bouts's paintings, and again in the representation of gems set in the hem of the garments and the halo of God the Father. The pictures adorning the wings also reveal the influence of Netherlandish painting.

MASTER GH

The Throne of Mercy. Central panel of the Holy Trinity triptych from Mosóc
1471

Tempera, transferred to a new panel; the upper corner restored.
137 × 107 cm
Inv. No. 52.645
Acquired in 1937 from the Lajos Ernst Collection for the Museum of Fine Arts
Bibliography:
Radocsay 1955: 99–100, 392

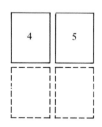

1 *The Holy Trinity*
2 *The Crucifixion*
3 *The Death of the Virgin*
4 *Angel from the Annunciation*
5 *The Virgin from the Annunciation*

The scene of the Annunciation extends over the outer side of two wings and could be seen in its entirety when the altarpiece was closed. The upper section of the inside wings, visible when the altarpiece was opened, represented the Crucifixion and the Death of the Virgin, both of which are also in the Gallery. (They became separated from the outer side.) The centre panel showed The Throne of Mercy (Plate 38).

The Annunciation is set in an interior with an open door and a row of windows overlooking an airy landscape of trees and hills. Gabriel greets the Virgin in the words *gratia plena dominus tecum* inscribed on the streaming banderole. The sharply broken shaded folds of the robes are used by Master GH to give a statuesque appearance to his figures which have the elongated faces characteristic of his work. The spatial effect is achieved not only through the chequered floor and realistically painted beams, the open door and the reading-stand, but also through an aerial perspective first applied in Netherlandish painting, in which the lower parts of the blue sky become gradually paler.

On the exterior of the wings of the altarpiece in Ghent created by the Van Eyck brothers (1432), the Annunciation is similarly given an indoor setting in a painting which extends over four panels. The Hungarian master modelled his work on this famous altarpiece not only with regard to arrangement and composition, but also in composing a low-ceilinged interior with a row of windows giving a view of a distant landscape. The altarpiece of Mosóc provides eloquent proof that the achievements of western European panel painting were being absorbed in Hungary in the late fifteenth century, and that painters were recomposing the well-known iconographic solutions in their characteristic fashion. (See Fig. at Plate 38.)

MASTER GH

Two panels of the Holy Trinity triptych from Mosóc
1471

Tempera on pine-wood panel,
64.5 × 51 cm
Inv. No. 52.647
and 64.5 × 51 cm
Inv. No. 52.646
Acquired in 1958
from the Lajos Ernst
Collection for the Museum
of Fine Arts
Bibliography:
Radocsay 1955: 99–100, 392; Radocsay 1963: 20, 49

39

The high altar of the church in Jánosrét was created, as was customary, to venerate the patron saint of the church. The carving in the shrine represents the titular saint while on the hinged shutters there are paintings depicting scenes from his life. One unique feature of the altar is that the central part does not consist of one single large shrine intended to house carvings. Only the figure of St. Nicholas stands in a niche; the rest of the shrine is covered by panels, as are the wings. The structure is interesting in that it represents a transition between the earlier type of altarpieces consisting merely of panel paintings and the later winged altars with a central section filled with carvings, the paintings being confined to the wings. The painted figures flanking St. Nicholas in the central shrine are independent of the narrative scenes of the wings and more related to the carving of the saint. The arrangement of the four small saintly bishops around St. Nicholas, the painted supporting brackets, the projecting carved tracery and columns, all tend to create the illusion that the standing figures are carved statues of the frame of the central shrine. This impression is enhanced by the suggestion of spatial depth created by the arrangement of the figures of St. Peter and St. Paul, and the plasticity of their garments. As parts of the central shrine—which demanded a sculptural solution—were in fact adorned with paintings, some art historians have concluded that the artist was first and foremost a painter whom they have named after this work the Master of Jánosrét.

THE MASTER OF JÁNOSRÉT

St. Nicholas high altar from Jánosrét
c. 1476

Central shrine:
carving in lime-wood, painted. 153 cm
Left fields on the shrine:
153 × 37.5 cm;
71.5 × 13 cm; 78 × 11.5 cm
Right fields on the shrine:
152.5 × 39 cm;
71.5 × 12.5 cm; 78 × 11 cm
The wings:
tempera on panel,
155 × 98 and 154 × 98 cm
The predella:
painted wood,
32 × 237 × 30 cm
Inv. No. 53.903.1–20
Transferred in 1939 from the Hungarian National Museum to the Museum of Fine Arts

Bibliography:
Radocsay 1955: 103–105, 337–338;
Stange 1961: 152;
Radocsay 1967: 73–74, 176

40

7	8		2		5		11	12
		1		I		4		
9	10		3		6		13	14

15	16

On the Jánosrét high altar there are eight paintings depicting the miracles of St. Nicholas. Of the four on the inside left wing the first picture shows the best known act of the saint: a gift of gold to the three daughters of the poor nobleman. St. Nicholas appears in full pontificals, a mitre on his head and a crosier in his hand. He is represented in a larger scale than that used for the other figures in the picture. Through a large window we can see the interior of a Gothic house where the three daughters are sleeping. The poor nobleman who in his plight was on the verge of forcing his daughters to pursue an illicit profession, prevented by St. Nicholas's gift, is represented by the painter in beggar's clothes.

The upper right panel shows the saint calming the tempestuous seas in answer to the prayers of storm-tossed voyagers. Although the realistic details, for example the sail, the barrel, the clothes and the lively gestures, all indicate careful observation, the huge half-length figure of St. Nicholas descending from the clouds and that of the devil breaking the mast, ensure the legendary atmosphere.

The story of the false swearing before the judge and the miracle of the gold hidden in a staff are closely connected and are therefore placed next to each other in the lower part of the left wing. The legend concerns a Christian who borrowed money from a Jew and swore before St. Nicholas's altar that he would repay the loan. But when the time came he swore before the judge on the Crucifix that he had already returned the money to the Jew. He had in fact cunningly handed over the staff containing the hidden gold—but only for the minutes when he was actually taking the oath, and his creditor had no idea of its contents. The last picture shows the consequences of this deceit. On his way home the Christian, overcome by fatigue, fell asleep on the road and was crushed to death by a passing coach. His staff broke and the gold coins rolled over the road. Passers-by advised the Jew to take what was due to him, but he wished only for the resurrection of the dead Christian. When this actually took place in answer to St. Nicholas's prayers the Jew, overcome by the miracle, decided to adopt the Christian faith. The scenes follow closely the text of the legend and the linear representation is illustrative in character.

THE MASTER OF JÁNOSRÉT

Scenes from the legend of St. Nicholas. Paintings on the inside left wing of the St. Nicholas high altar from Jánosrét
c. 1476

Tempera on panel,
155 × 98 cm
Inv. No. 53.903. 11–14
Transferred in 1939
from the Hungarian
National Museum
to the Museum of Fine Arts
Bibliography:
Radocsay 1955:
103–105, 337–338

The most successful of the paintings adorning the St. Nicholas high altar of Jánosrét, are those on the exterior of the panels. These represent the Agony in the Garden and the Crucifixion. Here the style is more mature than that of the legendary scenes represented on the interior. The impact of Netherlandish painting is clearly evident in the detailed landscape background—a feature unusual in earlier Hungarian panel painting—and also in some of the motifs adopted in Hungary from German art. The motif of the Mary Magdalen embracing the Cross, used by Eyck and Rogier, was transmitted to the Master of Jánosrét through one of the engravings of Master ES (Lehrs 30), while the figures of the Virgin and St. John on the left of the Cross and of the Captain on the right, bear witness to the influence and accurate imitation of Schongauer's engraving (Lehrs 10). In the late Middle Ages it was a general custom to copy the works of famous masters, taking over the whole composition or extracting details from it—a practice greatly facilitated by the development of wood-cuts and engravings in the fifteenth century. These borrowings facilitate the dating of any given altarpiece. The more conservative episodes from the life of St. Nicholas (Plate 41) were probably painted shortly before 1476; the Agony in the Garden and the Crucifixion are believed to be of a somewhat later date. The two latter panels may be the work of a gifted painter employed in the workshop of the Master of Jánosrét. He uses a great variety of shades rich in tone, and his style is softer and more painterly than that of the Master. In representing the landscape—which in his pictures does not form a detached background but, together with the figures, is an integral part of the composition—he applies the laws of aerial perspective, painting the distant mountains in paler shades.

THE MASTER OF JÁNOSRÉT

Crucifixion. Exterior of the right wing from the St. Nicholas high altar from Jánosrét
c. 1476

Tempera on panel, 154 × 98 cm
Bibliography:
Radocsay 1955: 103–105, 337–338;
Hoffmann, Edith: Jegyzetek a régi magyar táblaképfestészethez [Notes on old Hungarian panel painting]. AÉ I (1937), 8–9, 10–11, 26;
Lehrs: II. 30; V.10

Originally one of the side altars in St. Nicholas's Church, Jánosrét, together with the high altar and another altarpiece of the Passion from the same church, it can now be seen in the Gallery. In larger churches it was not unusual to have several altarpieces; the church at Bártfa, for example, is decorated with eleven winged altars even today.

Since the carvings of the Virgin and St. Dorothy resemble the female saints depicted on the right wing, it is most probable that the carvings and paintings were by the same artist. The carving and painting of the sharp folds of the garments are in contrast to the idealized faces reminiscent of works from the first half of the century. There is a naïve sentimentality in the elongated figure of the Infant clinging to His Mother's neck. The huge, richly carved crowns serve to break up the closed bulk of the figures, and also lend them a particular charm. The framework on the upper part of the shrine gives rise to the belief that the openwork pinnacles once embellishing the altarpiece must also have been richly carved.

The paintings on the outer side are of a later date and were made by changing a previous scene which is evidenced by the fact that the bust of God the Father was originally the portrait of a prophet. The floriate ornamentation under the Annunciation also dates from the time the other changes were made. The charming naïveté of the paintings and carvings are typical of the local style of the mining town.

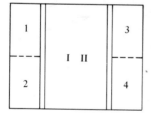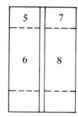

Altarpiece of the Virgin and St. Dorothy from Jánosrét

1470–1480

Carvings of the shrine:
painted lime-wood,
107 and 109 cm,
respectively
Interior of the left wing:
tempera on pine-wood,
each scene measuring
62 × 42 cm
Interior of the right wing:
tempera on pine-wood,
each scene measuring
62.5 × 40.5 cm
Inv. No 55.905.1–5, 7–8
Transferred in 1939
from the Hungarian
National Museum
to the Museum of Fine Arts
Bibliography:
Radocsay 1955:
105–106, 338–339;
Radocsay 1967: 74, 176–177

I The Virgin and Child
II St. Dorothy
1 St. Peter
    with a Bishop Saint
2 St. Bartholomew
    with St. John
    the Evangelist
3 St. Barbara
    with St. Dorothy
4 St. Margaret
    with St. Apollonia
5 Half-length portrait
    of God the Father
6 Angel
    from the Annunciation
7 Half-length portrait
    of a prophet
8 The Virgin
    from the Annunciation

43

Outside a medieval town masons working on the town-wall are depicted attacking a gentle-faced bishop with stones, trowels and hammers. A similar scene is represented on a panel from Újszandec in which heathen Prussians are seen driving away the evangelizer St. Adalbert with gestures similar to those of the masons, their arms raised to throw stones. The cult of St. Adalbert, a Prague bishop of the tenth century, spread quickly to Hungary and Poland. For instance, the cathedral in Esztergom was dedicated to him and his image is represented there on the ornate main portal, the twelfth century *Porta speciosa*. At his burial place in Gniezno (Poland), a twelfth century bronze gate in the local cathedral evidences his cult. However, it is comparatively rare to find representations of the life of this saint on surviving Gothic altarpieces.

The relationship between this panel and Polish painting of the period—very clearly evident on the altar of the Holy Trinity in the Cathedral in Cracow—has long been known, but research workers have not, so far, studied the significance of the unusually emphasized *veduta* that fills the greater part of the picture and seems to represent an ideal view of Cracow. *Vedute* depicted on panels can seldom be identified with any certainty and are never equal to engravings in respect of topographic accuracy. Nevertheless, in this painting, several emphasized motifs lead us to suppose that the picture represents Cracow: the clear representation of the castle hill, the Wawel, and the wall-enclosed town with its numerous churches, among them the one dedicated to the Virgin Mary, with a collapsed tower as described in the legend. On the badly damaged reverse of the panel are paintings of a Franciscan monk and a burning church reminiscent of the Franciscan church in Cracow.

The Expulsion of St. Adalbert. Provenance unknown
1470–1480

Tempera on pine-wood, 87 × 99 cm
Inv. No. 1638
Acquired by the National Museum from the Miklós Jankovich Collection

Bibliography:
Radocsay 1955: 324;
Lajta, Edit:
Két adalék a magyarországi középkori festészet ikonográfiájához
[Two commentaries on the iconography of medieval painting in Hungary].
MÉ VII (1958), 116–119;
Lajta, Edit:
Wygnanie świętego Wojciecha
[The Expulsion of St. Adalbert].
Biuletyn Historii Sztuki XXI (1959), 329–334

44

This representation of the Man of Sorrows *(Imago Pietatis)* is clearly intended for devotional purposes. It is completely detached from the events of the Passion. The intention, as in the Pietà, was to elicit sympathy for the sufferings of Christ among the faithful of the Middle Ages. As in thirteenth century Byzantine icons, the Man of Sorrows is depicted standing in a sarcophagus, crowned with thorns and displaying his wounds, while the Virgin caresses him gently, expressing her feelings by placing her cheek on that of her Son. The two angels in the background holding the brocade curtain are reminiscent of "angel Pietà" scenes, while the elaborate raised and gilded gesso of the frame and background are similar to those seen on the devotional Virgin pictures (Liptónádasd, Kassa, Plate 79). The panel in the Hungarian National Gallery is one of the finest examples of a type of painting which in the fifteenth century was popular throughout Europe. Other panels most closely akin to it are of Polish origin and come from Iwanowice, Biecz, Zbylitowska Góra and Ószandec. The style, seen in the realistic, stiff folds of the draperies, shows the influence of the Passion scenes painted for the high altar in Kassa in 1470.

Man of Sorrows from Kassa
1470–1480

Tempera on pine-wood, 47.5 × 36 cm; with original frame: 63 × 52 cm
Inv. No 55.911
Transferred in 1939 from the Hungarian National Museum to the Museum of Fine Arts
Bibliography:
Radocsay 1955: 118, 347;
Polak-Trajdos 1970: 153;
Cf. Walicki, Michał: Malarstwo polskie XV. wieku [Painting in Poland in the 15th century]. Warszawa, 1938. 19, 69, 132;
Walicki, Michał: Malarstwo polskie. Gotyk, renesans, wczesny manieryzm [Painting in Poland. Gothic, Renaissance, Mannerism]. Warszawa, 1961, Plates 22 and 40

45

It is not certain that the two figures are from Jánosrét; some sources mention the carvings as
originating from Besztercebánya. However, the two
communities are situated so close to each other that
the statues may have been made for the Jánosrét
church in a Besztercebánya workshop; they are, in
any case, products of the school of wood-carving
associated with the latter mining town. Carved Crucifixions, always showing the Virgin of Sorrows on
the left of the Cross and John the Evangelist on the
right, were very popular in Upper Hungary where
they embellished the triumphal arch of the churches.
As they were placed so high they were often made
larger than life-size; it would therefore seem that
these small carvings were made to stand in the shrine
of an altarpiece of the Passion arranged as described
above. Crucifixions of this type are known from
Bártfa and Bakabánya; the latter composition includes also the two thieves, the Mary Magdalen
kneeling at the foot of the Cross and the figures of
Longinus and the Captain. The Crucifixion group
from Jánosrét is characterized by graceful elongated
proportions. No other figures similar to these are
known, but a distant parallel may be drawn between
them and the statues of the Pipping Calvary created
by a prominent South German sculptor, Erasmus
Grasser, in the 1480s. The closed outlines of the Jánosrét figures are relieved by the softly flowing drapery, especially that of the mantle hanging over
St. John's left arm. The position of the Virgin's
hands and the curve in the middle of her cloak can
be traced back to an engraving by Schongauer. The
almost perpendicular fall of the drapery on her right
closes the outline of the slender figure like an ex-
clamation mark. The facial expressions of both the
Virgin and St. John are as undemonstrative as the
line of their garments; the elongated faces express
controlled grief.

**The Virgin Mary and
St. John the
Evangelist
from the Crucifixion
from Jánosrét (?)**
c. 1480

Painted lime-wood,
93 and 94 cm respectively
Inv. No. 55.835.1–2
Purchased by the Museum
of Fine Arts in 1934
Bibliography: Radocsay
1967: 77, 177;
Balogh 1957: 245

46

The God of the Bible is usually described as appearing out of the clouds. It is from the clouds that He speaks to the people in the Old Testament, and to the disciples at the Transfiguration of Christ. After the Ascension from the Mount of Olives, Christ is "carried up into heaven". When therefore a legendary episode selected for an altarpiece required the representation of Christ giving His blessing, the Saviour was depicted as a half-length figure emerging from a cloud. The subject for altarpieces was generally a vision seen by a saint or a miracle performed by a saint. The introduction of Christ was intended to convey to the faithful the lesson that the miracle was performed not by the saint personally but by the saint as an instrument of God's will. In this carving Christ's downcast eyes prove that it must have appeared above the main scene. The youthful character of the head excludes the possibility of its representing God the Father, though it is very similar to the carved figure decorating the Altar of the Annunciation at Kisszeben (Plate 109).

The same gesture of blessing can be seen in the left upper corner of the picture of St. Anthony (Plate 96) from Szepesbéla, and in the carved figure illustrated here the missing hand must also have held an orb.

The statue recalls the work of Master E S, the famous engraver of the Upper-Rhine region, whose prints served as models for numerous artists both in Hungary and in other countries. The wavy hair, soft drapery and rather dreamy eyes all point to Master E S, to some extent directly (see his engraving Lehrs No. 57/I) and also indirectly, through statues based on the engraving mentioned above. The most famous of these was carved by Nicolas Hagenower some years later, and is to be seen on the Isenheim altar with panels painted by Grünewald.

Christ,
Giving His Blessing.
Provenance unknown
c. 1480

Lime-wood,
painted but now worn;
38 cm
Inv. No. 59.1.11
Purchased
by the Museum of Fine Arts
from Mária Péter in 1959
Bibliography:
Radocsay 1967:
86, 172; cf. Lehrs: 57/I

47

The Master of the Szmrecsány high altar was an artist with an individual style manifest in both panels and statues which he made for numerous altars in the Szepes region. Such twofold activity was not rare in the Middle Ages when painters and wood-carvers co-operated closely within the guilds, and the painting of carved wooden statues required the same technical skills as panel painting. It was possible for the painting, gilding, carving and cabinet-work necessary for the creation of an altar to be completed by one man; but when commissioned to produce a large altarpiece the master would divide the work among his pupils and associates. The design and the most exacting techniques were done by the master himself whose style, adopted by his pupils, was then passed on to other artists. The altar of the Master of Szmrecsány may have been produced by a group of artists in this way. Two of his altarpieces are now in the Gallery: the Nagyszalók and the Szepeshely Virgin Mary altars. These are identical as to composition, and the figures are also very similar. The central narrow shrine contains a standing figure of the Virgin surrounded by small carvings or paintings of four female saints. The wings are adorned with scenes set one above the other. The interior of the left panel shows the usual fourteenth century iconography of the Annunciation with the Infant Jesus, which by the end of the fifteenth century must have appeared archaic, yet was well adapted to the painter's conservative style. The naïve simplicity of the work evidently contributed to its popularity and widespread influence.

THE MASTER OF THE SZMRECSÁNY HIGH ALTAR

The Annunciation from the altarpiece of the Virgin Mary in Szepeshely

c. 1480

Tempera on pine-wood,
83 × 68.5 cm
Inv. No. 55.913.6
Transferred in 1939
from the Hungarian
National Museum
to the Museum of Fine Arts
Bibliography:
Radocsay 1955:
128–129, 440

I   The Virgin and Child
1   St. Catherine
2   St. Dorothy
3   St. Barbara
4   St. Margaret
5   The Nativity
6   The Annunciation
7   The Adoration of the Magi
8   The Visitation
9   The Virgin of Sorrows
10 St. John the Evangelist
11 The Man of Sorrows
12 Mary Magdalen

An examination of the carved and painted figures shows that they are all of the same type—doll-like, gentle, with elongated faces, large eyes, high foreheads and curved eyebrows. These features are peculiar to the naïve style of the Master of the Szmrecsány high altar. The oval face is in harmony with the striking slenderness of the figure of the Virgin, an effect enhanced by the carefully carved long plaits of hair and the heavy drapery of her robes falling in parallel lines on the left side and at the front. Yet the figure is well balanced, for the cloak forms several deep hollow folds under the left arm and fans out at the lower edge to give stability to the figure. The little angels playing the lute as they peer out from the fluted hem, also the round-faced Infant illustrate the charming individual style which characterizes the work of the Master of the Szmrecsány high altar. (See Fig. at Plate 48.)

THE MASTER OF THE SZMRECSÁN HIGH ALTAR

Virgin and Child from the altarpiece of the Virgin Mary in Szepeshely
c. 1480

Painted
and gilded lime-wood,
153 cm
Inv. No. 55.919
Transferred in 1939
from the Hungarian
National Museum
to the Museum of Fine Arts
Bibliography:
Radocsay 1967:
85–86, 215

This figure of the angel Gabriel, also that of the Virgin now in the museum at Bártfa, were once part of a group representing the Annunciation. A similar composition has survived from the Kisszeben Annunciation Altar (Plate 109). Originally the archangel Gabriel may have held a rod and a banderole inscribed *Ave Maria gratia plena* in his left hand; his gesture and a whole series of analogous paintings suggest this possibility (cf. Plates 38, 39 and 101 of the Mosóc Holy Trinity altarpiece and of the Kisszeben high altar). The original arrangement of the figures was also similar in all these compositions: the angel appears to the left of the Virgin who is shown kneeling, holding a book, her head turned back in amazement. Although the group of the Annunciation comes from Frics in Sáros county, the deeply cut sharp folds point to a close relationship with sculptures originating from the Szepes region and the mining towns, particularly the carvings on the altarpiece of The Man of Sorrows at Lőcse and the high altar at Garamszentbenedek.

Restoration of the carving revealed the meticulous detail of the carefully painted face; also one can still see traces of a clasp on the gilded cloak lined with blue, and applied ornaments on the hem of the cloak. The dress, originally silver, is now dominated by the red bole used for grounding. The green lustre at the root of the wings—the ends of which had to be largely completed—suggests that they were once brilliantly coloured, like the wings in the Mosóc panel (Plate 39).

The Angel from the Annunciation from Frics

c. 1480

Painted and gilded lime-wood, 82 cm
Inv. No. 52.648
Deposited by the National Commission for Public Collections in the Museum of Fine Arts in 1937
Bibliography:
Radocsay 1967: 68, 77, 165;
Homolka 1972: Plates 114, 119-120

50

From the mid-fifteenth century the background of the Virgin Enthroned was more and more often closed with an ornamental curtain, generally held by angels. This was particularly suitable as a background on the central panel of a large triptych. In Hungarian medieval painting it was first used on the Mateóc high altar created after 1453. Behind the standing saints on the wings the background was usually a wall; this device, like the curtain on the centre panel, was particularly common in paintings from the Szepes region. In the centre panels of the Jánosfalva and Arnótfalva altarpieces—dating from the same period as that from Liptószentandrás—the Virgin Enthroned is depicted with a female saint on either side, but in the Liptószentandrás altar the large seated figure of the Virgin fills the whole composition. In executing this figure the painter was confronted by new problems and perhaps that is why at first glance the picture appears somewhat laboured. Yet the Master succeeded in his attempt, providing a foil for the large face of the Virgin by introducing the sweeping curves of her cloak with pale green lining and by a symmetric arrangement of the angels holding it in the foreground. A marked gift for the painterly can be seen in the representation of the precious stones and the Madonna's wavy fair hair; also in the shaded face of the Infant and the Virgin, and the emphasis on the broken folds of the cloak.

Triptych of the Virgin Mary from Liptószentandrás

c. 1480

Centre panel:
tempera on pine-wood,
162 × 171 cm
Interiors of the wings:
tempera on lime-wood,
each scene 78.5 × 55 cm
Predella:
tempera on pine-wood,
54 × 221 cm
Inv. No. 53.570. 1–6
Transferred in 1936
from the
Hungarian National Museum
to the Museum of Fine Arts
Bibliography:
Radocsay 1955:
129, 365

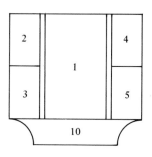

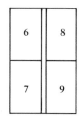

1 *The Virgin Enthroned*
2 *St. Barbara*
3 *Pope St. Martin*
4 *St. Dorothy*
5 *St. Leonard*
6 *The Agony in the Garden*
7 *The Crowning with Thorns*
8 *The Flagellation*
9 *The Crucifixion*
10 *The Veronica*

51

These two carvings are thought to have decorated one and the same altarpiece, but it is unlikely that they come from the superstructure or side-niches of the huge high altar of Kassa Cathedral. This assumption is also precluded by the great difference in style between these figures and the carvings of the shrine of the Kassa altarpiece. The two saints are realistically represented as old men with lined faces, circles under the eyes and with wrinkled necks—very different from the idealized main figures of the Kassa altarpiece. The garments are in the late Gothic style, the folds of the draperies deeply carved and falling in repeated sharply broken waves.

St. Jerome is represented as a Cardinal with a young lion clinging to his robes. It is thought that originally the saint held in his hand the thorn he had extracted from the animal's paw, for it was thus that the saint was frequently depicted. St. Gregory, one of the outstanding Popes of early Christendom, is shown wearing a three-tiered crown. He is holding an open book—a reference to his writings—and it is thought that originally a carved dove—his symbol —would have been perched on the open page.

**St. Jerome
and St. Gregory
from Kassa**
c. 1480

Lime-wood, painted,
79 and 78.5 cm,
respectively
Inv. No. 7183, 55.880
Transferred in 1939
from the
Hungarian National Museum
to the Museum of Fine Arts
Bibliography:
Radocsay, Dénes:
Der Hochaltar
von Kaschau und
Gregor Erhart. AHA VII
(1960) 28, 31, 37;
Radocsay 1967:
64, 179–180

52

Almost all the paintings and statues from the altarpiece have survived, but the former superstructure from above the shrine is missing. It is almost certain that this upper part of the altarpiece was embellished with three carvings from Cserény which are now in the museum in Besztercebánya. The sharply carved blocklike figures from the shrine are fine examples of the consistent development of the mid-fifteenth century Severe Style. In this respect they are related to the carvings of the Garamszentbenedek high altar and the Lőcse altarpiece of the Man of Sorrows, also created around 1483.

The inner and outer paintings (Plate 54) represent eight episodes from the life of St. Martin, a series obviously influenced by the Master of Jánosrét. However close the composition of these legendary scenes comes to that of the Master's work on the St. Nicholas high altar (Plate 40), the pictorial language is much more crude; indeed the Cserény painter's style is that of an apprentice. Yet the similarity between the two altarpieces leaves us in no doubt that they originate from the same workshop and demonstrate the close relationship between the art of the mining town and that of neighbouring Zólyom.

WORKSHOP OF THE MASTER OF JÁNOSRÉT

The St. Martin altarpiece from Cserény
1483

Statues in the centre niche: lime-wood, painted, 147, 135 and 147 cm, respectively
Inside panels of the wings: tempera on pine-wood.
Each scene 79.5 × 75 cm
Predella:
tempera on pine-wood, 45.5 × 197.5 cm
Inv. No. 3279
From 1880 in the Church of Our Lady, Buda Castle; later transferred to the Museum of Fine Arts, probably between 1901–1907
Bibliography:
Radocsay 1955: 105, 136, 286;
Radocsay 1967: 159

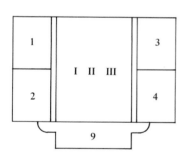
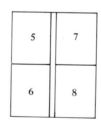

I St. Martin
II St. John the Evangelist
III St. Nicholas
1 St. Martin and the Beggar
2 The Temptation of St. Martin
3 St. Martin's Mass at Albenga

4 St. Martin Healing the Sick
5 St. Martin Taking Leave of His Disciples
6 St. Martin Healing a Child
7 St. Martin's Death
8 The Burial of St. Martin
9 The Veronica

The inscription in minuscules on the lower frame of the closed wings gives the date when it was made and the name of the donor, no doubt a worthy burgher of Cserény. *"Anno domini 1483 completum est hoc opus in die sancte barbare: istas tabulas iussit fieri honestus vir Georgius Petrovits"* (Completed on St. Barbara's day in the year of our Lord 1483. This winged altar was commisioned by the honorable György Petrovits). On the outer panels, as on the inner ones (Plate 53), there are fairly accurate representations of episodes from the life of St. Martin of Pannonia. In style and pictorial language they are closely related to those of the St. Nicholas high altar from Jánosrét (Plate 40). Yet, in spite of a similarity in the treatment of internal space, architectural detail and vividly evocative gestures, and even in the facial types, it is evident that the Master of Jánosrét was a more gifted and creative artist. The somewhat hard and less painterly style of the Cserény altarpiece is related to the panels of the Garamszentbenedek altarpiece of the Crucifixion, a product of the workshop of the Master of Jánosrét. (See Fig. at Plate 53)

WORKSHOP OF THE MASTER OF JÁNOSRÉT

The St. Martin altarpiece from Cserény (closed)
1483

Tempera on pine-wood.
Each scene 79.5 × 75 cm
Inv. No. 3279
For detailed data and bibliography see Plate 53

54

This altarpiece of the Passion was a small side-altar in St. Nicholas Church at Jánosrét. The superstructure and predella are lost. The artist who painted and carved the altar was clearly a member of the workshop of the Master of Jánosrét. The relief in the central shrine shows the Lamentation—the Virgin mourning over the deposed body of her Son. The paintings on the wings represent the story of the Passion. The figures in the relief suggest the distant influence of Veit Stoss's engravings, also the relief illustrating the same subject on the altarpiece of the Virgin Mary in Cracow (1477–1489). This influence is apparent in the seated figure of Christ, the ornamental head-dress characteristic of Netherlandish art worn by Mary Magdalen, the crown of thorns taken from the head of Christ and the rock indicated in the background. The drapery in the foreground, thrown open shell-like, also evokes the dramatic style of Veit Stoss. Another similarly composed relief of not much later date decorates the Brzezina altar in Poland; here there is a striking similarity in the figure of Nicodemus supporting Christ from behind. The realistic rendering of Christ's blood flowing down His body, as well as the stark features of painted Passion scenes, demonstrate the naturalistic trend in late Gothic art.

**The altarpiece
of the Passion
from Jánosrét**
1480–1490

The carving
of the central shrine:
painted
and gilded lime-wood,
95.5 × 83.5 cm
Inside panels of the wings:
tempera on pine-wood.
Each scene 54 × 38.5 cm
Inv. No. 55.904.1–9
Transferred in 1939
from the
Hungarian National Museum
to the Museum
of Fine Arts

Bibliography:
Radocsay 1955:
105, 339–340;
Radocsay 1967: 74, 176;
Polak–Trajdos 1970: 83;
Homolka 1972: 394

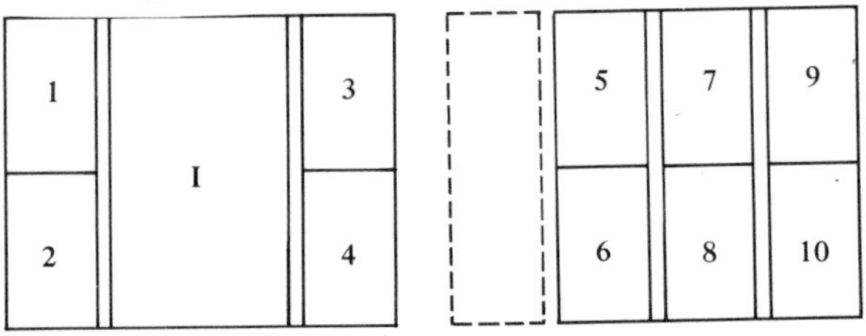

I The Lamentation
1 Christ Stripped
  of His Garments
2 The Resurrection
3 Christ Carrying the Cross
4 The Entombment

5 The Agony in the Garden
6 The Crowning with Thorns
7 The Betrayal of Christ
8 The Flagellation
9 Christ before Pilate
10 Ecce Homo

55

The composition, similar to the relief of the Passion altar (Plate 55) from Jánosrét, is a fine example of the relationship between the carvings produced in different mining towns; it also serves to indicate the popularity of this type of iconography in the late fifteenth century. It is carved in low relief and was undoubtedly attached to a painted background to decorate the wing of a small altar. The composition of the relief has been influenced by the Netherlandish painting. The position of Christ's body, turned sideways and lying in a diagonal line is similar to one of Veit Stoss's engravings and the relief on the Cracow high altar. The motif of the Virgin and the Mary Magdalen holding Christ's arm had already been used in the Jánosrét altar; however, by representing the left arm stretched out straight, the master of the Tájó relief added a distinct structural element to the composition. The straight line continues in Mary Magdalen's shawl, so that her standing, rather than kneeling figure becomes the corner-stone of the composition. St. John the Evangelist is holding Christ as he is usually shown holding the fainting Mary under the Cross or in scenes of the Last Prayer of the Virgin. The curve of his fluttering cloak is a quieter, more moderate version of Veit Stoss's draperies.

The Lamentation from Tájó
1480–1490

Painted lime-wood,
22 × 23.5 cm
Inv. No. 7939
Permanent deposit
by the Association
of Friends
of the Art Museums
with the Museum
of Fine Arts, 1940
Bibliography:
Radocsay 1967:
77, 220

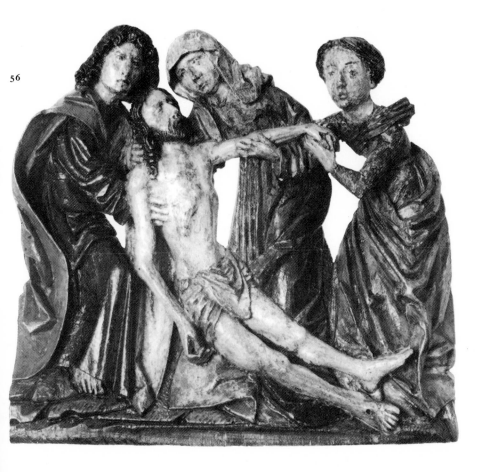

56

It is sometimes supposed that the altarpiece of the St. Mary Magdalen from Berki in Sáros County originated in Kassa. In style the relief in the shrine is directly related to the art of Kassa. However, the paintings on both the hinged and fixed lower wings are certainly the work of a lesser master. On the reverse of the panel representing St. Ursula, there is a painting of St. Margaret in which the script-like motif formed by the linear ornamentation of the floor was once thought to form the initials of the master, but this supposition has not been proved. The Death of the Virgin is represented according to the iconography of the last prayer—a type especially popular in the last quarter of the fifteenth century.

This mode of representation which, instead of the theme of death, emphasized the fact that during the Virgin's last prayer, she gives up her soul to Christ and thus goes to heaven, furnished an apt parallel to Christ's own ascension. These two paintings flank the relief of the Magdalen's ecstasy. The Crucifixion and the representation of the ten thousand martyrs face the martyrdom of St. Ursula and the eleven thousand virgins. When the hinged altar wings were closed, the fixed wings became visible, but only their fronts were painted. In this way, even when closed, the altar retained its width. The bottom picture of the fixed wing on the left represents Mary of Egypt who, like Mary Magdalen, retired from a life of sin to practise repentance. According to the legend, she took three loaves of bread with her into the desert, which she is holding here as her attribute.

The Ecstasy of St. Mary Magdalen. Altarpiece from Berki
1480–1490

The relief in the shrine:
painted
and gilded lime-wood,
161 × 121 cm
Inside paintings
of the wings:
tempera on lime-wood,
each scene 89.5 × 53.5 cm
Inv. No. 55.901.1–3, 6–7
Transferred in 1939 from the Hungarian National Museum to the Museum of Fine Arts

Bibliography:
Radocsay 1955: 120–121, 279;
Radocsay 1967: 70, 156;
Török 1973: 192

I The Ecstasy of St. Mary Magdalen
1 The Ascension
2 St. Ursula's Martyrdom
3 The Crucifixion and the Ten Thousand Martyrs
4 The Death of the Virgin
5 St. Barbara
6 St. Margaret
7 St. Catherine
8 St. Dorothy
9 St. Wolfgang
10 St. Mary of Egypt
11 The Tribute Money
12 The Miracle of the Bread

1		3	9	5	7	11
	I					
2		4	10	6	8	12

57

The relief from the centre of the St. Mary Magdalen altarpiece from Berki shows the penitent Magdalen living in seclusion at the moment when she was carried up by angels so that she might hear the song of the hosts of heaven. The composition follows a well-known example, an engraving by Master ES, though the representation of this scene was popular in German sculpture as early as the first half of the fifteenth century, as may be seen from Multscher's figure of St. Mary Magdalen (c. 1435). In the engraving by Master ES—nearer in time to the Berki relief—and in the Münnerstadt Riemenschneider altar the Magdalen appears in the nude, her body covered only by her long hair. However, the Hungarian sculptor has given the saint a splendid cloak, the nude being an unusual form of representation in that age. The Magdalen is usually shown supported by six angels; but here the sixth place is occupied by a winding stream which breaks the symmetry of the composition and enriches it with a new element. The artist evidently found pleasure in elaborating the background scenery in every detail, as a result of which Mary Magdalen's attribute, the jar of ointment in the lower right corner, is practically lost in the composition. The carving of the whirling stream, the duck diving for food, the sedge, the stork catching a lizard on the bank, the vegetation in the foreground represented with almost botanical fidelity, the leaves of a variety of trees, and finally, surmounting the relief, the figure of a shepherd with his flock and that of a goat nibbling the foliage of a tree, all go to show that the representation of nature was of considerable importance in sacral art at the end of the fifteenth century. The castles on the rocky hills, though realistic in detail, contribute to the mainly legendary atmosphere of the scene; and a similar effect is given by the two small feather-clad angels appearing as little birds of God. The Berki relief is an outstanding example of the art of wood-carving in Sáros County, and also bears witness to the artistic influence of Kassa. This is evident if we compare the carving on the Berki altarpiece with that of the high altar in Kassa.

The Ecstasy of St. Mary Magdalen. Relief of the altarshrine. St. Mary Magdalen altarpiece from Berki
1480–1490

Painted and gilded lime-wood, 161 × 121 cm
Inv. No. 55.901.1
Transferred in 1939 from the Hungarian National Museum to the Museum of Fine Arts
Bibliography:
Radocsay 1967: 70, 156; Balogh 1957: 240

58

Two wings, painted on both sides, and originally hinged, are the only surviving fragments of an altarpiece from Szepeshely. The paintings illustrated here are from the inside of the left wing; St. Jerome is represented on the exterior.

The Szepes region was one of the most significant centres of art in Northern Hungary, whence more panels have survived than from any other part of the country. The church of Szepeshely, an ecclesiastical centre, was decorated with a number of altarpieces. One of them, known as the altarpiece of the Coronation of the Virgin, comprised twelve panels splendidly illustrating the range and standard of the art of the Szepes region. This panel also illustrates the far-reaching influence of Upper Hungarian painting. It is from the facial types and the drawing of the hands that we can identify the artist as an associate of the master responsible for the Altar of the Coronation of the Virgin in the church of Szepeshely, although his style is somewhat harder and the problems of space had less interest for him. His talents, however, are well illustrated in the shading of the yellow and white draperies of the angel and the Virgin, suggesting sculptural firmness, and the bluish darkness of the nocturnal scenery in the background of The Nativity.

The Annuncation and The Nativity. Wing-paintings of an altarpiece from Szepeshely

1480–1490

Tempera on pine-wood, each scene 86 × 63 cm
Inv. No. 55.917.1–2
Transferred in 1939 from the
Hungarian National Museum to the Museum of Fine Arts
Bibliography:
Radocsay 1955: 125, 441;
Radocsay 1963: 26, 52–53

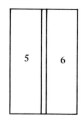

1 The Annunciation
2 The Nativity
3 The Adoration of the Magi
4 The Presentation
   in the Temple
5 St. Jerome
6 St. Augustine

This carving of St. Nicholas is representative of late fifteenth century carving, which yet indicates the trend that was to follow. The form suggests tranquillity both in the folds of the alb arranged over the saint's feet, and in that of the silhouette of the whole, while apart from the pastoral staff and the book, the figure is more or less symmetrical. There are few details intended to give animation to the composition—only the sudden widening of the mitre, the ribbons hanging from it and the space between the four little columns which once held the crook of the staff. The folds enlivening the chasuble are by no means sharp, being arranged in an even network over almost the entire front of the garment to give an impression of serenity. Nevertheless, one is made aware that it would require the merest suggestion of animation to turn the drapery into surging waves. A close examination of works by the Master of the Mateóc King Carvings (Plate 82) shows what little change suffices to produce this impression. Such an examination will also show that the carver of the St. Nicholas figure was one of the principal forerunners of the Master of the Mateóc King Carvings, a sculptor of widespread influence. The faces carved by the two masters are strikingly similar; the eyes scarcely differ at all, yet those of the kings are already more evocative.

The carver of St. Nicholas was evidently inclined to apply regular forms and decorative repetitions. The golden apples arranged on the book—the latter an area of geometric tranquillity, perfectly foreign to its surroundings—are identical in shape and size. Above them the bishop's beard and, still higher, the regular curls of his hair, are very similar in form. The one reflects the other, providing a suitable frame for the finely modelled smooth face, these circular forms balancing the large golden apples, which are as tranquil in form as the undulating surface of the chasuble.

**St. Nicholas
from Szlatvin**
1480–1490

Painted lime-wood,
135.5 cm
Inv. No. 53.372
Transferred in 1936
from the
Hungarian National Museum
to the Museum of Fine Arts
Bibliography:
Radocsay 1967:
86–87, 219

The finely carved marble is decorated with a ring flanked by ravens perched on branches and holding small rings in their beaks. The raven is the heraldic bird of the Hunyadi family, the Latin name *(corvus)* for this bird having provided the surname *Corvinus* for King Matthias. Next to the birds is a graceful floral motif and, on the right, a lion's head. These motifs probably occurred alternately round the frieze. The fragment, together with a lion's head, was found by the sculptor István Ferenczy in the nineteenth century, when builders were laying the foundations of his house on Buda Hill (No. 14 Országház Street). He made use of the motifs on this frieze when designing a base for the mounted figure of Matthias. Excavations in the Royal Castle of Buda have also produced a smaller fragment of the fountain, which proves that the fountain once adorned the castle of King Matthias. This is not the only fragment of a fountain originating from the castle of King Matthias. There are references in literature to a number of ornamental fountains in the Buda Castle grounds, and excavations have revealed the water-supply system. There were various kinds of both fountains and wells. We know, for instance, of a white marble fountain commissioned by King Matthias from the famous Florentine sculptor, Verrocchio, and praised in an epigram by Poliziano.

The standard of carving on this fragment matches that of the architecture and sculptural decorations of King Matthias's royal residence. The elegant floral motif next to the lion's head occurs also in a frieze decorated with putti and garlands attributed to Desiderio da Settignano—an attribution confirmed by a comparison with the carved floral decoration on the Marsuppini tomb in Santa Croce in Florence. The same motif was adopted by the nobility in what was known as "domestic embroidery", a type of needlework peculiar to Hungary.

**Fragment
of a fountain basin
with ravens
from Buda Castle**
c. 1480

White marble, 42 × 58 cm
Inv. No. 2272
Acquired by the Museum
of Fine Arts
from the István Ferenczy
Collection in 1902
Bibliography:
Balogh 1966: 121,
145–147; Balogh 1975: 168;
Török–Osgyányi 1981: 110;
Schallaburg: No. 202

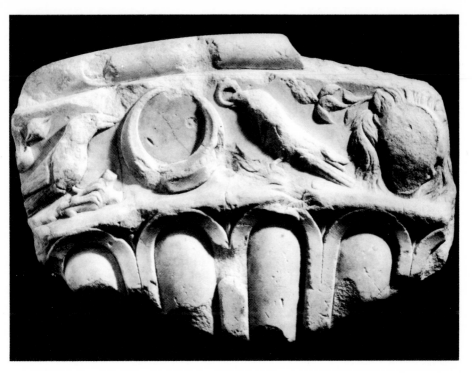

61

The centre section of this tripartite altar showed the Madonna enthroned with the Infant Jesus. Below them was a coat of arms with a mitre flanked by angels, fragments of which are still discernible. The figure on the left, placed in a Renaissance niche, may have been that of St. Lucia, the dish she is holding probably containing her eyes; while in the right niche is St. Catherine with a wheel.

The relief was found in the outer wall of the Pauline church in Diósgyőr. It was probably commissioned by the Bishop of Csanád, János Szakolyi (Johannes de Zokol), who became a monk and retreated to the Pauline monastery in Diósgyőr. His coat of arms showing a mitre indicates that he must have ordered the altar while still acting as Bishop of Csanád. The upper part of the altar comes from the chapel in Diósgyőr Castle—probably commissioned by Queen Beatrice. Some scholars believe that the two fragments belong together. Both are the work of Giovanni Dalmata, an outstanding sculptor engaged by King Matthias. This famous artist worked in Rome and created, among other things, the sepulchre for Pope Paul II. Later he was active in his native town, Trogir, before moving to Buda around 1486–1487. He was a favourite of King Matthias who showered him with decorations, gifts of property and land, and most probably commissioned him to design the royal sepulchre. A good many fragments of Buda Castle reflect the style of Dalmata. The composition of the Diósgyőr altar which comprises the figures of the Virgin and, on either side but rather lower, the figures of female saints, is characteristic of Dalmata's art; it is, for example, similar to the altar he created for the San Marco in Rome. The lively folds of the robes, the fine ornamentation of St. Catherine's garments and the formation of the niches decorated with acanthus leaves and flowers, are also typical of Dalmata's style. Works analogous with the relief illustrated here are the Madonna of the Roverella Monument in San Clemente Church in Rome, the lunette relief in Vicovaro, the Virgins in the Museo Petriano in Rome and the Museo Civico in Padua.

GIOVANNI DALMATA

Fragment of an altar from Diósgyőr

c. 1490

Greyish-white marble,
79 × 123 cm
Inv. No. 55.981
Transferred in 1939
from the
Hungarian National Museum
to the Museum of Fine Arts
Bibliography:
Balogh 1966:
282–283, 489–492, 727;
Balogh 1975: 184–187;
Török–Osgyányi 1981: 110;
Schallaburg: No. 337

62

The Renaissance style, gradually adopted in Hungary during the reign of Matthias Corvinus, continued to flourish there even after the death of the King. This is proved by numerous surviving remains, including architectural fragments from Bács Castle, built by the Archbishop of Kalocsa, Péter Váradi. Of these remains, now in the Gallery, the least damaged is the small baluster-pillar once part of a balustrade and adorned with the coat of arms of Péter Váradi. The shield is divided, the upper half containing two stars, the lower a stylized lily; above the shield is the archiepiscopal cross.

Péter Váradi received a classical education at Bologna University. Later he became a member of the Platonist circle active in Buda at that time, and King Matthias held him in such esteem that he entrusted him with the task of collecting the epigrams of Janus Pannonius. In 1479 he was appointed Privy Counsellor; later he became Lord Chancellor and in 1481 Archbishop of Kalocsa. In 1484, at the peak of a brilliant career, he was thrown into prison by the King for reasons unclarified to this day. He was released only after the death of Matthias. He then retired to his seat in Bács, where he remained as Archbishop of Kalocsa until his death in 1501. His letters written from Bács Castle are the finest relics of Hungarian classical correspondence. Váradi continued to apply all that he had learned during the reign of Matthias and it is very probable that Bács Castle was built with the co-operation of stone-carvers from the royal workshop in Buda, for the baluster is most closely related to the remains surviving from Buda Castle.

The baluster, composed of a small pillar and two spindle-shaped elements, is adorned with motifs of ribbons suspended in an illusory manner, passed through a ring and branching off in opposite directions; also shields placed crosswise, which tell of a revived interest in old trophies as decorative motifs. This type of baluster was most common in Italian Renaissance architecture. Almost contemporaneously with the building activites of Giuliano da Sangallo, it was adopted in Buda Castle whence it spread to the greater part of the country.

Small baluster-pillar showing the coat of arms of Péter Váradi from Bács Castle
1490–1501

Red marble
from the environs
of Buda,
78 × 36 cm
Inv. No. 55.1071
Transferred in 1939
from the
Hungarian National Museum
to the Museum of Fine Arts
Bibliography: Balogh 1966: 120, 699;
Balogh 1975: 150;
Török–Osgyányi 1981: 110;
Schallaburg: No. 637

Several fragments of Renaissance carving, dating from the first decade of the sixteenth century, identical in style and originating from one and the same workshop, have come down to us from the Inner City Parish Church. Originally, the huge tabernacles of parson András Nagyrévy and that of the City of Pest, still extant today, were located on the right and left of the Gothic sanctuary. These niches for the ciborium date from between 1505 and 1507. The centre of the sanctuary would have been the location of the Renaissance high altar of which only fragments now remain. On each fragment is a representation of a liturgical object: the platter for the host, the water and wine jugs, the incense boat with spoon and the aspergillum—all reminiscent of the kind of ecclesiastical vessels made of fine metal-work used at mass during the Renaissance. Bifurcating ribbons ending in tassels link the row of rhythmically alternating liturgical objects and garlands of fruit to a central cord hanging from a ring. Similarly arranged symbols associated with the celebration of the Eucharist can be seen on the pilasters of the altar donated by Corbinelli in the S. Spirito in Florence in the late fifteenth century.

The shaping of the sides of these fragments suggests that they were originally positioned on either side of a vertical column, which again adds weight to the theory that they formed part of the pilasters flanking the altar. On the red marble central part of the tabernacle there is also a decorative border carved in yellowish-white marl from Buda. The tabernacles are over eight metres in height which tallies with the already verified height of the altar.

The carvings from the high altar of the Inner City Parish Church are closely related in style not only with the lower fruit garlands on the two tabernacles in the church but also with a similarly embellished lunette frame which probably adorned the Esztergom archiepiscopal palace. The link with Esztergom is supported by the fact that the donor was András Nagyrévy, vicar of the Esztergom archbishop, Ippolito d'Este. Ippolito's records written from Eger mention a master called "Italus in Pesth", who carved Bishop Nicolas's figural tombstone in 1506. It is thought that these carvings were also produced in his workshop.

ITALUS IN PESTH

Fragments of a high altar from the Inner City Parish Church, Pest
c. 1500–1506

Marl
from the environs of Buda,
91 × 26 cm, 92 × 26 cm,
100 × 26 cm
On loan from the
Inner City Parish Church,
Pest

Bibliography: Balogh, Jolán:
I monumenti del
Rinascimento
della chiesa parrocchiale
di Pest. Rivista d'arte XX
(1938), 64–77;
Balogh, Jolán:
Későrenaissance kőfaragó
műhelyek. I. Közlemény:
Az előzmények
[Late Renaissance
stone-carving workshops.
Publication I: The precedents].
Ars Hungarica 1974/1, 42–44.
Cf. Balogh 1975: 149–150;
Török–Osgyányi 1981: 95;
Schallaburg: Nos. 727–730

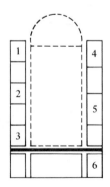

Reconstruction of the former high altar

64

This figure is frequently described, erroneously, as a representation of St. Anne. In fact the cowl covering the shoulders was worn by men, rather than women, at that time. Many saints are shown with a book in their hands, but St. Anne was seldom represented with this very ordinary and, therefore, least characteristic attribute. However, though the identity of the saint may be in doubt, the statue certainly shows a happy and fascinating mixture of materiality and ethereal lightness characteristic of sculpture in the Middle Ages. The powerful lines of the draped robe and the block produced by the closed outlines, make the figure most palpable and realistic, while the somewhat awkward posture, the heavy folds of the robe concealing the forms of the body, and the reserved expression of the face, all tend to strengthen the spiritual content. The figure suggests—appropriately enough since it was intended to decorate an altar—the victory of the spirit over the body. This was probably one of the last carvings to give expression in this way to the life of the spirit and the value of prayer, for sixteenth century art represented spiritual absorption in quite a different manner.

The style of the carving is unique in the art of the mining towns. The head, bent and turned, and the deep hollow producing a strong shadow on one side, are directly related to the work of the Viennese school developed after Nikolaus Gerhaert van Leyden, particularly to the work of the more extreme members of the school with its special stylistic marks. The sculptor of the statue illustrated here applied what he had learned from the Viennese in a very original way, for his flat carving, resembling a low-relief, and his astringent tone are quite unknown in Austrian territory and do not appear in the work of Master Nikolaus's followers.

The carving of a Saint from Selmecbánya
c. 1490

Lime-wood
with traces of paint,
107 cm
Inv. No. 7638
Donated to the Museum of Fine Arts
by Antal Géber, 1939
Bibliography:
Radocsay 1967: 77, 208–209;
Homolka 1972: 72, 345

65

The panel represents a legendary scene from the life of St. Martin. The Bishop, having given his clothes to a needy man, celebrates mass in poor, hastily acquired garments. At the elevation of the Host angels descend to cover his bare arms.

The altar table in the sanctuary, shown in great detail, is decorated with a picture within the picture: a horizontally arranged retable with a scene of the Crucifixion. This is of special importance in the history of the development of winged altars in Hungary, for it demonstrates that this early type of retables of which very few examples have survived, was still in use at the end of the fifteenth century. Seen against the embroidered white altar-cloth the shadows are effective. The artist's representation of the missal is most realistic; also the representation of the mitre and the Gothic style objects made of precious metals, the ciborium between two candlesticks, the chalice and the paten, the latter only just visible under the edge of the communion cloth. Realism was not, however, an end in itself; the painter introduced these details to create an atmosphere of wonder before the legendary scene. The realistic characters are also imbued with piety. The portraitlike features of the male figure kneeling on the right suggest that it was he who commissioned the altarpiece. The painter's endeavours to represent the interior in perspective, the sharp folds shown almost in relief and the subtle colour effects all place the master of this panel among the finest Hungarian painters active in the late fifteenth century.

Bishop St. Martin's Mass. Of unknown provenance
c. 1490

Tempera on pine-wood, 101.5 × 89.5 cm
Inv. No. 1637
Acquired in 1875 by the Hungarian National Museum from the Miklós Jankovich Collection; transferred in 1939 to the Museum of Fine Arts
Bibliography:
Radocsay 1955: 327;
Benesch, Otto: Der Meister des Krainburger Altars. In: Benesch, Otto: Collected writings. III. New York, 1972. 221–222.
Kunst der Reformationszeit. Staatliche Museen zu Berlin. Berlin, 1983. Exhibition catalogue B 37.

This painting, together with that of Bishop St. Martin's Mass (Plate 66), decorated the inner side of one wing of an altarpiece; an exterior painting representing St. Nicholas and the three daughters of a poor nobleman, was the work of a minor master. This was often the case with winged altars: since they were open most of the time, the inner panels were painted by a master painter, the exterior by a member of his workshop.

The scene is set in the open air. The winding road disappearing into the distance serves to integrate the group of figures into the imaginary landscape. St. Nicholas stands out against the group of fashionable turbaned, worldly-looking men, not only as the central figure in the composition, but also owing to his striking and transfigured countenance. From among the worldly members of the group, the man shown with his back turned towards us, has clearly been painted by a highly gifted master. His posture is one often seen in Netherlandish art and accounts partly for the spatial arrangement of the whole group. The turbaned figure in yellow is noteworthy for the plastic shading of the rich folds of his garment, reminiscent of Gothic carving. The glittering sheet of water surrounding the small town, fabulous on the whole but not without realistic elements, the forest with its colourful foliage and the fox with a bird running towards the thicket, are some of the finest and most painterly details in the picture. The delicate shading of the faces must be the work of a very talented master of the late fifteenth century.

St. Nicholas Raising Three Dead.
Provenance unknown
c. 1490

Tempera on pine-wood, 102 × 94 cm
Inv. No. 183
Acquired in 1875 by the Hungarian National Museum from the Miklós Jankovich Collection; transferred in 1939 to the Museum of Fine Arts
Bibliography:
Radocsay 1955: 327;
Benesch, Otto: Der Meister des Krainburger Altars. In: Benesch, Otto: Collected writings. III. New York, 1972. 221–222.

The panel represents the best-known episode from the legend of St. Martin. The young knight at the town-gate of Amiens cuts his cloak in two and gives half of it to a beggar. In the interior represented on the left side of the picture another episode from the legend can be seen. Christ appears at night to Martin, who suddenly realizes that it was the Saviour himself who put him to the test in the guise of a beggar. He is then baptized.

The building on the left, decorated with statues mounted on brackets, and the room into which we can look, show the distant influence of Netherlandish art. This building, a fantastic edifice of many storeys, is an imaginative feat on the part of the painter. Although it seems the painter had some difficulty in representing the figure on horseback, his skill is amply demonstrated in the symmetrical composition, the distressed expression of the faces, the careful treatment of such details as the hair and the beard, and also the freshness of the colours. The scene, set against a gilded background, decorates the inside of a panel which may have been part of a large winged altar, possibly dedicated to St. Martin. On the exterior of the panel is a representation of Christ crowned with thorns. Some scholars have noted that the style of the master—especially in the scene of the crowning which depicts a vast number of figures with expressive movements—is related to late Gothic Austrian painting, and is particularly close to the style of the Styrian *Master of the Divisio Apostolorum*.

St. Martin and the Beggar. The inside wing-painting of an altarpiece. Provenance unknown
c. 1490

Tempera on panel,
88 × 91 cm
Inv. No. 179
Acquired in 1875
by the Hungarian
National Museum
from the Miklós Jankovich
Collection;
transferred in 1939
to the Museum of Fine Arts
Bibliography:
Radocsay 1955:
328–329; Stange 1961: 71

68

Surprisingly few medieval paintings have survived from the Transdanubian region (Western Hungary). We have only two wings from the church at Nagytótlak, other than the panels from Alsólendva and Németújvár, which illustrate the development of painting in south-west Hungary, although several winged altars produced in that region are mentioned in the literature.

The inner side of the wings from Nagytótlak depict scenes from the life of the Virgin; on the exterior are the figures of St. Stephen, St. Emeric, St. Ladislas and St. Nicholas. Owing to their geographic origin, the panels are in some ways related to Austrian painting, especially to the Upper Austrian works surviving from the late fifteenth century. The iconography of the Death of the Virgin, in which the kneeling figure of the Virgin Mary is surrounded only by the apostles, became generally adopted around 1500. The same composition was very popular in Austrian relief sculpture. It should therefore be borne in mind that the absence of a detailed interior is characteristic of this iconographic type and not a shortcoming in the representation. This work is distinguished by the artist's fine brush-work; his figures are simple and graceful, his colours light and bright. The fresh green tints in the background and the violet shadows in the Virgin's white cloak are particularly effective.

The Nativity and The Death of the Virgin. The inside wing of an altarpiece from Nagytótlak
c. 1490

Tempera on pine-wood.
72 × 53 and 76 × 53 cm respectively
Inv. No. 182
Donated in 1864
to the Hungarian
National Museum
by Ferenc Szenczy;
1939–1973
in the Museum of Fine Arts
Bibliography:
Radocsay 1955:
129–130, 407–408;
Stange 1961: 103;
Török 1973: 192–194

1 *The Annunciation*
2 *The Adoration of the Magi*
3 *The Nativity*
4 *The Death of the Virgin*
5 *King St. Ladislas*
6 *St. Emeric*
7 *King St. Stephen*
8 *St. Nicholas*

The high altar from Kisszeben is the largest and most elaborate in the Gallery; it is, in fact, the finest of all the altars which have survived from the former Hungarian territories. The principal figures are large, in keeping with the whole structure, but it is not merely size that makes them so impressive. The strict appearance, meaningful glance and richly gathered folds make John the Baptist an impressive figure, one that commands respect, although it can hardly be called powerful. His unrealistically slim hands—expressive like his eyes—and his bony feet enhance his ascetic looks. The folds are extremely plastic but static, seldom exposing the inner surface of the garments. The locks of the beard and the tufts of fur of the lambs are arranged in an almost ornamental way. All this would have been unimaginable when Veit Stoss's sweeping bold style was exerting so powerful an influence on Hungarian sculpture of the sixteenth century. We must therefore turn to the conclusions of earlier scholars and endorse the opinion of Károly Divald, who dated the altar from before 1510–1516, i.e. the years suggested by more recent authorities. During the troubled period following the death of King Matthias, Kisszeben was for years in the hands of the Polish crown prince John Albert. Thus the Polish coat of arms carved on the predella may well indicate that work on the altar was begun during this time, which makes the absence of Stoss's influence all the more surprising. The high altar is related in style to Silesian sculpture; this applies particularly to the three statues—three figures which stand apart from the mainstream of Hungarian art. In the late fifteenth century, when the altars for the Kassa and Eperjes churches had been completed, the Kisszeben high altar became the third major project to be undertaken in the region.

MASTER ANS

St. John the Baptist from the high altar at Kisszeben
1490s

Painted
and gilded lime-wood,
190 cm
Inv. No. 3916
Transferred in 1909
from the Museum
of Applied Arts
to the Museum of Fine Arts
Bibliography:
Radocsay 1967:
115–117; 183–184;
Polak-Trajdos 1970: 156;
Homolka 1972: 257–259, 405;
Ziomecka, Anna:
Śląskie retabula szafowe . . .
[Altarpieces from Silesia].
Roczniki Sztuki Śląskiej X
(1976), 91

70

One of the masters of late fifteenth century sculpture in the mining towns was the quaint, undeniably provincial, yet extremely fascinating anonymous carver of the Necpál Virgin and Child. The figure is somewhat stocky, the posture simple and relaxed, thus balancing the animated drapery of the robes. These fall in deep folds, forming furrows divided from each other by hard ridges which suggest the brittle quality of glass. The vigorous lines continually lead the eye to the base, where they converge as in a calm pool and break up into small ripples. Of the crescent supporting the Virgin Mother, only the right horn is fully visible; in form it corresponds with the sharp-cut lively lines of the drapery; the end curves outward and upward to balance the downward and inward line of the robe. The animation is produced mainly by the hem of the cloak, whether we take the line running almost straight down from under the right hand, or the one between the wrists forming a very effective V-shape that reaches right down to the crescent. The smoothness of the upper part of the carving is in quaint contrast to the animated folds. The mass of evenly flowing hair is broken only by surface furrows; the folds of the kerchief showing under the crown and draped behind the Infant are quite flat, while the bodice of the robe fits tightly round the shoulders. The Virgin's face and the Infant's body are even more strikingly smooth. They are composed of large, tranquil forms, so that the lines on the Infant's body—round the ankles, above the round belly and on the upper arm and neck—seem inconsistent. Among these forms the Virgin's protruding chin is all the more significant: it is a mark that reliably relates the statue to the Virgin of Körmöcbánya and the altar of the Coronation of the Virgin in Bakabánya, also to a somewhat later Madonna of unknown provenance now in the Slovak Gallery.

The Virgin and Child from Necpál
Late fifteenth century

Lime-wood, painting and gilding damaged; 135 cm
Inv. No. 4034
Acquired
for the Museum of Fine Arts
between 1911–1913
Bibliography:
Radocsay 1967: 80, 203–204;
Homolka 1972: 257, 394

71

On the reverse of this panel—the wing of an altarpiece—there is a picture of Abraham preparing to sacrifice Isaac, a subject rather rarely represented in late Gothic altarpieces. Abraham, holding a candle, is seen walking in verdant country followed by Isaac carrying a bundle of brushwood. Perhaps owing to the unusualness of the subject, it is not as successfully represented as the Nativity, in which the artist was helped by numerous earlier examples. The antique ruin, which often appears in the iconography of the Nativity, is indicated here by part of a column, possibly of marble, placed conspicuously behind St. Joseph. In the Liptószentmária representation of this subject (Plate 31) the antique column, indicating Bethlehem, forms an important element of the building. In this panel Jesus is shown lying in a manger, as in the Németlipcse altarpiece (Plate 28). In the background, as was usual in representations of the Nativity, we see the shepherds hearing the good tidings brought by angels. The atmosphere of wonder at the miraculous Nativity is ensured by the hovering cherubim holding a banderole with the inscription *Gloria in excelsis deo*. The realistic representation of the Infant and of St. Joseph's gesture protecting the candle, bear witness to the influence of Netherlandish painting; in the kneeling figure of Joseph there is an echo of the art of Rogier van der Weyden. The Nativity has survived in good condition except for the gilded background which has been worn off exposing the red bole ground.

The Nativity.
Provenance unknown
1490–1500

Tempera on pine-wood,
90 × 66 cm
Inv. No. 1641
Acquired in 1875
by the
Hungarian National Museum
from the Miklós Jankovich
Collection;
transferred in 1939
to the Museum of Fine Arts
Bibliography:
Radocsay 1955: 329

Gloria · in excelsis · deo

The frail figure of the Virgin is depicted kneeling in prayer, surrounded by the twelve apostles, supported by St. John the Evangelist. Facing her is an elderly apostle, probably Peter, reading prayers for the dying. He holds the stump of a candle in his left hand. The apostle standing on the extreme left holds a holy-water stoup and, judging by the position of his left hand, he must also have held an aspergill, while the puffed out cheeks and raised right arm of the younger apostle on the extreme right suggest that originally he was shown blowing on the thurible. The iconographic significance of this Death of the Virgin like the Last Prayer lies in the fact that the Virgin is not shown lying on her death-bed as a mere mortal, but kneeling in prayer and giving up her soul to Christ, thus suggesting the Assumption to come. This type of representation of the Last Prayer was equally widespread in painting and sculpture in Central and Eastern Europe from the last third of the fourteenth century. In the Austrian territories a similar treatment of the subject is found from the last third of the fifteenth century mostly in the relief carving on winged altars reflecting the influence of painting. It is for this reason that, even in reliefs in which the Virgin is shown kneeling, a bed was often represented in the carving. In Poland and Hungary, on the other hand, the brilliant artistic solution of Veit Stoss's high altar in Cracow (1477–1489) popularized carvings in which the Virgin was represented only with the apostles. The form of the kneeling Virgin, shown in left profile, was inspired by the Cracow high altar. Her left hand, now missing, may also have been drooping limply. Although this carving cannot be compared with the work of Stoss, it does not lack artistic inventiveness and is well suited to a small altarpiece. His individual touch is seen in the shaping of the heads of the apostles. There is a dramatic quality in the facial expressions of Stoss's figures, but the naïve alarm and manifest frailty of the Kassa apostles gives them a more intimate and human character.

The Death of the Virgin from Kassa
1490–1500

Painted and gilded lime-wood,
80 × 100 cm
Inv. No. 55.922
Transferred in 1939 from the
Hungarian National Museum to the Museum of Fine Arts
Bibliography:
Radocsay 1967: 67, 83–84, 180;
Török 1973: 192–194

In style and in modelling, these two carvings are more or less isolated. From among the carvings which have come down to us from Szepeshely the figures they most closely resemble are those decorating the Szepeshely altar of the Coronation of the Virgin. The relationship between the two statues themselves is puzzling. Their size, gestures and workmanship leave no doubt as to their affinity and that they must have been created as counterparts; but we cannot be certain of the scene in which the Virgin and St. John the Baptist are depicted side by side. Medieval iconography does not show them together except in representations of the Last Judgement and related scenes. These are to be found, although rarely, even on winged altars, for instance on the Ghent altar by the Eyck Brothers. In these compositions, however, the Virgin and St. John are always shown kneeling, as mediators. However, there is some reason for assuming that these figures were part of a Crucifixion group, for the postures and gestures are similar to those seen in an engraving of this subject (Lehrs, 31) by an artist from the Upper-Rhine regions who signed his works with the initials ES. The forward movement of St. John is a stance frequently used by ES, and the carriage of the figures which seem almost to emerge from the foot of the Cross, is also to be seen in Master ES's engravings. His influence is also reflected in the thick-set, closed shape and the rigid folds of the drapery—unusual features in the art surviving from this area. These details, however, while assisting us to classify the style of the statues, provide little clue to the theme. For although the upward pointing gestures seem to corroborate the view that they were originally part of a Crucifixion group, the fact is that it was customary to depict John the Evangelist, and not John the Baptist at the foot of the Cross. Although John the Baptist does indeed figure in a very famous Crucifixion scene of a somewhat later date—and from Master ES's country too—namely the Isenheim altar by Grünewald, this is so unusual that it cannot be regarded simply as an analogue.

**The Virgin Mary
and St. John
the Baptist
from Szepeshely**
1490–1500

Painted and gilded wood,
118 and 122 cm respectively
Inv. No. 55.921
Transferred in 1939
from the
Hungarian National Museum
to the Museum of Fine Arts
Bibliography:
Radocsay 1967:
84–85, 215; Homolka 1972:
176, 407; Lehrs: 31

74

In the late fifteenth century the most important centre of painting in the Szepes region was the Szepeshely provostry (today episcopal see). One of the outstanding painters active there was known as the Master of Szepesváralja after an altarpiece—the only one among all his surviving works. Like other great artists of the age, he worked alone, remaining aloof from the efforts of fellow painters to solve such exciting problems as spatial composition, the rendering of individual character or the expression of emotion, nor did he wish to augment the number of subjects worthy of a painter's brush. He dared to retain a concise style in an age when artists and public were avid for works full of decorative detail, animated compositions and a life-like representation of the principal figures depicted against a rich background. Yet his gifts enabled him to produce an equally powerful effect by the use of vivid colours which convinces us of his standing as an artist.

The master of the panel is not represented in our collection by any work of his own, but this panel from a small altarpiece, acquired for the National Gallery from the Franciscans of Gyöngyös, was painted by one of his pupils. It is thought that the Franciscan monks received the panel from fellow-members of their Order in the Szepes region. Sophia and her three daughters, Faith, Hope and Charity, are known as early Christian martyrs, but there is a belief that they do not represent historic persons but are allegorical representations of the Christian virtues. However this may be, the family group linked to these virtues, was widely represented on panels in medieval Hungary.

The painting illustrated here is a characteristic work by a pupil: it bears the marks of the master's style but is dominated mainly by external features easy to master. The undemonstrative, yet in some places powerful colouring produces an almost monochromic overall effect. The figures command respect by their restrained gestures and seeming immobility. The shapes of the heads and the wide, staring eyes, provide convincing proof of the influence of the Master of Szepesváralja. A recent supposition that the painter was a follower of Márton, known by his panel from Jánosfalva, appears to be unfounded.

**St. Sophia
from Szepeshely**
1490–1500

Pine-wood, 67.5 × 40 cm
Inv. No 3181
Acquired in 1901 for the Museum
of Fine Arts
from the Franciscans
of Gyöngyös
Bibliography:
Radocsay 1955:
127, 442; Glatz 1975: 37

The picture shows the Virgin as a child entering the Temple in which she was to spend her girlhood. In this episode she is generally represented escorted by various figures which, however, are never depicted beyond the steps. Here they are replaced by two angels, thus emphasizing the solemnity rather than the miraculous nature of the event. The interior, entered through an opening in a low rail at the top of a flight of unusually narrow steps, is reminiscent of the sanctuary of a Romanesque church raised over an undercroft; the pillars and the vaulting supported by them are also evocative of the age. According to the symbolic language developed by contemporary Netherlandish painters this outmoded architectural style indicated a reference to the Old Testament. In this panel it was intended to suggest the interior of an ancient temple. As Netherlandish painting was held in such high regard and attracted so many followers, this kind of symbolism was understood all over Europe. In this particular panel, however, the painter wanted to present an unequivocal picture of the Temple in Jerusalem, thus an indirect allusion did not satisfy him. The head of the high-priest turned towards the Virgin is covered with a shawl embroidered with a pattern resembling Hebrew letters; behind the Christian-type altar covered with a white cloth two stone tablets of the Ten Commandments rather like late Gothic winged altars rise almost to the arched ceiling of the Temple.

The painting represents an attempt to depict an elaborate internal space, a difficult task beyond the ability of the artist. The perspective is clumsy and the two groups of figures are placed too far apart, though this makes each group in itself more effective. The figures of the two angels provide the most charming motifs of the composition.

The painting is unquestionably in the characteristic style of the Szepes region. The painter chose cleverly, if in an eclectic way, from the stylistic elements associated with the Master of Szepesváralja and the painter Márton. His inclination to emphasize beautiful but superficial features shows that his closest links were with Márton. Consideration of style, however, is insufficient basis for the recurring conjecture that the painting was created by Márton.

The Virgin Entering the Temple from Szepeshely
1490–1500

Panel, 77 × 45.5 cm
Inv. No. 53.383
Transferred in 1936
from the Hungarian
National Museum
to the Museum of Fine Arts
Bibliography:
Radocsay 1955:
127–128, 213, 441;
Glatz 1975: 37

These three life-size statues were originally placed high on the ridge of the north transept of St. Elisabeth's Church in Kassa. Supported by brackets, they were spaced at equal distances across the width of the transept. St. Stephen stood on the left, St. Ladislas a little higher in the centre, and St. Emeric on the right. A photograph from the last century clearly shows the slender pinnacles which rose above them. The statues were removed from their original position during the reconstruction of the cathedral in 1859–60 and replaced by new ones.

Although the usual attributes are lacking, the facial types fully correspond with traditional representations of the saintly Hungarian kings generally portrayed together. The aged, bearded St. Stephen probably held in his right hand a sceptre, the mark of which is still discernible; the orb in his left hand and the lower part of his crown have survived intact. An old drawing shows the king standing with his legs crossed, in the same way as St. Ladislas. The younger king, St. Ladislas, is also clad in armour below which we can see the lower part of a mail shirt. The king may have held a battle-axe in his right hand while in his left hand there is still the fragment of an orb. The youngest royal figure, prince St. Emeric, has a rather girlish face and wears a loose cloak with a broad collar. His tilted head and the crosswise curving line of his cloak enhance the dance-like posture characteristic of all three statues. Similar representations of saintly Hungarian kings were made for the high altar in Szepeshely in the 1470s; the contemporary carved wooden statues on the superstructure of the high altar in Kassa were also analogous in composition. Among the remains now in the Gallery the carvings of St. Stephen and St. Ladislas from Mateóc (Plate 82), are comparable in respect of posture and armour to the Kassa figures. St. Emeric's cloak, however, is not so rich in folds as that of its Kassa counterpart; it is rather dominated by an asymmetric arrangement of large curves similar to those found on the sepulchre of Casimir Jagiello made by Veit Stoss in the 1490s. The dance-like posture, which in the 1480s became exaggerated to the grotesque, can be traced back to Nikolaus Gerhaert. Both Stoss and the sculpture in Kassa had strong connections with Gerhaert's art earlier too.

St. Stephen of Hungary, St. Ladislas and St. Emeric from the Cathedral in Kassa
1490–1500

Liparite-tuff, 136, 170 and 170 cm respectively
Inv. No. 55.1573–55.1575
Transferred in 1939 from the Hungarian National Museum to the Museum of Fine Arts
Bibliography:
Mihalik, József:
Három kassai kőszobor
[Three stone statues from Kassa],
AÉ XXX (1910), 213–;
Marosi, Ernő:
Tanulmányok
a kassai
Szent Erzsébet templom
építéstörténetéhez
[Studies on the architecture of St. Elisabeth's Church in Kassa]. III. MÉ XX (1971) 261–291

77

The Pietà from Keszthely is undoubtedly the most beautiful of all the statues originating from the interior of the country, especially remarkable in that it comes from a place occupied by the Turks, unlike the other places in Upper Hungary or Transylvania from which medieval works of art have come down to us.

The Pietà is an elaborate representation developed from the most tragic theme in the religious art of the period—the Virgin Mary mourning over the dead body of Christ. The composition comprises only the two main figures—Mary and her Son—from the group of mourners at the foot of the Cross. In the Keszthely Pietà the figure of the Virgin is large in proportion to that of Christ. This oddly matched pair is often found in medieval art, the intention being to remind the spectator of the figure of the Virgin holding the newborn or Infant Jesus on her lap. The horror of the crucifixion is intensified by the realization that the dead body is that of the young man whom we also know as the charming Infant that gave serenity to so many representations of Mother and Child.

In this Pietà the Virgin seems to tower over her Son. The carving is shallow, almost relief-like; Mary's face is sketchy and superficial, the folds of the mantle which covers her head and shoulders, also the folds of the robe from knees to hem, are all large and irregular in arrangement. Here the single aim is to emphasize the frailty of her Son. On the figure of the Virgin there are no finely carved details such as the hair and beard of Christ, which serve to enhance the nobility of His features. His face, turned towards the spectator, is the most important part of the composition from the point of view of both content and form. It is on the face that the main lines of the composition converge: the hanging arm, the body, the stiffly upheld left arm and the mantle draped over the Virgin's head are all connected with the most distant parts of the surface. The carving of the hands and feet, executed with loving care, are worthy of the noble face. As we dwell on the accurate and slightly idealized modelling, we become aware that even the knees and ankles help to express a deeply-felt message.

Pietà from Keszthely (?)
c. 1500

Lime-wood,
the painting damaged,
89 cm
Inv. No. 52–641
Acquired in 1941
by the Museum
of Fine Arts
from the Keszthely Museum
on an exchange basis
Bibliography:
Radocsay 1967:
126, 181–182

78

This charming panel exemplifies the traditional half-length representation of the Virgin; considering the date of creation, it is a fairly conservative painting, for the gracefully curving ornamental foliage in the raised and gilded background from gesso completely isolates the two figures from their environment. The rose, "Queen of the flowers" in the centre of the composition, befits the "Queen of Heaven". Her splendid lilied crown and the stylized but definitely plant-like ornamental foliage in the background, so pleasingly entwined round the Virgin's halo and enfolding the figure of the Infant, indicate the same celestial relationship. The foliage derives from the type of representation known as "The Virgin in the rose hedge" and, like the flowers creeping into the bower, symbolizes heaven.

The style of the painting points to the Szepes school. Around the turn of the century the art of painting in Kassa revived under the impulse it received from the Szepes region—although only a short time earlier the richest winged altar in Hungary had been produced in Kassa. Now the main sources of influence were the workshop of the painter of the Szepeshely altarpiece known as the altar of the Coronation of the Virgin and that of the Master of the St. Anthony Legend. The master of the Virgin and Child illustrated here clearly learned his art in the Szepeshely workshop, though we have no means of knowing whether or not he also painted the wings of the altar of the Visitation in Kassa. Since the style of the panel strongly resembles that of the Kassa altar, some scholars attribute both works to one master, while others consider them to be the work of two different artists. It will probably never be possible to determine with certainty whether one single master could have produced two works in which the differences are as marked as the similarities.

The Virgin and Child with Roses from Kassa
c. 1500

Pine-wood, with original frame
71 × 60.5 cm
Inv. No. 55.911
Transferred in 1936 from the Hungarian National Museum to the Museum of Fine Arts

Bibliography:
Radocsay 1955: 164–165, 347;
Stange 1961: 130;
Radocsay 1963: 26, 53;
Glatz 1975: 45

79

The altar must have been created shortly after 1500, for it was then that statues were used to decorate the centre shrine of altars instead of the earlier painted figures. As a result, the tracery above the heads of the figures and especially the brocade pattern filling in the space behind them to increase the illusion of its being the back of the altar shrine, became gradually obsolete. Although the female saints have a more imposing appearance than the earlier figures, they are still quite slender in build.

St. Anne, represented as a grandmother, holds in her arms both her daughter, the Virgin, and the Infant Jesus. With her on one side is Mary Magdalen, on the other St. Elisabeth of Hungary. This type of St. Anne has its origin in Byzantine art where the Hodegetria, Mother of God, is represented holding the Infant in a similar way. The rigid symmetry of the composition, and the lack of any sense of scale in depicting the saints and the Child indicate the origin of the motif.

The upper part of the left wing shows St. Helen with the Cross she had found, the lower portrays another saint of the Holy Land, St. Mary of Egypt. It was once thought that the latter figure was a representation of St. Elisabeth, a clearly erroneous interpretation, for it is most unlikely that a saint would be represented twice on one and the same altar. The fact that the saint is shown with bread in her hand must have given rise to this mistaken identification. However, in this picture the bread represents the food which Mary of Egypt took with her when she retreated into the desert to live the life of a recluse. This supposition is corroborated by the corresponding figure in the Berki altarpiece where the veil thrown over the saint's shoulders shows that she scarcely allowed herself the garments to cover her nudity. But the painter of Berzenke must have felt that even a hint of such deprivation would affect the dignity of the figure. The right wing of the altar represents St. Sophia and her three daughters, and St. Hedwig with the chapel she founded.

The altar owes its beauty mainly to the pictorial language which contrasts with the brilliance effected by the use of lively local colours. Besides the dominant reds and greens there are many subtle variations which can hardly be defined.

St. Anne with the Virgin and Child. Altarpiece from Berzenke
c. 1500

Central panel: Lime-wood.
144 × 103 cm
Inside panels of the wings:
Lime-wood,
69 × 46.5 cm each
Inv. No. 55.834. 1–9
Transferred in 1936
from the Hungarian
National Museum
to the Museum of Fine Arts
On temporary loan
in the Budapest
Historical Museum
Bibliography:
Radocsay 1955:
129, 281
800 Jahre Franz von Assisi.
Franziskanische Kunst und
Kultur des Mittelalters.
Krems, 1982. 10. No. 51, ill.
32

1 *St. Anne with the Virgin and Child between Mary Magdalen and St. Elizabeth of Hungary*
2 *St. Helen*
3 *St. Mary of Egypt*
4 *St. Sophia with Her Three Daughters*
5 *St. Hedwig*
6 *Angel from the Annunciation*
7 *The Virgin of Sorrows*
8 *The Virgin from the Annunciation*
9 *The Man of Sorrows*

80

2		4	
	1		
3		5	

6	8
7	9

For a work of this period the panel is strikingly archaic in character. The calm, seemingly immobile figures, the effective silhoutte of the decorative crowns, the spatial depth scarcely emphasized in spite of the tiling of the floor and the gilded background, are characteristics of fifteenth century pictorial art. On the other hand, the manner of painting and the arrangement of the figures filling the space without overcrowding it, link the panel to a later period. This inconsistency serves to enhance the solemnity of the meeting between the saintly women and their queen. Barbara, seen holding a tower in the lower left corner, Catherine sitting above her with a broken wheel in her lap and, on the other side of the Virgin, St. Dorothy with a basket of flowers, and Margaret leading a dragon on a leash like a dog, are the noblest of the martyr virgins. St. Catherine having been regarded as the highest ranking among them, it is on her finger that the Infant Jesus slips the engagement ring with a playful boyish gesture. This unstressed yet very important detail illustrates an episode from a characteristically medieval legend that probably owed its birth to a misunderstanding. It is thought that Catherine's original attribute, the wheel, as represented in a small picture, was mistaken for the engagement ring symbolizing devotion to the Saviour. As the role of a betrothed would not have befitted the adult Christ, He is represented here as an Infant in his mother's lap, an ingenious idea hinting at the irrationality of the event.

The style of the picture is directly related to that of contemporary Austrian painting, a link frequently found in Western Hungary in several periods. The Rottal panel in the Alte Galerie in Graz, often referred to as an epitaph, can be regarded as its most direct parallel. This is strikingly evident in the arrangement of the figures and even in the facial expressions. The Németújvár panel is, however, more severe in its effect; it lacks the elegance of the Graz panel in which the figures are depicted in sumptuous costumes. The Graz panel is characterized by the cool elegance of the costumes and the carriage of the figures, while the Németújvár panel, a narrative painting expressing warm feelings, shows a quite different approach.

The Mystic Marriage of St. Catherine from Németújvár
c. 1500

Pine-wood. 101.5 × 73 cm
Inv. No. 52.657
Acquired
for the Museum of Fine Arts
from the
Batthyány Collection
Bibliography:
Radocsay 1955:
130, 411

The carvings after which the Master was named originate probably from Mateóc. They show the two canonized Hungarian kings—the royal saints most often represented in Hungarian art—clad in late Gothic mail. The idea of a war-lord king was well suited to the contemporary mood, although it was not a very fortunate one from the artist's point of view, for he clearly found pleasure in carving elaborate drapery and even endeavoured to envelop these armoured figures in cloaks. He must have delighted also in the carving of the kings' hair and beard. The light and unerring touch evident in these details demonstrate his great technical skill and effectively draw the spectator's attention to the sharp-featured faces and compelling glance of the saints. Some of the folds follow the same regular spiral lines as St. Ladislas's hair, but some are more erratic and resemble rather his thick—though never rugged—beard. Although the central figure of the original altarpiece is missing, it is evident that the artist composed the pair of canonized kings together with the missing carving. The two surviving outside figures not only turn towards each other (which in most cases is the sole proof of relationship between similar altar carvings), but are smoothly enclosed on the outer sides, the main purpose being to emphasize the liveliness of the inner sides. (The absence of the central figure, probably a Madonna, is the more regrettable as it must surely have provided the focal point for the animation produced by all the spiralling folds.)

The search for tasks permitting a display of technical skill must have spread to the Szepes region from Cracow, where the marvellous altarpiece of the Virgin Mary had already been produced by Veit Stoss some ten or twenty years before the creation of the Mateóc saintly king figures. At the same time it may have been from Vienna that artists learned to attempt the dissolution of traditionally closed compositions and also to make use of more independent forms. The Master of the Mateóc King Carvings was the earliest representative of Veit Stoss's style in the valley regions below the Tátra mountains, and the only outstanding follower of Veit Stoss who did not belong to the loosely defined workshop of Master Pál of Lőcse.

MASTER OF THE MATEÓC KING CARVINGS

St. Stephen and St. Ladislas from Mateóc (?)
c. 1500

Lime-wood with traces of paint; 114 and 106.5 cm respectively
Inv. No. 55.894, 55.895
Transferred in 1939 from the Hungarian National Museum to the Museum of Fine Arts
Bibliography:
Radocsay 1967: 109–110, 198;
Homolka 1972: 172

82

This picture is a detail sawn out from a larger panel, and the identity of the figure is therefore uncertain, but it is generally believed to be the Virgin. The dignified appearance and the crown support this assumption. However, it was customary to indicate that the Virgin was the Virgin Mother by representing her with a crown placed over a mantle and not over flowing tresses as worn by maidens; it is therefore also possible that the figure is that of a female saint entitled by royal descent or by her saintly life or martyr's death to wear the celestial crown. The attribute held in her hand cannot be seen, and her identity must therefore still remain a matter for speculation.

The fine shape of the face, moderately detailed painting of the jewels, animated outline of the crown and loosely flowing hair, are all details indicating that this is the work of a talented master. Although the general effect of the colour-scheme is somewhat sombre, almost monochromatic, we can assume that it was originally brighter. (Here we should remember that it is not a complete painting but only a detail which, in the interest of the overall colour effect, may have been purposely painted in dull shades.) Both the head and shoulders are rounded and voluminous, as if they were a section of a wooden statue represented in a painting.

The style of the picture is so close to that of the Medgyes high altar that the painter may reasonably be considered as a pupil of the Master of Medgyes. Risky though it is to draw far-reaching conclusions from one small detail, it would appear that the pupil was no less gifted than the master. However, since so little of his work has survived, our evaluation must remain largely a matter of conjecture.

Half-length painting of the Virgin (?) from Marosvásárhely
After 1500

Pine-wood, 46,7 × 37 cm
Inv. No. 3713
Acquired in 1908
by the Museum of Fine Arts
Bibliography:
Radocsay 1955:
180, 388

The figure of St. Nicholas exemplifies the sculptural art of Szepes region at the beginning of the sixteenth century, when artists in small workshops began to be dominated by the influence of Veit Stoss who was active in Cracow before. Indeed it is on this altar that we find the earliest evidence in this region of the new style, manifest especially in increased animation. The vivacious appearance of the saint is effected by deep cuts representing the bold opening of the cloak, the edges turned back to reveal the inner side. The smooth surface covering the left leg sets off the deep groove formed in front of the right leg, while the conch-like fold exposes the inner side of the cloak. The saint is shown gazing upwards in an unusual manner, into the distance, instead of at the faithful, thus producing a dreamy, lyric atmosphere reminding us of the important role this motif was to assume in Master Pál of Lőcse's school hardly a decade later. (This to some extent accounts for the belief which gained ground some forty years ago, that the St. Nicholas carving was the earliest work by Master Pál of Lőcse to have survived.)

The pictures on the wings are by the Master of St. Anthony's Legend, the painter who exerted the strongest influence in the Szepes region between 1500–1510. The comparatively narrow field represented in each of these pictures, also the small but extremely plastic figures and the uniformly bright landscape so admirably suggesting an open vista, are all characteristic of his art. However, as the artist did not work alone, it is difficult to determine which of the pictures are his own. In each picture there is a gold background above the horizon.

The asymmetric shape of the predella indicates that originally the altar must have stood along the right wall of the church. The way in which the Virgin, the Infant Jesus and St. Anne are placed in the horizontal field, and especially the choice of colours, is so different from that seen in the pictures on the wings that the relatedness of the works may be questioned. However, when the wings are closed, we find a uniform colour scheme. From these differences of style we conclude that the external panels of the wings and the painting on the predella are not the work of the master in charge of the workshop.

The St. Nicholas altar from Nagyszalók
1503

The carving
in the shrine:
lime-wood,
repainted, 133 cm
The wings: pine-wood,
67 × 37 cm each
Predella: pine-wood,
44 × 176 cm
Inv. No. 53.541.2–11
Transferred in 1936 from
the Hungarian
National Museum
to the Museum
of Fine Arts.
On temporary loan
to an exhibition
of the National Museum
Bibliography:
Radocsay 1955:
169–170, 213, 404–405;
Radocsay 1967: 85, 86, 203;
Homolka 1972: 232;
Glatz 1975: 46

1 St. Nicholas
1 St. Nicholas Abating the
   Storm
2 St. Nicholas Prevents the
   Execution of Three Youths
3 The Miracle of the Corn
4 The Charity of
   St. Nicholas
5 St. Francis
6 St. Stanislaus
7 St. Wolfgang
8 St. Florianus
9 The Virgin, the Infant
   Jesus and St. Anne

84

This is rightly recognized as the most popular work in the Gallery, a superb achievement illustrating in one composition a variety of pictorial approaches adopted by artists in the late Middle Ages —a search for the picturesque detail in the drawing and an emphasis on figures and landscape. It is the creation of one of the very best painters of the period, gifted in the use of powerful and effective colour schemes. The linear effect is also important in his pictures, especially the now softly fluttering, now stiff and broken, but always cleverly designed curves of the folds. An especially interesting feature of his work is his meticulous way of painting. His manner of representing with loving care even the smallest detail can only be compared to miniature painting.

The two figures fill the field harmoniously. The landscape reflects a whole world of luxuriant vegetation, barren rocks, gently sloping hills, soaring peaks, trodden paths through meadows scattered with flowers, a river, a bridge, a castle and a city—the world in miniature. Searching the distant horizon one is surprised to find that above this luxurious landscape there is no blue sky but a golden folio as seen in preceding centuries. However, the golden lustre, glinting also from the garments of the saints, has its own important purpose—to add to the lofty spiritual atmosphere which pervades the picture. The two women show a gentle, but not over-familiar attitude towards each other. Elisabeth, who is the elder, kisses the hand of Mary to express her reverence. This eloquent action is symbolic and was used to express feudal subservience.

The flowery meadow may be the main source of the overall lyric atmosphere. Large, surprisingly flat flowers—each one a symbol of the Virgin—grow profusely at the feet of the saints. Thus, as our eyes are drawn from these flowers to the Virgin and Elisabeth we find them also blossom-like, delicate and beautiful. This impression plays a significant part in producing the exquisite harmony and clarity of the composition.

The panel was made for Selmecbánya, one of the most important mining towns in Hungary, where it decorated the high altar of the Castle Church.

MASTER M S

The Visitation
1506

Lime-wood, 140 × 94.5 cm
Inv. No. 2151
Purchased in 1902
by the Museum of Fine Arts

Bibliography:
Radocsay 1955:
150–152, 155–156, 422–425;
Radocsay, Dénes:
450 Jahre Meister M S.
AHA IV (1957) 203–230;
Stange 1961:
147, 152–153;
Radocsay 1963: 29–32,
54–56;
Urbach, Zsuzsa:
Die Heimsuchung Mariä,
ein Tafelbild des Meisters MS
(Beiträge
zur mittelalterlichen
Entwicklungsgeschichte
des Heimsuchungsthemas).
AHA XI (1964), 69–123,
299–320;
Feuchtmüller, Rupert:
Die Auswirkungen
der Donauschule in Ungarn.
Alte und Moderne Kunst X
(1965), Heft 80, 31;
Mojzer, Miklós:
Die Passionsbilder
des Meisters M S.
Budapest, 1978; Mojzer, Miklós:
Les panneaux
de Maître M S conservés
à Budapest,
Hontszentantal (Antol)
et Lille. Annales
de la Galerie Nationale
Hongroise 3 (1980), 5–40;
Schallaburg: No. 768;
Mojzer, Miklós:
Um Meister M Z. II. Teil.
AHA XXVII (1981), 248, 274

There is little doubt that the sculptor of this statue is the master who carved the king statues illustrated in Plate 82. This is evident from the lack of stability of the figure, the facial expression (especially the comparatively broad nose and the wrinkle over the bridge), the proportions of the body and the way the hair and beard are carved. However, the folds of the cloak are more animated and fall in broader ripples, so that by comparison the drapery of the king statues appears to be broken up into too many small surfaces. The effectiveness of the flowing line of the cloak is enhanced by the fact that the undulations are strictly limited to the part of the figure they envelop; the closely patterned lines of the hair-shirt, also St. John's smooth naked arms and chest, are clearly separated from the rest of his body covered by the cloak. The head, rather decorous, is covered with thick hair and the facial expression is somewhat wry. The pensive distant look of the eyes almost anticipates the sweet lyricism which, through Master Pál of Lőcse's workshop, was generally adopted in the Szepes region hardly a decade later. The activity of this artist may have greatly contributed to the rapid spread of the new style which, only a few years after its first appearance, dominated the art of the entire county.

MASTER OF THE MATEÓC KING CARVINGS

St. John the Baptist from Szlatvin
1500–1510

Lime-wood,
losing its paint. 112 cm
Inv. No. 53.373
Transferred
in 1939
from the Hungarian National Museum
to the Museum of Fine Arts
Bibliography:
Radocsay 1967:
109, 219;
Homolka 1972: 172

This panel, depicting the death of King Boleslo, together with two other panels now in the Gallery, was part of an altarpiece illustrating the legend of St. Stanislaus. The position of the carved wooden trellis decorating the upper part of the gilded background on all three pictures indicates that these scenes must have adorned the inside panels of the wings. The other panels show the martyrdom of St. Stanislaus and the unchaining of Peter.

St. Stanislaus lived in the eleventh century, and became Bishop of Cracow in 1072. This popular Polish saint was greatly venerated in Hungary where there are early references to several altarpieces dedicated to him. He was also revered in Bohemia and Austria. The earliest representations of the legend may be found in the fourteenth century Hungarian illuminations of Anjou legends; there his story is illustrated in eight pictures which, however, do not include the scene of King Boleslo's death.

Legend has it that King Boleslo, having killed St. Stanislaus with his own hands while the Bishop was celebrating mass, undertook a pilgrimage to visit the Pope, who absolved him from his sin. During the last ten years of his life he lived incognito, doing penance in a monastery, the site of which is variously indicated in the sources—sometimes in Hungary and sometimes quite positively in Ossiach. When the King felt that he was nearing his end, he disclosed his secret. The panel shows Boleslo in his four-poster bed telling his story with lively gestures to a group of monks and laymen. The details in the foreground—the tub, the table with costly vessels, the book, the writing materials and the document, also the dog gnawing a bone—all bear witness to the increasingly realistic approach found in late medieval painting. On the basis of the broad faces, rough features and some similarities in the composition, Hungarian scholars relate the panel both to works by the Master of the Passion scenes on the Kassa high altar and to those of the Master of the Martyrdom of the Apostles, also active in Kassa. Since these painters were members of the Kassa school which developed under Polish influence, the panel illustrated here may be regarded as an important example of the link between Poland and Hungary in painting.

The Death of King Boleslo. Provenance unknown
1500–1510

Tempera on pine-wood.
85 × 77.5 cm
Inv. No. 906
Acquired
for the Hungarian
National Museum
from the Miklós Jankovich
Collection;
transferred in 1939
to the Museum of Fine Arts
Bibliography:
Radocsay 1955:
118, 326; Lajta, Edit:
Szent Szaniszló
legendájának
három jelenete
[Three scenes
from the legend
of St. Stanislaus].
BMH 5 (1954), 107–110;
Śnieżyńska-Stolot, Ewa:
Ze studiów
nad ikonografią legendy
św. Stanisława Biskupa
[Iconographical motifs
of the legend
of St. Stanislaus].
Folia Historiae Artium VIII
(1972), 161–182

87

In the sanctuary of medieval churches it was the custom to place a crucifix in an elevated position above the heads of the congregation, usually assisted by figures of the Virgin and St. John the Evangelist. In well-endowed churches the two thieves were also represented, animated figures as described in the New Testament, "their legs broken" (to hasten their death before the Sabbath). This mode of representation not only fulfilled the artist's desire to interpret as realistically as possible the words of the Scriptures, but was also significant from the point of view of composition: the convulsive jerks and agony of the thieves makes us more aware of the eternal nature of Christ's sacrifice, His death to bring salvation to all men.

In style the Szepesbéla figures bear little resemblance to the indigenous carvings of the Szepes region. In fact some scholars relate them to The Angel from the Annunciation (Plate 50) from Frics – a comparatively distant place, also to the statues of the high altar in Bakabánya, which is even further from Szepes. This undeniable link between works originating in different areas serves to caution us against too readily attributing works to local artists.

The Crucifixion from Szepesbéla
1500–1510

Lime-wood, painted and gilded; the figure of Christ 140 cm, that of the thieves 75 and 65 cm respectively
Inv. No. 53.562, 55.898.1–2
Transferred in 1939 from the Hungarian National Museum to the Museum of Fine Arts
Bibliography: Radocsay 1967: 111, 214; Homolka 1972: 170

88

Late Gothic art is generally characterized by an increased degree of animation. There are exceptions, the best-known in the field of panel painting being the works of Memlinc, Zeitblom and Hans Holbein the Elder. It is possible that the Master of Okolicsnó, the most prominent artist in Liptó County in the 1500s, may have had something in common with these masters. His work was outstanding, even measured by the high standards of the neighbouring Szepes region; his style, however, is a completely isolated phenomenon in that area. Although his manner of painting is extremely individual and therefore easily recognizable, only two other works apart from the altarpiece in Okolicsnó can be attributed to him, namely two side-altars in the neighbouring church of Szmrecsány. It was not only a standard that the Szepes region provided for him; it was from Szepes that he drew his earliest inspiration. His art, without parallel in Liptó, had great affinity with the panels decorating the altar of the Coronation of the Virgin in Szepeshely, an influence clearly originating during his years of apprenticeship there.

His pictures are lucidly composed, the figures arranged in simple geometric forms. The sombre colours, completed here and there with patches of stronger reds, yellows and greens, the immobility of the figures suggesting controlled grief, their angular carriage and the deserted landscape all contribute to the general atmosphere. Had no other creation of the Master come down to us, we could content ourselves with stating that he used his means to express sorrow and mourning. However, comparing the work with the panels from Szmrecsány, it is evident that these characteristics are features of his individual style. His ideal in painting must have been an undemonstrative, somewhat austere solemnity which he could best achieve in this type of composition.

THE MASTER OF OKOLICSNÓ

The Lamentation from the high altar in Okolicsnó
1500–1510

Tempera on pine-wood,
133 × 100 cm
Inv. No. 184
Purchased by the Hungarian National Picture Gallery in 1880
Bibliography:
Radocsay 1955:
176–177, 412–413;
Radocsay 1963:
33, 57–58;
Glatz 1975: 45;
Schallaburg: No. 771

From his arrangement of figures and painterly approach we might describe the work of the Master of Okolicsnó as reticent and even conservative. However, the art of Memlinc shows that by deviating from the general trend an artist does not necessarily create works of inferior value. Although ways of representing space was one of the major problems faced by artists in Central and Eastern Europe at that time, the Master of Okolicsnó remained fairly indifferent to it and bestowed little care even upon the landscape in his Lamentation. In the panel illustrated here the figures are carefully placed side by side as on a relief, hardly covering each other. The suggestion of recession is enhanced by the golden background and brocade altar-cloth, both with a pomegranate design. The Master was aware that this style of painting could to some extent produce an illusion of depth. It is in the placing of the Infant that he most successfully suggests the roundedness of the human form and the arrangement of the figures one behind the other. At the same time he emphasizes the importance of the Child in this composition. At that time it would have been unimaginable to depict an altar without a central shrine or niche, but since in the Temple of Jerusalem a winged altar would have been quite out of place, the master has placed the stone tablets of Moses on the altar as a retable. One of the tablets serves to frame the small central figure. The powerfully painted male heads are particularly effective. Although they are by no means portrait-like, the features are so marked that even in the absence of a definitely demonstrable Italian or Netherlandish influence, they can well be compared to contemporary painting in those countries.

THE MASTER OF OKOLICSNÓ

The Presentation in the Temple from the high altar in Okolicsnó
1500–1510

Tempera on pine-wood.
133 × 100 cm
Inv. No. 184
Purchased
by the Hungarian National Picture Gallery in 1880
Bibliography:
Radocsay 1955:
176–177, 412–413;
Radocsay 1963: 33, 57–58;
Glatz 1975: 45;
Schallaburg: No. 772

These statues are so small that they must surely have been made for a rather small altar. They represent young men and this, together with the liturgical, dalmatic robes, suggests diaconal saints; St. Stephen and St. Lawrence were the ones most often represented. St. Stephen having been stoned, is usually made recognizable by the fragments of rocks held in his hand or on his lap, while Lawrence is usually shown with the grate on which he was roasted to death. Here the grate is not held by the figure on the right, but the details suggest that he must have held this instrument of his martyrdom in his left hand, and it would therefore seem that this is indeed the figure of St. Lawrence.

Calmness of modelling, as seen in these two figures, is rare in works dating from the early sixteenth century, especially in the modelling of loosely hanging parts and folds of the garments seen on late Gothic statues. When we consider the silhouette, these statues surpass in quality many others which owe their animation to the carving of robes. The indication of movement similarly adds to the plasticity of the figures. In both figures the trunks are twisted; the saints turn their heads aside and gesticulate with their hands; their hair has a life of its own. In wooden statues of the then flourishing Danube School we often see hair represented as if blown by the wind. Here, however, the master obviously considered such a solution as exaggerated, although there is no doubt that, in addition to local traditions, he received stylistic incentives from Austria. He avoided all externals and solved the task of suggesting movement in his figures without availing himself of the then fashionable tumble of draperies.

St. Stephen the Protomartyr and St. Lawrence (?) from Kassa
c. 1510

Lime-wood, the painting and gilding damaged; 45 cm and 45.5 cm respectively
Inv. No. 55.870.1–2
Transferred in 1939 from the Hungarian National Museum to the Museum of Fine Arts
Bibliography:
Radocsay 1967: 125, 180

These figures of the Virgin of Sorrows and St. John the Evangelist may have decorated a side-altar in the cathedral at Kassa (then still only a parish church). In 1556 the city was badly damaged by fire, and many of the altars perished, so that it is no longer possible to tell which one they belonged to. Judging by the folds of the garments, the Crucifixion comes from the workshop responsible for the carvings on the high altar, a contribution to the status of the city as an important centre of late Gothic sculptural art, even by European standards. The figures illustrated here are flatter and more stereotyped than those on the high altar, though it was on the latter that they were undoubtedly modelled. The creases in the garment on the horizontally held lower arm are evocative also of the solution seen on the Visitation—an altar similarly modelled after the high altar. Some of the deep cuts —for example those behind the left elbows on both figures—show that the master was not totally committed to the use of flat elaboration.

On the other hand, certain more external marks than those enumerated so far, indicate that the master's interest was not confined to local traditions. Certainly he had also remarked the style then emerging along the Bavarian-Austrian section of the Danube. This is evident especially in the facial expressions and St. John's luxuriant hair. It is interesting to note the application of the two styles —parallel rather than coalescing in these works.

Figures from the Crucifixion in Kassa
c. 1510

Lime-wood, repainted.
56 cm
Inv. No. 55.928. 1–2
Transferred in 1939
from the Hungarian
National Museum
to the Museum of Fine Arts
Bibliography:
Radocsay 1967:
125, 180;
Homolka 1972: 52
(mentions them erroneously
as in the Košice Museum)

The kneeling posture in representations of the Death of the Virgin was intended to emphasize the piety of Mary: she was praying until the very moment of death. The apostles, brought together by the news that she is dying, surround her so closely that practically nothing can be seen of the room in which she kneels. They are alone together, as on the occasion of the pentecostal miracle. The simplicity of the representation, which excludes many interesting small painterly details and leaves the main part of the room in obscurity, without indicating the outer world through the door or the window, is believed to show the influence of the relief on painting. The most famous example of this type of composition is the Cracow altar by Veit Stoss, but there are numerous other reliefs of various sizes modelled after the Cracow altar, including works of Hungarian provenance (Plate 73). On the panel illustrated here the impact of Cracow is unmistakable: this may be seen in the arrangement of the apostles in two rows, one behind the other, in the hand supporting the weary body of the Virgin from behind, and in the figure of St. Peter on the right holding a thurible. Rooms with barrel vaults often figure on sixteenth century panels from the Szepes region; the arcaded window and door intensify the effect of an interior, but this effect is not enhanced by the broader window in the longitudinal axis which, placed above the Virgin, serves to emphasize her role as the central character. This window is too large in proportion to the rest of the room and seems to pierce the ceiling; thus it belongs rather to the visionary aspect of the picture. Christ appears behind it with a newborn babe in his arms—symbol of the Virgin's soul as it ascends to heaven. Thus the window actually permits a glimpse of heaven. At the beginning of the sixteenth century, however, the realistic trend was already so strong that the artist did not dare simply to portray an opening in the wall: illogically, but in a way characteristic of his age, he painted a true window with a stone frame, sill and jamb, the latter foreshortened in perspective.

CIRCLE OF THE MASTER OF KÁPOSZTAFALVA

Death of the Virgin from Szepeshely
c. 1510

Panel, 103 × 74 cm
Inv. No. 53.377
Transferred in 1936
from the Hungarian
National Museum
to the Museum of Fine Arts
Bibliography:
Radocsay 1955:
172, 443–444;
Glatz 1975: 44

This panel represents the awed amazement of the apostles when they are visited by the Holy Ghost. They give expression to their feelings by making startled gestures, or by adopting an elated, reserved attitude. The facial expressions are highly individual, but only James standing on the extreme left has any other special distinguishing mark. It is also possible to identify Peter and John standing at the back. The Virgin is shown seated and dignified, praying amidst the apostles.

The apostles are solemn but by no means rigid; the group is characterized by bright but not glaring patches of colour. In fact the colour scheme is one of the attractive features of the panel which is rightly considered to be the most characteristic painting of the Csík region. The style, though obviously related to that of the German schools of the early sixteenth century, is not so close to any one of them that the work might be attributed to a German artist or an artist trained in Germany. The enrichment of the traditional formal idiom with certain contemporary solutions demonstrates the independence of Csík painting. The altar—like the local school as a whole —is basically conservative; this may be seen in the arrangement of the planes, the detailed drawing and the important part played by the contour lines. The modern solutions came partly from the Danube School, but they are to be seen only in the carriage and beards of some of the figures. (The snow-covered mountain peaks in the Passion scenes on the wings are generally attributed to local influences. This may be right, but the example was surely set by the Danube School which took so much delight in representing peaks reaching to the skies, see Fig. at Plate 94b.)

The high altar from Csíkszentlélek

c. 1510

Pine-wood, 170 × 134 cm
The wings:
82 × 60.5 cm, each;
the predella: 38 × 210 cm;
the lunette: 82 × 74 cm
Inv. No. 53.370.1
Transferred in 1936
from the Hungarian
National Museum
to the Museum of Fine Arts
Bibliography:
Radocsay 1955:
188, 292–293;
Radocsay
1963: 34–35, 59;
Feuchtmüller, Rupert:
Catalogue of the
"Kunst der Donauschule"
exhibition.
St. Florian–Linz, 1965:
150;
Schallaburg: No. 786

94 a

Special mention should be made of the splendid embossed and gilded tracery. At first sight one has the impression that it is composed of Gothic motifs dissolving into the Italian Renaissance style; more careful observation reveals, however, that they are less rigid and rather more restless and sensitive. They are in fact motifs derived from the formal idiom of the Danube style, as also are the alternately long and short rays emanating from the dove —the symbol of the Holy Ghost—their purpose being to express the dynamism and all-pervading power of God's grace. When we consider that in 1510 the Danube School had not long been established, we may well be amazed that its influence was already visible in work originating in the valleys below the Eastern Carpathian mountains.

The Descent of the Holy Ghost from the high altar in Csíkszentlélek *c.* 1510

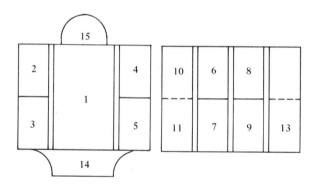

1 The Descent
   of the Holy Ghost
2 St. Francis Receiving
   the Stigmata
3 St. Blasius,
   St. Augustine
   and St. Nicholas
4 St. Anne, St. Elisabeth
   and Mary Magdalen
5 St. Catherine, St. Barbara
   and St. Dorothy
6 The Seizure of Christ
7 Christ Carrying the Cross
8 Christ before Pilate
9 The Crucifixion
10 The Agony in the
   Garden
11 The Crowning
   with Thorns
12 The Flagellation
13 The Resurrection
14 The Virgin,
   the Man of Sorrows,
   St. John the Evangelist
15 The Coronation
   of the Virgin

94 b

The setting is an urban interior with many interesting objects represented in great detail. This accurate, realistic representation was evidently important to the artist. To create an illusion of space in the room, for example, he built up a network of lines, using the floor-tiles as his starting point. The foreshortenings are excellent, yet the final result is a rather dry appearance. This, however, is offset by the rich tones of the painting and the light and vivid representation of certain details.

The picture shows much stir and bustle in the somewhat crowded room after the delivery of the Child. Anne, exhausted, is spooning up her broth while still lying in bed, but the midwives are busy bathing the baby. The midwife on the left, pouring water into a basin, wears an unusual cap, a somewhat simplified version of the truncated cone-shaped Burgundian headdress. The mantle worn by the two other women is more in keeping with the contemporary style of the middle-class; Anne's mantle has become loose while lying in bed. The readily recognizable items of furniture are also worthy of note. The events foreshadowing the birth can be seen through the window. Anne, for long barren, is told by an angel that she will have a child; she is to go and meet her husband, who can be seen returning through the open city gate.

Considering the colour scheme and tonality of the panel, as well as the proportions of the figures with their comparatively large heads, the work is absolutely unique among the early Hungarian paintings which have survived. Lippa being a town at the edge of the Hungarian Plain, its geographic situation may account for the unusual quality of the work. Apart from the panels which have come down to us from Csegöld, which was spared by the Turks, this is the only painting that does not originate from the mountainous areas.

The painting on the reverse is severely damaged. From the name "SIMON", uncovered in the course of recent restorations, we already know that originally it must have decorated an altar dedicated to St. Anne; the other panels also represented members of Christ's kinship. On the reverse of the panel showing the Birth of the Blessed Virgin there was a picture of "Simon Zelotes".

Birth of the Blessed Virgin. Wing-painting of an altar from Lippa (?)
1510–1515

Lime-wood, 80.5 × 55 cm
Inv. No. 3403
Purchased in 1907
by the Museum
of Fine Arts
Bibliography:
Radocsay 1955:
186, 365

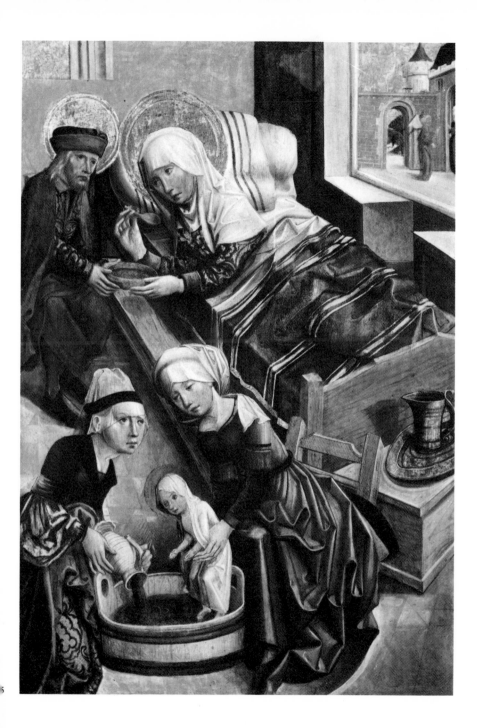

The Danube School of painting, very influential in the first decades of the sixteenth century, dominated the art of Bavaria and Austria along the banks of the river Danube, an area easily accessible from the Szepes region. The distance is not great, even if expressed in kilometres, and appears still less so when we consider that trade and cultural relations were very close between the inhabitants of the areas at that time. It is, therefore, a striking fact that the influence of the Danube School is scarcely discernible in the development of painting in the Szepes region —at least as evidenced by the works that have come down to us. It did however help to stimulate interest in landscape painting, as may be seen in this work with its towering rocks, forests and scrub, and the castle with bastions and gate-houses in the background. It is a deserted landscape, by no means as desolate as the deserts of Egypt but as in Flemish models, uninhabited apart from the central figure. But while late medieval painters were content to exclude the human figure from their landscapes, they depicted buildings and townscapes in the background. (There are landscapes without buildings in some works by members of the Danube School.) The manner in which the figure and the landscape —especially the foliage of the trees—are painted, links this picture with the panel from the high altar in Lőcse; in fact certain parts of the castle appear in practically the same form in both pictures.

The panel represents a scene from the legend of St. Anthony, depicting him when he has resisted all temptation. Christ's blessing in recognition of the sufferings endured by the Saint, is inscribed on the banderole, the words being taken from the most famous medieval collection of lives of the saints called the *Legenda aurea*. Translated into English it reads: "As you have held out manfully, I will make your name known to the whole world." It is interesting that the Saviour emerging from the clouds gives His blessing with His left hand. This somewhat awkward gesture is evidently a make-do solution: Christ being in the left corner of the picture, He would have covered himself by raising His right hand.

**The Vision
of St. Anthony
the Hermit
from Szepesbéla**
c. 1510–1520

Lime-wood, 94 × 70 cm
Inv. No. 53.565
Transferred in 1936
from the Hungarian
National Museum
to the Museum of Fine Arts
Bibliography:
Radocsay 1955:
166, 174, 213, 434–435;
Glatz 1975: 46–48

The altar is one of the finer products of the Liptó workshops which, however, failed to evolve any markedly individual style. The carving in the shrine is, in fact, similar to the main figure decorating St. Anthony's altar in Szepesszombat, a work by the same hand. Animated in the late Gothic style and carved with deep undercuts, it could well be the work of one of the more conservative sculptors of Szepes. Traits showing a more contemporary approach result from the scarcely perceptible influence of Veit Stoss's art, weakened by a series of transmissions and manifest only here and there in the artist's inclination. The position of the carving in the shrine is strange, for there would have been room for two additional figures, one on either side, but from the very beginning it always stood alone. By leaving most of the shrine empty, the artist wished to emphasize the importance of this particular figure. The raised platform within the shrine is also unusual. The panels on the wings reveal more of the contemporary trends of the second decade of the sixteenth century. They are reminiscent of the products of the Danube School, but being more laboured and quite lacking in animation, they are in fact only distant variants. The influence of the school was probably conveyed by Lucas Cranach who was then becoming rather popular among the painters working east of Saxony.

The St. Andrew altarpiece from Liptószentandrás (open)
1512

The carving in the central shrine of the altar: lime-wood, the painting and gilding damaged; the garment originally decorated with a gilded brocade pattern, 123 cm
The carving in the upper part with pinnacles: lime-wood, the painting and gilding damaged, 72 cm
The wings: pine-wood, 73 × 57.5 cm each
The predella: pine-wood, 48 × 190 cm
Inv. No. 53.569.1–8
Transferred in 1936 from the Hungarian National Museum to the Museum of Fine Arts
Bibliography:
Radocsay 1955: 177, 366;
Radocsay 1967: 110, 189;
Homolka 1972: 174

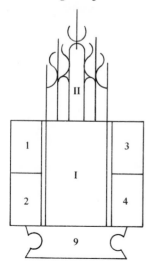
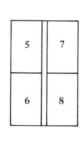

I   St. Andrew
II St. Bartholomew
1   The Crucifixion
2   The Resurrection
3   The Tormenting
    of St. Andrew
4   St. Andrew on the Cross
5   St. John the Evangelist
    and St. Peter
6   St. James the Less
    and St. Simon
7   St. Barbara
    and St. Catherine
8   St. Margaret and
    a Female Saint
9   The Sudarium
    with Two Angels

This panel is one of the problematic works now in the Gallery. The emphasis on the cruel details of The Flagellation is in keeping with the period indicated by the date, but the origin of the panel has always been a matter for speculation among the experts. The style is based on a mixture of elements taken from Dürer and the Danube School; the colours are as bright as those of Albrecht Altdorfer or Wolf Huber. These characteristics are enhanced by unrestrained animation. The figures seem to be unable to move in the low, squat space filled with an unnecessarily large number of columns, so that their gestures seem all the more violent. The columns suggest a grand portico, rather than a torture chamber; the head of a person lurking in the left upper corner could be that of the proconsul himself. At the beginning of the sixteenth century columns were a rarity in architecture north of the Alps; for this reason, they did not often figure in paintings. Thus their presence here adds an element of grandeur to the chamber, giving it a more contemporary Italianate appearance. At the same time, however, the queer, ring-shaped ornaments appearing at intervals on the stem of the columns, make them look awkward and primitive.

This picture is identified in the literature as one of several panels originating from Transylvania, the most likely breeding ground for the joint manifestation of such a variety of influences. However, this argument is no longer considered to be conclusive, for very similar panels originating from Salzburg and Hessen have now been found.

The Flagellation.
Provenance unknown
1514

Pine-wood
109 × 102.5 cm
Inv. No. 1639
Acquired
by the Hungarian
National Museum
from the Miklós Jankovich
Collection.
Transferred in 1939
to the Museum of Fine Arts

Bibliography:
Radocsay 1955:
186–187, 332;
Feuchtmüller, Rupert:
Die Auswirkungen
der Donauschule
in Ungarn. Alte
und Moderne Kunst
X (1965), Heft 80, 32;
in the Catalogue of the
"Kunst der Donauschule"
exhibition.
St. Florian–Linz,
1965, No. 364;
(See Feuchtmüller's views
also on page 149
of the same catalogue);
Stange, Alfred: Die Kunst
der Donauschule
—Würdigung und Kritik
der Ausstellung
des Landes Oberösterreich
in St. Florian und Linz.
Alte und Moderne Kunst X
(1965), Heft 82, 49;
Spätgotik in Salzburg.
Die Malerei 1400–1530.
Salzburg, 1972, 168–169;
Végh, János:
Spätgotik in Salzburg.
Die Malerei 1400–1530.
Anmerkungen
zur Ausstellung.
AHA XX (1974), 340;
Schallaburg: No. 788

1514

98

This rather small altar would hardly have been effective in a church or any other large interior. Most probably it was used for private prayer. It may have stood in a small chapel, perhaps in a castle or a nobleman's mansion, and it is possible that it was not used for the celebration of mass but only for prayer. The shrine of the altar is now empty but it is assumed that it once contained a statue of the Man of Sorrows, or perhaps the Virgin of Sorrows, the figures most appropriate to the angels on either side holding emblems of the Passion. Their position is somewhat unusual, though not rare. It was customary to employ a smaller scale for subsidiary figures, though these were generally carved in the same way or perhaps in a lower relief; if a less expensive solution was required, paintings were substituted for sculptural works. Incidentally, it would seem that whoever commissioned this work was not particularly exacting: the reverse of the wings showing St. Bernardine of Siena and St. Giles were simply left unpainted. Nor was he fastidious in the choice of the master: this is obviously a work of only average quality typical of provincial painting in Sáros. Yet it cannot be said that the painter had no ambition. Nowhere in his work can he be accused of having sought the easy solution: he attempted spatial representation in his placing of the figures and tried to give anatomical reality to their gestures, also adding sharp features to the faces. But his efforts were not always successful. His strong point was colouring: the combined effect of his extraordinary browns and violets is truly attractive. It recalls faintly the fascinating colour scheme of the Danube School and some of the facial features also point to this source.

Small altar from Hervartó
1514

Pine-wood;
the panels measuring
81.5 × 22 and 82 × 22 cm,
respectively
Inv. No. 53.902.1–53.902.3
Transferred
in 1939 from the
Hungarian National Museum
to the Museum of Fine Arts
Bibliography:
Radocsay 1955:
178, 315

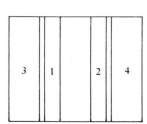

1 *Angel with Sword and Lance*
2 *Angel with Column and Sponge*
3 *St. Bernardine of Siena*
4 *St. Giles*

99

Figures for the decoration of large winged altars were always the joint work of several members of one workshop. This accounts for the heterogeneous style of the carvings, especially evident if the workshop was not managed by a strong personality or by a master who deliberately allowed the members considerable freedom of style. The result of such circumstances is clearly discernible on the high altar from Kisszeben, where the slightly rough style of the three main figures is in sharp contrast to the style of the four martyr virgins. The latter, if not definitely smiling, are still gentle, baby-faced figures and in their original position their charm was enhanced by the fact that they were half the size of the statues in the shrine of the altar. The folds of their garments, compared to those of the central carvings, are less deep, their glances less fixed, and it would be hard to credit that they are from one and the same altar had we not reliable data available regarding their origin. It is undeniable that the gentler, more charming style, so different from that of the main figures, plays the more important role in the character of the winged altar as a whole. Placed on either side of the altar shrine in superimposed niches, these milder figures serve to create a transition between the powerful effect of the central figures and the gaiety of the bright panels.

There is a certain morphological conformity between the side carvings and the pictures on the wings by which they are linked beyond doubt. The carvings and most of the figures on the panels are graceful; they all have long fingers on which the joints, however, are unusually thick, almost gnarled. As these large medieval winged altars were usually produced by a number of carvers and painters in close co-operation, these artists may have influenced one another, and all of them may have adopted apparently insignificant but revealing details. These details allow us to determine more accurately the date when the side figures were created: the modelling of the hands in the manner mentioned above is not found on the central carvings; it follows, therefore, that the figures of the martyr virgins were produced at a later date, probably simultaneously with the painting of the wings. (See Fig. at Plate 100b.)

Carving of St. Catherine from the high altar in Kisszeben
1510–1516

Lime-wood, painted and gilded.
92.5 cm
Inv. No. 3916
Transferred in 1909 from the Museum of Applied Arts to the Museum of Fine Arts
Bibliography:
Radocsay 1967: 116, 183;
Homolka 1972: 259

100 a

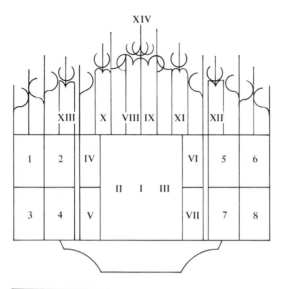

**Carving
of St. Dorothy
from the high altar
in Kisszeben**
1510–1516

Lime-wood, painted and
gilded. 92 cm

The open altar:
- I   *The Virgin and Child*
- II   *St. John the Baptist*
- III   *St. Peter*
- IV   *St. Barbara*
- V   *St. Margaret*
- VI   *St. Catherine*
- VII   *St. Dorothy*
- VIII   *Mary*
- IX   *St. Elizabeth*
- X   *King St. Stephen*
- XI   *King St. Ladislas*
- XII   *St. Martin*
- XIII   *The Man of Sorrows*
- 1   *Zacheriah's Offering*
- 2   *The Birth of St. John
  the Baptist*
- 3   *The Baptisme
  of Christ*
- 4   *St. John the Baptist
  before Herod*
- 5   *St. John the Baptist
  Preaching*
- 6   *St. John the Baptist
  in the Desert*
- 7   *The Decapitation
  of St. John the Baptist*
- 8   *The Delivery
  of the Head of St. John
  the Baptist to Herod*

The closed altar:
- 9   *The Annunciation*
- 10   *The Nativity*
- 11   *The Last Judgement*
- 12   *The Virgin Entering
  the Temple*
- 13   *Ecce Homo*
- 14   *The Crucifixion*
- 15   *Christ the Savior (?)*
- 16   *Blessing
  of an Unknown Man*
- 17   *Christ Walking upon
  the Water*
- 18   *The Transfiguration*
- 19   *The Ascension*
- 20   *The Holy Trinity
  with Music-making
  Angels*
- 21   *Christ in Limbo*
- 22   *The Resurrection*
- 23   *Trumpeteers
  of the Last Judgement*
- 24   *The Coronation
  of the Virgin*

100b

This is one of the fascinating paintings which once decorated the vast high altar at Kisszeben. Panels, each one almost 1.5 metres in height, once covered the surface of the altar in two rows one above the other. When the wings were closed, sixteen large pictures representing scenes from the New Testament, from the Annunciation to the Last Judgement, could be seen together. The series is at present undergoing restoration. It was restored during the baroque period when, as was customary at that time, the panels were completely repainted: although the medieval compositions were preserved in a recognizable form, no part of the pictures remained untouched. The present project, undertaken with the aim of restoring the panels to their original appearance, was begun several years ago and is still far from being completed. The style cannot be assessed until the work is finished, especially as the series was evidently painted by several masters. However, it is already clear that the painting can be traced back partly to the Szepes region and partly to Poland.

The arrangement of the figures in the Annunciation is not the artist's own idea; he took it from a very popular and much copied earlier composition by Schongauer (B.3), adapting it in combination with Master ES's engraving (Lehrs 13), in order to suggest the corner of a room. By enlarging the figures, however, he introduced into the original works a new and peculiar character: for scarcely one square inch is left empty in the picture, the floating figures, so important for Schongauer, being replaced here by weighty ones arranged side by side. The strength of the figures is enhanced by the severely simple background: it is rather unusual for medieval painters to so greatly simplify an interior in an endeavour to concentrate the spectator's attention on the figures. (See Fig. at Plate 100b.)

The Annunciation from the Kisszeben high altar
1510–1516

Lime-wood, 144.5 × 73 cm
Inv. No. 3916
Transferred in 1909
from the Museum
of Applied Arts
to the Museum of Fine Arts

Bibliography:
Radocsay 1955:
355–356;
Radocsay 1963:
26–29, 53–54;
Glatz 1975:
37; Lehrs: 13

The Kisszeben church was dedicated to St. John the Baptist, scenes from his life being therefore represented on the interior panels of the altar-wings. The first panel of the series depicts Zechariah's offering, as was usual in all St. John series. According to the Gospel, Zechariah was burning incense in the temple when Archangel Gabriel appeared to him and prophesied that though already an old man, he was to have a son. Yet Zechariah's vision of Gabriel is almost hidden by the numerous figures standing about in the foreground. Both the prophet Zechariah and the Archangel are singularly small in the picture, smaller than the perspective would justify. The most holy place in the temple was similar to the sanctuary of a Gothic church, although the windows were not ogival. The Ark of the Covenant on the altar, resplendent like a reliquary, is set off by a canopy of golden brocade. The men in the foreground are the faithful who wished to be present while the priest performed his office but as they were not admitted to the Holy of Holies, they are waiting to receive his blessing when he emerges. One of the group on the right is shown wearing a strikingly ornamented high Jewish cap, while the figure in front of him is dressed, like Zechariah, in gold brocade. It is no accident that the painter placed these figures with their backs to the sanctuary where the offering is taking place. It was his intention to indicate thereby that they are only in the porch of the temple whence they cannot see into the Holy of Holies. The gilded upper part of the panel was originally decorated by applied tracery to increase the effect of splendour and solemnity when the altar was opened. (See Fig. at Plate 100b.)

Zechariah's Offering from the Kisszeben high altar
1510–1516

Lime-wood, 145.5 × 73 cm
Inv. No. 3916
Transferred in 1909
from the Museum
of Applied Arts
to the Museum of Fine Arts
Bibliography:
Radocsay 1955: 355–356;
Radocsay 1963:
26–29, 53–54;
Glatz 1975: 37

The winged altar, widely adopted in the fifteenth century, was preceded, among other things, by the reliquary placed on a communion table. The earliest of the north German winged altars consisted precisely of a row of busts or statuettes containing relics. Later the reliquaries were removed to the lower ledge of the altar, the predella. On paintings of the Virgin with Child, too, the small reliquary caskets were mostly concealed in the frames (Plate 37). By the beginning of the sixteenth century a further development had taken place: the small busts—once made of precious metal and later often carved of wood—were now replaced by half-length figures such as those decorating the Leibic predella.

In a typically medieval manner, a whole series of events—in this case the story of the redemption—is indicated by the representation of Christ risen from the sepulchre, His fatal wounds clearly visible, still sorrowing but having gained eternal life. Praying beside Him is the sad figure of the Madonna, and John, the favourite pupil. The predella of the other altar in Leibic also represents the death of Christ (Plate 116). It would appear that the then parish priest or patron found the representation of this subject important. The folds of the clothes worn by the figures are less ruffled than those of St. Anne, to whom the altar is dedicated, and those of two other figures above the predella. There is, however, no doubt that they are all the work of the same hand. The gifted, though not outstanding sculptor has been identified as Georgius Salienarius whose name is scratched into the cloak of Mary, one of the figures in the shrine. As, however, medieval masters signed their names in a different style, it is possible that the inscribed name is that of a contemporary church-goer.

Man of Sorrows with half-length figures of the Virgin and St. John the Evangelist on the predella of St. Anne's altar, in Leibic
1510–1520

Lime-wood,
painted and gilded,
44.5, 46.5 and 42.5 cm
respectively
Inv. No. 53.574.3–5
Transferred in 1936 from the Hungarian National Museum to the Museum of Fine Arts
Bibliography:
Radocsay 1967: 109, 188

I St. Anne with the Virgin and Child
II St. John the Almsgiver
III St. Christopher
IV St. Lawrence (?)
V The bust of Christ
VI The bust of St. John the Evangelist
1 St. Ursula
2 St. Elisabeth
3 St. Apollonia
4 St. Barbara
5 St. Anne, Salomas, Joachim, Cleophas
6 Esmeria, Efraim, Elisabeth, Eliud
7 Mary, Joseph and the Infant Jesus
8 Eliud, Emerencia, Enim
9 Mary, Cleophas, Simon, James, Judas Taddeus, Joseph, Alpheus
10 Emerenciana, Stollanus, Anne, Esmeria
11 Mary Salome, Zebedeus, St. John the Evangelist, St. James the Greater
12 Enim, Menela, Servatius

103

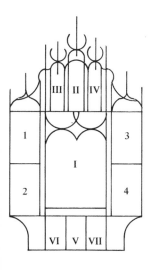

The figure stands in the upper part of the altar-piece which is crowned with arches, some regular, others much elaborated with pillars, ornamental foliage, creepers and tracery; the superstructure of very large altars usually extended to the ceiling of the church and statues of saints were often incorporated into the richly gilded carving. They represented saints not seen in the altar-shrine with the titular saint and the characters closest to her, nor in the relief or painting decorating the wings, yet they could not be altogether excluded. They were much smaller than the main figures, yet at the same time more distant from the spectator, a problem only to be solved by simplifying the forms of the details.

Typical of such figures is the small statue of St. John the Almsgiver illustrated here. The mortal remains of the patriarch of Alexandria were brought to Buda in 1489 as a gift from the Turkish Sultan who hoped in this way to win the goodwill of King Matthias.

The relic was placed in the chapel of the royal palace where it stimulated a cult of the saint in Hungary. He soon became known all over the country and was represented on the winged altars produced in large numbers at that time. Much was written about him, legends gained ground, and here he is shown wearing the garments of a cardinal, although as a patriarch of Alexandria he had no right to such robes; in fact, the office of cardinal was established only much later. He carries a money-bag in his hand from which he distributes alms. The figure from Leibic is typical: St. John is shown in the pontificals or *cappa magna* worn by cardinals, with the hood pulled over his head.

The shape of the beggar's skull deserves special notice. It is neither beautiful nor regular; apparently the sculptor wished to suggest by this detail the beggar's afflicted state and need for help. From the sculptural point of view, this individually carved head is much more interesting than the regularly carved smooth ones of the large principal figures below, which look almost as if they had been turned on the lathe. (See Fig. at Plate 103.)

St. John the Almsgiver from the superstructure of St. Anne's altar in Leibic
1510–1520

Lime-wood, gilded and painted, 85.5 cm
Inv. No. 53.574.6
Bibliography:
Radocsay 1967: 109, 188; Végh, János: Alamizsnás Szent János a budai várban [St. John the Almsgiver in Buda Castle]. Építés–Építészettudomány IX (1980) 455–467

The panel shows St. Anne in the company of her three daughters born of her three marriages and her many grandchildren. It is noteworthy that none of the husbands are present. The matriarch shares her bench with the Virgin who—to emphasize the difference in age—is seated without a cushion. The figure of the Infant Jesus between them is comparatively large. Of the women only Mary is represented with flowing hair—to indicate the miracle of her lasting virginity. It is a scene that had been often depicted earlier on icons; the hieratic solemnity of those works is absent here, the arrangement of the bustling figures and the narrative motifs now giving a realistic atmosphere.

The style of the painting is unique; there is no similar work known from the mining towns around Dubravica; it is related more closely to Bavarian and Frankish art. The figures, although more crude and powerful, are reminiscent of the types seen in Hans Suess von Kulmbach's works. The restless undulation of the drapery, the luxuriant hair of the children tossed on one side, are details known to us from pictures by followers of the Danube School but the indoor setting is wholly alien to their approach. A genuine Danube School master would have set the scene in the open air, and filled in a background of magnificent trees and mountain peaks reaching to the sky.

So many paintings originating within the early boundaries of Hungary have perished that it would be rash to conclude that no similar work has ever existed; nevertheless it does seem that this work is unique. For we know that the squires of Dubravica village, László and Márk Dubravicky, held important positions at Court during the Jagiellon dynasty, and Márk even had the title of Master of the Horse. The name John was common in the family and the emphasis on the Evangelist—in the picture the only child dressed like a grown-up, sitting at the feet of St. Anne with his attribute, the book, under his arm —was no doubt intended to draw attention to a child relative. As they moved in court circles at Buda, the Dubravickys may easily have become acquainted with a court painter and commissioned him to execute this panel. This seems to be the most obvious explanation of the unusual style.

The Holy Kinship from Dubravica
1510–1520

Pine-wood, 101 × 102 cm
Inv. No. 8133
Purchased in 1942
by the Museum
of Fine Arts
from György Tornyai
Bibliography:
Radocsay 1955:
160, 299;
Radocsay 1963: 32–33,
56–57;
Exhibited
at "Kunst der Donauschule",
St. Florian–Linz, 1965,
Catalogue No. 368
(See also comments
by Rupert Feuchtmüller
in same Catalogue,
p. 149); Löcher, Kurt:
St. Florian. Die Kunst
der Donauschule (Malerei).
Pantheon XXIII (1965), 344;
Feuchtmüller, Rupert:
Die Auswirkungen
der Donauschule
in Ungarn.
Alte und Moderne Kunst
X (1965), Heft 80, 31;
Zolnay, László:
A régi zólyomi ispánság
építkezéseinek történetéhez.
Közlemény
[A study on the history
of the building activities
of the old Zólyom
stewardship].
Ars Hungarica VII
(1979), 47–48;
Schallaburg: No. 760

105

The gruesome scenes of the Apocalypse were a constant source of inspiration to medieval artists. The crescent under the feet of the earlier representations of Mary was an established way of hinting that the female figure was identical with the Virgin. Dürer's series of woodcuts published in 1498 ensured the popularity of the subject. The gloomy, fatalistic beliefs of the period also contributed to its persistence. It is owing to the artistic genius and effective techniques of reproduction developed by the Nuremberg master that sixteenth century representations—even such large altarpieces as the one from Szentbenedek—were modelled after his woodcuts.

Judging by the drapery and the colour-scheme, this Transylvanian painter must have acquired his skill at one of the Danube School art centres. His picture is a powerful painterly elaboration of Dürer's work. The painterly approach was important, for although he did not depart much from his model—except by including a belligerent angel in the upper right corner and an evangelist in the lower left, and made the background look more like a landscape—the small size and more airy arrangement of the figures weakened, rather than improved the composition. The presence of the evangelist can be accounted for by the fact that the painter did not have enough space to depict the whole series. The large but comparatively narrow panel suggests that he may have elaborated only one other scene to represent the triumphant end of the story, the two panels thus forming the wings of an altar.

The Woman of the Apocalypse with the Dragon from Szentbenedek
1510–1520

Pine-wood, 120 × 74 cm
Inv. No. 7639
Donated to the Museum of Fine Arts
by Rudolf Bedő in 1939
Bibliography:
Radocsay 1955:
186, 432;
Feuchtmüller, Rupert, in the Catalogue of the "Kunst der Donauschule" exhibition. St. Florian–Linz, 1965: 149

The peculiar style of this panel may possibly be due to the fact that it was painted for the high altar of the Franciscan church in Csíksomlyó. It should be noted that while Hungarian scholars acquainted with local developments in art date the picture to the second decade of the sixteenth century, the author of the most comprehensive analysis of German panel painting, who evidently did not regard this picture as specifically Transylvanian, or a product of Csík, gives the date of origin as around 1480, his calculation being based on the average age of German panel painting. The conservative style, the hardness of the figures and the decisive role of the drawing, are all striking features of the work. As the number of medieval paintings destroyed in Franciscan churches in Hungary exceeds those of the parish churches, it is difficult to make definitive statements about their style. However, as the Franciscans were active among poor, uneducated people whose taste was probably fairly conservative, it is most likely that paintings owned by the Franciscans were not characterized by the latest trends.

Nevertheless a careful examination of this picture reveals numerous details of great beauty. Especially charming are the painterly bagatelles, also the highlights carefully placed to increase the effect of the brocade of Mary's dress and even to suggest its texture. They, and not the rainbow-coloured wings of the angels, form the focal point of the picture. Surprising as it may seem at first glance, this master had a gift for pictorial presentation: particularly interesting are the thick, curving impasto lines forming the crowns of the angels and the leather belt of the Virgin plaited from loose strips. The Virgin's crown, intended to be a central motif, is painted in more or less the same way, yet with less success: it is unfortunately not colourful enough to dominate the rest of the composition. The figures of Peter and Paul are both rather elongated, probably to give a more monumental impression but this does not affect their sombre, yet vigorous appearance. The distant reserved expression of their faces is highly characteristic. On the whole we see in the quaint style of the picture a definite rejection of the grace and subtlety proper to Gothic art.

**Virgin and
Child with
Angels and Saints.
At her feet:
St. Francis
and St. Dominic**
1510–1520

Lime-wood, 167 × 121 cm
Inv. No. 181
Purchased in 1891
by the Hungarian
National Museum;
transferred in 1936
to the Museum
of Fine Arts
Bibliography:
Radocsay 1955: 137,
188–189;
Stange 1961: 156;
Radocsay 1963: 32, 52–53

In the early sixteenth century, the most prominent sculptor after Master Pál of Lőcse was the Master of the Altars of St. Anne, whose style, like that of the famous Lőcse carver, had its origins in the variant of late Gothic art represented by Veit Stoss which originated in Cracow. The real name of the Master is not known; his work can be identified only on the basis of style. The name by which he is known in the literature was given to him because he carved two large altars dedicated to St. Anne. The earlier of these comes from Kisszeben, a town in the former Sáros County.

In the Kisszeben altar shrine the figures are not placed rigidly side by side in the customary manner at that time, but are arranged turned towards each other to form a group. Although this might seem an obvious arrangement of an altar depicting Anne with two companion figures, here it is perhaps permissible to recognize in it the individual style of the Master, since almost all his works comprise two or three figures. The altarpiece illustrated here shows St. Anne, her daughter, the Virgin Mary, and her grandchild, the Infant Jesus; however, standing on the knees of the Virgin, the Child actually divided the scene into two halves. The shrine of the altar is logically adapted to this arrangement: the closing upper part suggests two niches. The Gothic ogee arches adorned with minute carvings are, however, rather high above the heads of the main figures, so there is room also for the dignified figure of an angel holding a decorative shawl who stands out against the pomegranate pattern adorning the back panel of the altar box; another piece of decorative fabric is suspended behind the main figures by a second angel. Splendid though the altar is, it is on this fabric, with its beautiful design, that the eye lingers. The design continually departs from the regular, suggesting the spontaneity of free-hand drawing, and adding to the animation characteristic of late Gothic painting. This apparently lightly painted surface is actually produced by the sgraffito technique: the brilliantly polished uniform silver field was covered with a layer of white paint through which the pattern was then scratched out.

THE MASTER OF
THE ALTARS
OF ST. ANNE
The group of the
altarshrine
of the St. Anne
altarpiece
from Kisszeben
1510–1515

The statues and carving:
lime-wood;
the altarshrine:
pine-wood,
painted and gilded,
91 and 93 cm, respectively
Inv. No. 52.757.1,
52.757.4–5
Transferred
in 1934 from the Museum
of Applied Arts
to the Museum of Fine Arts
Bibliography:
Radocsay 1967:
111–115, 183;
Homolka 1972: 276;
Schallaburg: No. 770

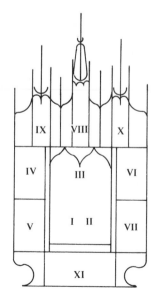

108

This group of carvings is the Master's finest and most effective creation. Here, with his unerring feeling for plasticity, he succeeded in uniting the reticent elegance characteristic of all his works with a refined type of stylization. These features are enhanced by his carving of the faces—full of feeling but never sentimental—and the meticulously carved regular windings of the drapery—in the style of the age yet individual in the application. (The beauty of the facial expression is enhanced by the fact that the paint on the faces and hands is the original layer and that on the clothes, though of a later date, is in the original colours.) The movements are studied, but the Master knew where to draw the line between the elaborate and the affected. Perhaps the tress of hair falling on the shoulder and upper arm of the Virgin most clearly demonstrates his ability to exercise restraint: he stylized just enough to effect the balance between the naturalistic and the geometric. The tress of hair is splendidly set off by the plain background formed by the cloak, but this plain surface is important also from other points of view: it follows the new stylistic ideal which spread steadily in the second decade of the century, making the forms more closed and quiet.

THE MASTER OF THE ALTARS OF ST. ANNE

Figures from the shrine of the Annunciation altarpiece in Kisszeben
1515–1520

Lime-wood, painted and gilded, 104 and 105 cm
Inv. No. 52.756.4–5
Transferred in 1934 from the Museum of Applied Arts to the Museum of Fine Arts
Bibliography:
Radocsay 1967: 112–113, 184;
Homolka 1972: 276, 411;
Schallaburg: No. 769

   I Angel from
     the Annunciation
  II The Virgin
     from the Annunciation
 III God the Father
 IV Angel with Violin
  V Angel with Lute
 VI St. Dorothy
 VII St. Barbara
VIII St. Margaret
 IX St. Catherine
  X A Female Saint
 XI St. Agnes
XII A Female Saint
XIII The Virgin;
XIV Two Kings and
XV The Saracen King
    from the Adoration
    of the Magi
 1 Death of the Virgin
 2 The Nativity
 3 Coronation of the Virgin
 4 Circumcision of Christ
 5 The Visitation
 6 Flight into Egypt
 7 Christ among
   the Doctors
 8 Christ Taking Leave
   of His Mother

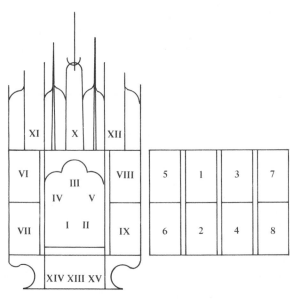

Originally, the figure of God the Father, His hand raised in blessing, accompanied by angels playing musical instruments, was to be found in the upper section of the altar shrine above the scene of the Annunciation. One of the angels is carved with a viol, the direct ancestor of the violin, the other touching the strings of a lute. The suggestion of music provided a suitable addition to the solemnity of the scene. This moment marked the beginning of the earthly life of Jesus, which was to end in the Crucifixion, by which He would redeem mortal sinners. The music-making angels seem to be offering to the faithful a glimpse of heaven indicating the peace and glory of the life to come. The figures of the angels, unlike those of Gabriel and the Virgin, are carved in the more animated late Gothic style. This follows partly from the fact that they are represented seated on cumuli suggesting that they are spiritual beings, which the Master was able to demonstrate by the simple means of placing them on supports that would move in the slightest current of air, instead of on fixed braces. The Gothic style is also seen in the loose composition of their clothes and hair and the shaded surface forming a veritable small cavity between the musical instruments and the bodies. In the original state of the altar the effect of the shading would have been even more marked because the rich carving decorating the upper part of the shrine almost enclosed the angels leaving them in a dim, mysterious light. (See Fig. at Plate 109.)

THE MASTER OF THE ALTARS OF ST. ANNE

Angels playing musical instruments from the Annunciation altarpiece in Kisszeben
1515–1520

Lime-wood, painted and gilded, 32 and 34 cm respecitively
Inv. No. 52.756.7–8
Transferred in 1934 from the Museum of Applied Arts to the Museum of Fine Arts
Bibliography:
Radocsay 1967: 112–113, 184;
Homolka 1972: 276, 411;
Schallaburg: No. 769

Here, as on fifteenth century winged altars, the subsidiary figures are the four most popular martyr virgins: Dorothy, Barbara, Margaret and Catherine. The frequency with which they were represented is demonstrated by the fact that altars on which they were to be seen were given a special name: the quaternion, after the German "Viereraltar". The crowns are not an indication of royal descent but rather that by suffering a martyr's death these virgins had earned the crown of eternal life. However, on the quaternion-type altars the figures were placed at either end of the shrine closely fitted into niches scarcely larger than themselves, while on the altar from Kisszeben they take up the whole inside of the wings. St. Dorothy fits admirably into the available space, the carver having solved the formation of the figure with great skill. Carved in relief, the figure gives a rounded and realistic impression: even the knees are turned outwards in a naturalist manner. Although the virgin saints on the wings are stockier and more robust than the principal figures, they are similar in type, with similarly expressive faces and a studied carriage of the head. The link with the figures illustrated in Nos. 108–110 is also evident from the slight but clearly recognizable asymmetry of the composition. Dorothy is shown turning her face towards the altar shrine and lifts her attribute also in that direction; her cloak, of which the hem describes the same curve as that of the Virgin in the central group, divides her figure, leaving one half darker than the other. Nor is the familiar tress of hair missing from her right shoulder. We can be confident that the reliefs, even if somewhat rough-and-ready in execution, are the work of the master-carver responsible for the whole altar. (See Fig. at Plate 109.)

THE MASTER OF THE ALTARS OF ST. ANNE

St. Dorothy from the inside wing of the Annunciation altarpiece in Kisszeben
1515–1520

Lime-wood, painted and gilded, 77.5 cm
Inv. No. 52.756.15
Transferred in 1934 from the Museum of Applied Arts to the Museum of Fine Arts
Bibliography:
Radocsay 1967: 112–113, 184;
Homolka 1972: 276, 411;
Schallaburg: No. 769

According to theological interpretations on the life of Jesus, the Annunciation marked the moment of Christ's Incarnation, while the Adoration of the Magi was the first expression of man's veneration for the Saviour, symbolized by the prostration of the wise men before the Child who even as a newborn Infant was mightier than any one of them. Even in the Middle Ages, the triad of the Magi was already associated with the three then known parts of the world—Europe, Asia and Africa. In the fifteenth century it became customary to represent one of the Magi as a Moor.

The wise men are shown presenting themselves to the Virgin who is seated on the left; they are carved advancing, one after the other, in the manner known from the sarcophagi of the early Christians. The Infant almost slips from His mother's lap as, curious, He reaches for the box—evidently containing gold coins—held by the old king who is already kneeling. In this scene the Infant is sometimes represented as dignified and remote, in others He is very vivacious. The most famous contemporary example of the type of Infant seen here is in Dürer's picture of the Three Magi, now in the Uffizi Gallery in Florence, and in his woodcut dated 1511. In the background the other two kings are seen bringing their gifts of frankincense and myrrh. The three gifts were added when the predella was restored.

These figures are the Master's finest creations. He alone must be responsible for the subtle facial expressions, the regular curly beards, the regal effect of the drapery. The faces of the men are strikingly similar to that of God the Father represented above the Annunciation. Compared to the other figures on the altar, those on the predella are more animated which bears witness to the versatility of the sculptor as well as to the consistency of his artistic approach.

The painting executed to form a background to the scene deserves special attention. It is finished with as much loving care and attention to detail as any panel picture, its secondary role is indicated only by the fact that it contains few definite motifs. Meticulous as the Master was, he did not want to waste his time by painting details that would be concealed by the statues. (See Fig. at Plate 109.)

THE MASTER OF THE ALTARS OF ST. ANNE

The Adoration of the Magi from the predella of the Annunciation altarpiece in Kisszeben
1510–1520

Lime-wood, 54, 59 and 62 cm respectively
Inv. No. 52.756.2, 12–14
Transferred in 1934
from the Museum
of Applied Arts
to the Museum of Fine Arts
Bibliography:
Radocsay 1967: 113;
Homolka 1972: 276, 411;
Schallaburg: No. 769

112

The figure, which has come down to us in very good condition, is in the style of the Master of the Altars of St. Anne, although it cannot be attributed to him. The large flat folds of the garments, the inclination of the head and the curves of the shawl covering the head, point to his influence. This is also clearly to be seen in a less obvious but nonetheless characteristic feature, namely the flat, almost relief-like modelling, which gives to the Master's sculptural art such individuality in the Szepes region and in Sáros. These special traits are even more readily discernible in other works, which have not been acquired by the National Gallery but which can still be seen in their places of origin—for instance the figures on the high altar in Héthárs and the Crucifixion in Igló. It is clear that another hand has been responsible for the harsh and grave expression of the face and the stocky and bony shape of the figure of the Virgin in Budapest, emphasized, in the contemporary manner, by unusually sharp breaks in the crumpled drapery, reminiscent of breaks in crystals. These specific traits are particularly evident on the Igló Virgin whose movements are so strikingly similar to those seen on the Budapest statue. However, the face of the Igló Virgin is more full of feeling; the Virgin in the National Gallery seems to show more restraint in her grief.

The Virgin from the Crucifixion. Provenance unknown
1515–1520

Lime-wood, painted and gilded, 100 cm
Inv. No. 57.14.M
Donated in 1957
to the Museum
of Fine Arts
Bibliography:
Radocsay 1967:
115, 175

In a votive picture donated by Senator János Hütter this subject is more fully represented: the painter also included portraits of the donor and his sons. Behind him his patron saint, John the Evangelist, is seen standing with his right arm resting on the shoulder of the praying figure. Another rare addition is the figure of St. Joseph behind the Virgin. The interior may have been inspired by a Dürer print: the spacious effect produced by the barrel vault and the ample use of Renaissance style architectural decorative elements were surely meant to create an atmosphere of solemnity. The balusters of the terrace railing closely resemble those of the outside staircase of the Town Hall in Bártfa, completed in 1509 and considered a novelty in the whole neighbourhood at that time. The main motif of the skilfully painted landscape in the background, namely the mill to which people are seen carrying corn for grinding, is evidently not just a charming genre-scene but is also of symbolic significance. Just as the corn has to be ground between mill-stones to make flour which thus is the basis of the bread for the Eucharist, so Jesus, held with anxious care and great reverence between the two saintly women and touched by them only through a clean white veil, has to die a bitter and painful death to bring about the redemption of mankind.

The panel—which reminds one of the old Hungarian altar of St. Anne in Lőcse—is strikingly Augsburgian in style, for it aspires to a very Italianate appearance which the master tries to attain with his putti, architectural details and other small motifs. The face of the Senator, the only portrait in the medieval collection, of the National Gallery recalls Dürer's Fugger portrait. This odd resemblance may be due to the fact that the Thurzó–Fugger mining and trading company was at the height of its power and activity in those years and it may have been through this family that the master was subjected to this otherwise rare artistic influence.

St. Anne with the Virgin and the Infant from Eperjes
c. 1520

Pine-wood, 124 × 84 cm
Inv. No. 53.566
Transferred in 1936
from the Hungarian
National Museum
to the Museum of Fine Arts
Bibliography:
Radocsay 1955:
161, 300–301;
Glatz 1975:
51–52;
Schallaburg: No. 759

MATER MEA HIC SVNT FRATRES MEI QVI VERBVM DEI AVDIVNT ET FACIVNT

Legend has it that the saint was condemned by the emperor to die on the wheel, and when God's angel destroyed this instrument of torture, she was then beheaded. The picture shows the destruction of the wheel and the beheading side by side. The composition and the details demonstrate unequivocally that the master modelled his work on a painting by Lucas Cranach the Elder who from the second decade of the century exercised a steadily growing influence on the painters of northern and eastern Germany, Poland, Bohemia and Hungary. The altar to which the panel originally belonged, dates from the beginning of this period of Cranach's influence. It is characteristic of the master that of the Cranach pictures devoted to the subject he chose the two earliest as his models, namely the picture in Budapest (in the Collection of the Calvinist Diocese on the Danube) and the one in Dresden (in the Staatliche Kunstsammlungen). The wonderful animation, the romantic atmosphere of the landscape and the impression of the heavens rent by lightning, all characteristic of the German master, can be seen here simplified, tamed, with almost no sense of distance; and some of the movements have no organic link. The picture is a simple work by a provincial master painted with a care that deserves respect. It is clear that he wished to follow the formal idiom of Cranach, which he considered modern. He was anxious to depict the fashionable clothes, the style of moustaches, the crowns, seen in pictures of the Danube School; however, we have to remember him chiefly because of the great artist he chose to follow and whose style he helped to disseminate. The history of art is indebted to him if only for the fact that in this series he preserved the memory of an altar by Cranach which has disappeared without trace. The anonymous artist of Szepes lacked the imaginative powers necessary to have composed these scenes, and the original series cannot be traced among surviving woodcuts by the German master. Thus it seems that somewhere there must have been an altarpiece by Cranach which our painter saw on one of his study tours and remembered when his employer demanded just such a picture from him.

St. Catherine's Martyrdom from the Szepes region
1520

Pine-wood,
104.5 × 99.5 cm
Inv. No. 55.914.4
Transferred in 1936
from the Hungarian
National Museum
to the Museum of Fine Arts
Bibliography:
Radocsay 1955: 444;
Végh, János: Ismeretlen
Szent Katalin-sorozat
a Szepességből
[An unknown
St. Catherine series
from the Szepes region].
MÉ XIII (1964), 79–88

115

The figures in the shrine, after which the altar is named, are a later addition; the original sculptural decoration may be deduced from the relief on the predella. The somewhat hesitant movement of the soft figures is similar to that seen on the earlier Leibic altar (Plate 103). Yet the relief of The Lamentation can hardly be the work of the same master; the presence of identical stylistic marks does not mean that the two works are identical in quality. Knowing the custom of medieval workshops, it is no surprise to find that the leading master did not execute every detail of the winged altar himself. In this case he very likely produced the lost central figures for the box, and entrusted to one of his assistants the execution of the smaller ones for the surface of the predella which would have been obstructed from the view of the congregation by the officiating priest. This particular assistant was certainly not without talent. The three main figures are beautifully grouped as they bend over the heavy-limbed prostrate body of Christ, while the line of figures in the background is pleasingly rhythmic. The model followed by the master was evidently the relief on the predella of the altar of St. John in Lőcse; the whole of the composition and the movements of the more important figures are so much in keeping with this influential work that probably the sculptor was charged to follow it faithfully. Nevertheless he succeeded in giving the relief his own characteristic touch, changing some details which, though minute, are not without significance. He placed the body of Christ more in the foreground, nearer the lower edge of the predella, made it larger than his model and suggested the setting by introducing small details such as the rocks in the upper left corner.

It is no accident that this scene is so often found on the predellas of winged altars. The subject is suitable for the low broad surface to be decorated and is in keeping with the function of the altar where, according to the teachings of the Church, at the daily mass, the bread and wine was changed into the blood and body of Christ. This scene is one of the most suitable ones for conveying in a horizontal composition the religious significance of the Crucifixion.

The Lamentation from the predella of the Leibic altar of Two Bishop Saints
1521

Lime-wood,
painted and gilded,
51 × 100 cm
Inv. No. 53.578.4
Transferred in 1936
from the Hungarian
National Museum
to the Museum of Fine Arts
Bibliography:
Radocsay 1967: 108–109,
188–189;
Schallaburg: No. 762

  I St. Nicholas
 II A Bishop Saint
III St. James the Greater
 IV St. Florianus
  V A Male Saint
 VI The Lamentation
  1 St. Ottilia
  2 St. Margaret
  3 St. Apollonia
  4 St. Ursula
  5 The Flagellation
  6 Christ Carrying the Cross
  7 The Crowning with Thorn
  8 The Crucifixion
  9 The Agony in the
     Garden
 10 Ecce Homo
 11 Pilate Washing his Hands
 12 The Resurrection

116

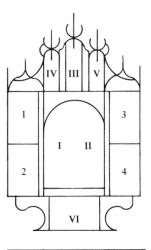

The panels clearly show the influence of the members of a workshop who, under the guidance of the Master of Káposztafalva, were responsible for the high altar of Lőcse, and who acquired considerable influence in the Szepes region in the 1510s. Both in the cast of the features and in the scale of the scenes as related to the picture surface there is a hint of the altar at Lőcse; however, the two altars are by no means identical in quality. In the panels illustrated here the faces are less sharp-featured than at Lőcse, and the arrangement of the figures and their movements within the available space are generally vague, though anatomically plausible, especially the nudes. The painter composed his scenes with a few characters. Even in Christ Carrying the Cross he refrained from including a large crowd. The movements of the figures are distinct and easily apprehended; the faces are expressive, those of the henchmen distorted but not grotesque. However, the master did not owe all his results exclusively to his own talent and the influence of the Lőcse workshop: his paintings show motifs and solutions taken from Altdorfer. The panel showing the Crucifixion is modelled directly after the high altar in Káposztafalva (although the trees and the grass show the influence of the Lőcse altar); but the three other panels contain motifs taken from Altdorfer's work: in the two upper panels these motifs appear to have been copied with slavish accuracy. As the panels date from 1521, and the woodcuts after which they were modelled date from 1513, the presence of such motifs is not surprising. Nevertheless, they are especially worthy of attention as originating from the Szepes region where painters were for the most part influenced by the work of Dürer's pupils and Cranach. The chief value of the series lies in the light but powerful colouring. This applies especially to the Crucifixion. With his sweeping brush-strokes the painter could counteract the difference which separated him from the Master of Káposztafalva who was inclined to emphasize fine, carefully elaborated details. (See Fig. at Plate 116.)

Paintings on the altar of Two Bishop Saints from Leibic. Outer sides of the hinged wings
1521

Lime-wood, 83 × 52 cm each
Inv. No. 53.578.12–15
Transferred in 1936
from the Hungarian
National Museum
to the Museum
of Fine Arts
Bibliography:
Radocsay 1955:
175, 363–364;
Schallaburg: No. 762

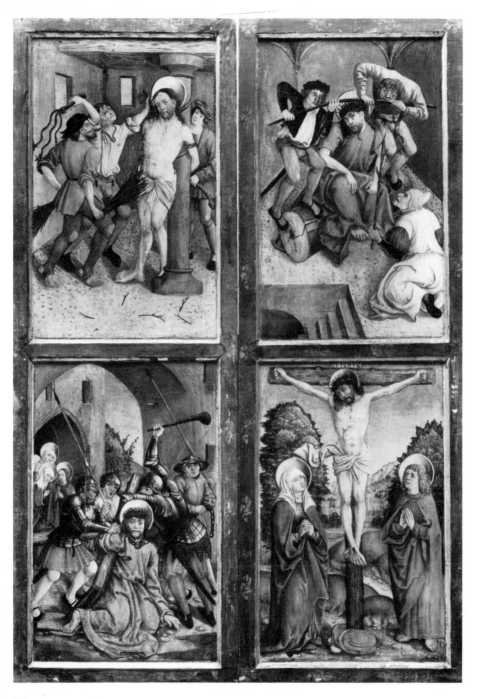

This relief was originally carved for the shrine of an altar. The background pattern connected the outline of the figures. The style is remarkably similar to that of works by the Master of the Altars of St. Anne, especially to the reliefs fixed to the inner sides of the wings. The flat carving, the odd dough-like folds, even the undulating headshawl over St. Anne's brow and the tress of hair falling on the Virgin's shoulder and upper arm, are characteristic of works illustrated in the preceding pages. These similarities have caused some scholars to attribute the work to the Master of the Altars of St. Anne; however, the vacant expression of the Virgin's face and the awkwardness of the posture, deprive this supposition of credibility. The facial expression would have been more effective if the original layer of paint had survived. There are some excellent de-tails, such as the cross-legged posture of the Infant on his little cushion, and St. Anne's somewhat bony, anxious face, but these are insufficient to raise the general level of the work.

St. Anne with the Virgin and the Infant from Monyhád
c. 1520–1530

Lime-wood, originally painted, 71.5 × 71 cm
Inv. No. 55.896
Transferred in 1939 from the Hungarian National Museum to the Museum of Fine Arts

Bibliography:
Radocsay 1967: 115, 199;
Homolka 1972: 276, 411–412

118

Neither the canonical, nor the apocryphal texts refer to the leave-taking of Christ—an episode usually represented directly before the Passion scene. In a fourteenth century meditation, however, we are told that, before entering Jerusalem, Christ bade farewell to his mother, to Mary Magdalen and other saintly women, who begged Him not to leave and expose Himself to danger. The special iconographic significance of this relief lies in the fact that here, as in the *Noli me tangere* scenes, the Virgin touches Christ's garment, as if to detain him. The figures of the Virgin and of Christ, and especially Christ's head, show that the artist must have known Dürer's woodcut of the same subject in his series of the Small Passion scenes; Mary Magdalen, looking sorrowfully to heaven with her arms crossed, also bears witness to the influence of Dürer's pictures of the Virgin of Sorrows. However, the master of the relief adapted these models to suit his own style. The well-balanced composition, and Christ's cloak similar to those of classical Greek rhetors with its long folds and quiet surfaces, demonstrate effectively the strengthening of the Renaissance influence, also seen in the plasticity of the face and the sweeping lines of the figure of Mary Magdalen.

There are also certain parallels between this work and the work of the German Renaissance artists Hans Daucher and Peter Vischer. This mixture of the Gothic heritage with Renaissance elements is also found in Hungary: the figures are set before a background of painterly delicacy. This comparison also attests that by creating such a refined plastic composition and by conveying throughout his work a profound sense of grief the Nyitra master has bequeathed to posterity a work of art matched by few of his contemporaries. The relief is one of the finest examples of northern Renaissance art which in Hungary developed parallel with the Renaissance trends of the age of King Matthias Corvinus directly influenced by the Italian Renaissance. From the subject it would seem that the relief must originally have formed the central part of a commemorative monument together with three apostles on the right side, of which only fragments of figures remained in Nyitra. The monument was probably in the Nyitra Episcopal Cathedral.

Christ Taking Leave of His Mother from Nyitra
1520–1530

Limestone, 117 × 103 cm
Inv. No. 55.1594
Transferred in 1939
from the Hungarian
National Museum
to the Museum of Fine Arts
Bibliography:
Török, Gyöngyi:
Abschied Christi
von seiner Mutter—
Ein Relief aus Neutra.
AHA XXIV (1978), 219–232;
Schallaburg: No. 773

119

This relief, the finest Hungarian Renaissance sculpture of its kind, is directly related to a type of Virgin and Child developed in Italy, especially in Florence. The serenity of the Virgin and the charm of the Infant with His hand raised in blessing, strengthen our first and lasting impression of solemnity and monumentality which in sixteenth century art so greatly fascinated those living outside Italy. The Virgin's garments are strikingly Italianate; the robe, especially the line and embroidery of the neckline is, for instance, highly reminiscent of that worn by Mona Lisa. The solemnity of the work is enhanced by the elaborate moulding enframing it, also the straight and very definite line of the cord which so pleasingly relieves the emptiness of the background. A similar purpose is served by the gentle angels holding the crown. It is true that to see so large a crown held by such diminutive angels must provoke a smile, but the overall solemnity remains. The fluttering wings and undulating folds of the angels' robes are the most animated parts of the whole relief, a liveliness enhanced by a marked effect of light and shade. The crown held by the angels is a local motif of late Gothic sculpture, witnesses the deep undercut, which is not a Renaissance characteristic, nor even appropriate to stone cutting, but a typical wood-carving technique.

András Báthory, who commissioned the Virgin, was a member of the illustrious family who provided for the building of the Nyírbátor church and who were great patrons of late Gothic and Renaissance art. In the inscription engraved along the lower edge of the relief he rightly called it a "masterpiece". Originally the work may have been destined to surmount the door of a church or chapel, for the inscription also includes the words: "Peace be with those entering here."

András Báthory's Virgin and Child

1526

Marble, 68 × 51 cm.
Reading of the inscription:
ORA · PRO · NOBIS
SANCTA · DEI
GENITRIX
VIRGO · MARIA
PAX · INGREDIENTIBVS
EGREGIVM · HOC · OPVS
FECIT · FIERI
ANDREAS · FILIVS
ANDREE · DE · BATHOR
Inv. No. 55.982
Transferred in 1939
from the Hungarian
National Museum
to the Museum of Fine Arts.
Currently exhibited
in the Hungarian
National Museum
Bibliography:
Balogh, Jolán:
La Madone d' András
Báthory
BMH I (1947), 8–14;
Białostocki, Jan:
The Art of the Renaissance
in Eastern Europe. Hungary,
Bohemia, Poland.
Oxford, 1976, 9;
Schallaburg: No. 655

The ceiling is a special product of that amalgamation of the Gothic and the Renaissance which gave rise to so many variants of style at the beginning of the sixteenth century. It shows a splendid combination of figural and ornamental elements comparable to those adorning the finest letters patent of the age. It had long been a custom to board in the gaps between the beams supporting the attics, and to decorate these with ornamental or figural paintings. In the late Middle Ages these decorations acquired a special significance: the ornamental foliage suggesting luxuriant vegetation symbolized the garden of Eden. Such beauty in their church inspired the faithful with awe as if they were already in heaven. The trend towards decorated ceilings gained new impetus from Italian examples of Renaissance-style coffered ceilings with strong beams and gilded rosettas.

A splendid series of ceilings started with one in Gógánváralja, commissioned by Miklós Bethlen of Betlen. As far as we know this was the first in Hungary to be divided into square fields. The Renaissance style which, from its beginnings in the early sixteenth century, soon became the dominant influence in art, is immediately recognizable here. The artist must have seen an Italianate coffered ceiling in one of the larger towns, probably in nearby Gyulafehérvár. It is not enough, however, to appreciate only the Renaissance influence in this ceiling, for the details of both the figural and the ornamental motifs are characteristic of the late Gothic; they are very similar to those seen in German engravings, for instance the decorative foliage designed to fill in the spaces in Martin Schongauer's compositions and the figures placed in circles formed of vegetal motifs in the works of Master ES or Israel van Meckehem. From the technical point of view the task of painting a ceiling was comparable to that of creating an altarpiece. The artist was obviously active in both fields. In style the Gógánváralja ceiling comes closest to those which have survived in small and remote Polish villages (Kozy, Libusza, Krużlowa) on the northern slopes of the Carpathian mountains.

Details of a ceiling from Gógánváralja
c. 1501–1519

Pine-wood;
the squares average
90 × 90 cm each
Inv. No. 55.966
Purchased by the Museum
of Fine Arts from the
Gógánváralja church in 1903
Bibliography: Balogh, Jolán:
Az erdélyi renaissance
[Transylvanian Renaissance]
I. Kolozsvár, 1943:
118–121, 297–300;
Radocsay, Dénes:
A gógánváraljai
festett famennyezet
lengyel rokonsága
[Polish relations of the
Gógánváralja coffered
ceiling]. A Magyar
Tudományos Akadémia II.
Társadalmi-Történet-
tudományok
Osztályának Közleményei.
Series 3, II (1951), 61–65;
Tombor, Ilona:
A magyarországi
festett famennyezetek
és rokonemlékek
a XV–XIX. századból
[Coffered ceilings and related
remains in Hungary
from the fifteenth-nineteenth
centuries]. Budapest, 1968:
22, 79–80, 134–135;
Wolff-Łozińska, Barbara;
Malowidła stropów polskich
I. polowiny XVI w.
Dekoracje roślinne
i kasetonowe [Polish ceilings
from the first half
of the sixteenth century,
coffered and with floral
ornaments].
Warszawa, 1971, 84, 106, 111;
Schallaburg: No. 790

121

Though traditional in form, this altarpiece is an extremely late work. It is of the quadripartite type, created in accordance with the tradition. (Note the very slender supports on which the figures rest in the side shrines; the small altar from Hervartó [Plate 99] shows how the illusion of support could be given by the painter.) The outer panels seem dull in comparison to the inner panels, the lunette and the predella which are all brilliantly painted in the traditional manner. The paintings are based on Dürer's work which still exerted a powerful posthumous influence all over Europe. The unknown master of the Csíkmenaság altar has in most cases simplified Dürer's compositions, adapting them to suit the smaller areas he had to cover. However, the ornamental carving of the framework of the altar already reflects the Renaissance trend. The rustic simplicity of the figures is characteristic of the style in its declining years. Yet these popular figures have a freshness that should by no means be underrated. The angels holding the crown above the Virgin's head, for example, have been taken from a Dürer engraving of 1518 or from a woodcut of the same year, but this is evident only from their carriage and the way they are holding the crown on high. While in Dürer's works they have a certain grace and dignity, here no trace of these qualities can be found. The pert carriage of their heads, their sturdy bodies like those of healthy children, and their chubby little faces give them a character all their own.

The Virgin Mary high altar from Csíkmenaság
1543

The carving in the altar-shrine: line-wood, painted and gilded, 132 cm
The angels: painted lime-wood, 35 and 30 cm
Carvings in the left side shrine: lime-wood, painted and gilded, 60 and 56 cm
Carvings in the right side shrine: lime-wood, painted and gilded, 56 cm.
The inner side of the wings: pine-wood, 85 × 53 cm
The lunette: pine-wood, 85.5 × 117 cm. The predella: pine-wood, 47 × 125 cm
Inv. No. 53.540.1–13

Bibliography: Radocsay 1955: 189, 288–289;
Radocsay 1967: 130, 159;
Schallaburg: No. 787

I   Virgin and Child
II Angels Holding the Crown
III A Male Saint
IV St. Barbara
V   A Male Saint
VI St. Margaret
1   The Annunciation
2   Adoration of the Shepherds
3   The Visitation
4   The Adoration of the Magi
5   The Arrest of Christ
6   Christ Carrying the Cross
7   Christ before Caiaphas
8   The Crucifixion
9   Agony in the Garden
10 Crowning with Thorns
11 The Flagellation
12 The Resurrection
13 St. Anne with the Virgin and Child
14 The Lamentation

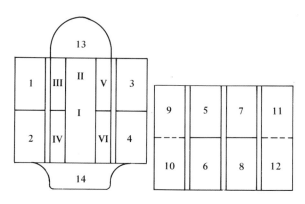

In this altar, the provincial, though individual tone of the carvings is least obvious in the pictures on the outer panels of the wings. When closed, the altar shows only scenes from the Passion, creating a Lenten atmosphere, and these scenes are invariably closely modelled after Dürer. The scenes are more or less faithful replicas of various prints by the great master, though the female heads bear witness to the artist's attachment to Csík traditions. The power of this local influence is especially evident in the faithful preservation of the graphic character of the prints. Flat linear representation always attracted the painters of this region more than soft painterly effects. This preservation of the graphic character—especially of Dürer's drawings—may have been important for them for another reason too, namely that it increased their power of expression, a quality always regarded as essential by the artists of Csík. The predella also points to Dürer's art; not so much to his prints as to one of his paintings. There is no doubt that the *Glimm Lamentation,* now in Munich, was in the artist's mind when painting his own version, although the unusual horizontal composition necessitated numerous changes. However, the choice of this particular work as a model proves that the painter must have travelled far, for the work he chose as a model was not easily accessible. To know it as well as he did was no mean achievement. In the semicircular lunette surrounded by rich Renaissance ornamentation, figures of St. Anne and Mary with the Infant remind us that the altar, though dominated by scenes from the Passion, is actually a Lady-altar. This is the picture which, of the whole series, least resembles any of Dürer's compositions. Panels closed by a semi-circle are not unusual on fifteenth century altars; here, however, the Renaissance influence is seen in the quiet form, totally enframed, with a volute of acanthus on either side. (See Fig. at Plate 122.)

The Virgin Mary high altar (closed) from Csíkmenaság
1543

Pine-wood,
outer panels 86 × 53 cm
The fixed wings:
195 × 70 cm
The lunette:
pine-wood, 85.5 × 117 cm
The predella:
pine-wood, 47 × 125 cm
Inv. No. 53.540.8–9, 14–21
Transferred in 1936
from the Hungarian
National Museum
to the Museum of Fine Arts
Bibliography: Radocsay
1955: 189, 288–289;
Schallaburg: No. 787

This painting which surmounts the altar is chiefly noteworthy because, of all the compositions modelled after Dürer, it is the one least reminiscent of the great Nuremberg master's works. Whereas the narrow panels give an effect of pictorial flatness, this painting has a vigorous landscape background. This in itself directs our attention not to Dürer but towards the Danube School.

The blades hanging down at the left end of the grassy bank are unequivocally Danubian in style, while other details of the landscape owe less to this source. However, if we consider that the altar was produced as early as the middle of the century, that is when the style of the Danubian artists was already declining, we understand why the forest is devoid of that characteristic mysterious atmosphere. In the painting we can recognize the very principle which guided the artist in composing the wings. Thus he cut out from his composition as many trees as possible, so that he could more effectively represent one or two "protagonists" by employing all his skill to produce a three-dimensional effect. He followed the same principle of simplification in the rest of his compositions modelled after Dürer's engravings, but in these, however, he had to reduce the number of the figures. In certain places, where the paint has worn off, the priming and even the sketch can be seen.

St. Anne with the Virgin and the Infant Within the lunette of the high altar from Csíkmenaság
1543

Pine-wood, 85.5 × 117 cm
Inv. No. 53.540.8
Transferred in 1936
from the Hungarian
National Museum
to the Museum of Fine Arts
Bibliography:
Radocsay 1955:
189, 288–289;
Schallaburg: No. 787

The illustrated broadsheets made in Hungary about the Turkish battles furnished news to foreigners. One of these preserved for us the first authentic portrait of Zrínyi by Matthias Zündt. His series of portraits continue on single-sheet prints and illustrations to epigrams and poems written in praise and remembrance of Zrínyi. With this collection Forgách wished to describe Zrínyi to his contemporaries as a model of heroism and self-sacrifice. Similar reasons motivated the patron of this picture as well. The visual and thematic parallels of Christ on the Cross and the idealized depiction of Jerusalem in the background are the Christian hero and Szigetvár, the scene of Zrínyi's heroic death. On the bottom the incomplete text mentions Zrínyi as Emperor Maximilian's soldier and provides accurate details on the siege of 1566.

VIENNESE (?) MASTER last third of the sixteenth century

Allegorical scene with Miklós Zrínyi, the hero of Szigetvár

Oil on canvas,
87.5 × 152 cm
Inv. No. 75.3 M.
Bibliography:
Buzási, Enikő:
Késő reneszánsz és
kora barokk művészet
[Late Renaissance
and Early Baroque Art].
Budapest, 1980.

124

125

Of the Hungarian kings St. Ladislas is perhaps the one most often represented in post-medieval frescoes, altar paintings and statues. In the Middle Ages he was associated with the ideal of chivalry and the legends which gathered around him determined the manner of his representation. Thus the knightly armour and the battle-axe have become permanent attributes, in addition to the crown and the orb. The painting illustrated here, dating from the late sixteenth century, is only superficially linked with medieval portraits of St. Ladislas. The king is shown seated on a throne wearing an ample, richly embroidered cloak studded with pearls round the hem. In the foreground is a voluted and foiled shield with the national emblem, stylized in harmony with the throne. The background is designed to suggest the interior of a Renaissance palace. Through opening on either side of the wall behind the throne—draped with embroidered hangings—there is a view of the landscape. A similar motif was often used to fill in the background in north Italian Madonna paintings of the fifteenth and sixteenth centuries. The monochrome landscape on the left is a topographic reference to one of St. Ladislas' most important church activities, the foundation of the Cathedral in Nagyvárad, while the one on the right shows his legendary defeat of the Cumanian abductor. This evocation of two popular episodes from the story of the king's life is intended partly to identify St. Ladislas as a ruler of worldly power, and partly to indicate the ideal unity of the Christian king and the Christian knight. St. Ladislas is shown as a historical personage, without a halo—a fact indicating that the painting was destined for a secular building. The episodes from the king's life or, to be more accurate, from legends associated with his name, are treated as historical facts. The same approach characterized the series of prints of royalty and other notabilities which became so popular all over Europe in the course of the sixteenth century. It may be assumed that such prints served as models for the painted portrait of St. Ladislas and the two related pictures of St. Stephen and St. Emeric.

HUNGARIAN PAINTER
c. 1600

St. Ladislas

Oil on panel,
103 × 101.3 cm
Inv. No. 55.967.3
Formerly
in the Hungarian
National Museum
Not previously
published.—*cf.*:
Rózsa 1973: 16–19

126

Since the Middle Ages this had been a traditional way of representing the Holy Trinity. The underlying idea was taken from a text in the Old Testament (Hebr. 9,5) in which there is a reference to the "thronum gratiae" or "Throne of Mercy". Luther was the first to translate the expression into German as "Gnadenstuhl", the name generally adopted since then for this kind of Holy Trinity picture. Similar pictorial compositions of the subject occurred even in the eighteenth century. The figure of God the Father is shown enthroned on a marble bench, usually drawn in a larger scale than that of Christ whose cross He holds in His hands. It may be that the dove representing the Holy Ghost was at one time in the upper part of the panel now damaged.

The picture is characterized by a special mixture of northern and Italian styles. The painter's vision is medieval in spirit, the figures rigid and the drapery heavy, yet the forms and colours are a provincial version of Italian late Renaissance. The crucified figure of Christ is carefully elaborated. In depicting the body the painter may have had recourse to a Roman example of Mannerist art. The landscape attests to his knowledge of North Italian painting and there can be no doubt that he had either visited Italy or studied under an Italian master. Paintings similar in style and spirit are known to have come from Carniola (now Slovenia) and from Croatia. This panel was probably painted by a local artist who was either active in the Transdanubian region at some time, or who was commissioned to paint the picture for someone living there.

CARNIOLIAN (SLOVENIAN) OR CROATIAN PAINTER, first quarter of the seventeenth century

The Holy Trinity

Oil on larch-wood, 109.5 × 90 cm
The panel damaged on top and at bottom.
On the reverse:
St. Louis of Toulouse (?), St. Peter and St. Christopher
Acquired for the Hungarian National Museum from the Jankovich Collection;
in 1939 transferred to the Museum of Fine Arts
Bibliography:
Mojzer: MÉ 1981

From 1568 to the year of his death in 1584, János Rueber held the official title of "Captain-General of Upper Hungary", which was simplified to "Captain of Kassa" after the name of the town from which he administered his territory. In several counties of the royal territory of Hungary, from the mining towns to the upper reaches of the Tisza, he was the highest ranking representative and the commander of the armed forces of the monarch then residing in distant Vienna, yet he was a devout Protestant. This was still possible in the troubled and constantly changing situation in Hungary in the sixteenth century; but after Rueber's death the Habsburgs took good care to appoint only Catholics to such important posts. In those days St. Elisabeth's Church in Kassa was in Protestant hands; thus the fervid protector of the new faith was buried in one of its dignified side-chapels belonging to the Szathmári family and today forming the prebendal sacristy.

The sepulchre has not survived in its entirety. It was demolished in 1733 and only the main figure was preserved. It must have been a large wall structure with a niche, the archetype of the sepulchral monument most often commissioned by members of the Hungarian nobility at the beginning of the seventeenth century. Medieval sepulchres usually took the form of a stone effigy of the deceased lying on the sarcophagus or death-bed, or maybe kneeling in prayer awaiting the Last Judgement, but this statue from János Rueber's sarcophagus is in the typical style of the Renaissance. A statue of the deceased serves as his own memorial—an upright and dignified figure in full armour, one hand resting on his helmet and gauntlets, the other holding out his commander's staff.

Rueber's nationality is truly reflected in the style, which is in the Austrian-South German Renaissance manner. The stone monuments which have come down to us from one or two generations earlier tended mainly towards the Italianate but with the advance of the sixteenth century the Renaissance style, filtered through the German taste, reached Hungary.

Sepulchral monument of Captain-General János Rueber of Pisendorf from Kassa

Late sixteenth century

Marble, 185 cm
Inv. No. 55.1593
Transferred in 1939
from the Hungarian
National Museum
to the Museum of Fine Arts
Bibliography: Wick, Béla:
Kassa története és műemlékei
[History
and monuments of Kassa].
Kassa, 1941, 79[37]

Paul Juvenel, a Nuremberg painter of Flemish origin, was a pupil of the prominent German landscape painter, Adam Elsheimer. He was not, however, interested in painting evocative landscapes and rather learned from his master a way of representing costumed figures in genre-scenes in a historical setting. To enhance the period atmosphere of his narrative pictures he placed his figures against some architectural background corresponding to the taste of the age. This necessitated, as in this picture, a spacious background composed of architectural elements of classical Antiquity. The male figures are represented wearing classical or eastern robes, while the women are dressed in the contemporary bourgeois fashion. The subject of the painting ("Suffer little children to come unto me," Matthew 19, 13–15 and Mark 10, 13–16) was particularly popular in Juvenel's time. Another painting by the same artist, dating from 1630 and with many similar details, found its way to the Castle of Pommersfelden.

After his return to Nuremberg, Juvenel became very popular. He was commissioned to decorate the façade of numerous houses, and the council room of the Town Hall, with historical and architectural paintings. His work aroused the interest of the Emperor himself, and it must have been at his invitation that the painter settled in Vienna in 1638 and in Pozsony shortly afterwards. As King of Hungary, Ferdinand III commissioned Juvenel to paint the great series of allegorical and historical works in the Castle of Pozsony. The pictures were meant to appeal to the Hungarian nobility for sympathy and loyalty to the monarch. The series was in fact Juvenel's most important work. Although the paintings were lost some time in the eighteenth century, descriptions and prints have fortunately survived. They were interesting allegorical genre pictures which express the general bourgeois belief that by carrying out his official duties the king was demonstrating a peculiarly royal virtue. It was of course not yet possible to apply the idealized type of representation adopted later.

PAUL JUVENEL
(Nuremberg
1579–1643 Pozsony)

"Suffer little children to come unto me"

Oil on iron plate,
37.5 × 24.5 cm,
with illegible signature
and date on the step
in the bottom right corner
Inv. No. 79.3 M
Purchased in 1979
from the heirs
of Anastas Tomory
who brought the picture
to Hungary from Poland
Bibliography:
Mojzer: MÉ 1981;
Juvenel pozsonyi műveiről
[On the Pozsony works
of Juvenel]; Rózsa 1973

Willmann was a highly gifted artist active in Berlin, Prague and Silesia. His influence extended throughout the northern parts of Central Europe and he was in many respects the intellectual and artistic forerunner of Maulbertsch. In his youth he studied in Amsterdam. His work consisted mainly of large frescoes and paintings of religious subjects; his smaller panel paintings are rare.

The picture illustrated here may be one of his early works. The theatricality of the composition, and the glowing, vibrant colours, show the influence of Flemish painting, while the details reveal the influence of Rembrandt (then still alive). In no other work by Willmann do we find a detailed representation of Palladian architecture; its presence in this painting reflects the deep impression made on the artist by the neo-classic Town Hall then being built in Amsterdam as well as the impact of the contemporary taste in architecture. The scene, reminiscent of an episode from a baroque opera, was taken by the artist from Virgil's *Aeneid*. The Greek hero, Aeneas, is shown taking leave of his lover, Queen Dido, who after his departure kills herself in despair. The Queen, seated on a throne, is both dignified and resigned; the hero and lover strikes a theatrical attitude. Members of his suite and the two young women seated in the foreground are akin to the figures in the artist's later and larger works representing legends and the torturing of martyrs. Willmann in fact showed great skill in representing the suffering almost sublimated into sensual pleasure. It is possible that during his early activities in Holland his imagination was greatly stimulated by theatrical performances.

MICHAEL LEOPOLD WILLMANN (?)
(Königsberg 1630–1706 Lubiaz)

Dido and Aeneas

Oil on panel,
73.5 × 50.4 cm
Worn in many places;
the figure bending forward
from behind the throne
is irreparably damaged
Inv. No. 75.8 M.
Purchased in 1975
from a private collection
Bibliography:
Mojzer: MÉ, 1981

An interesting form of art connected with seventeenth century burial rites was the epitaph. The inhabitants of northern and western Hungarian cities, for the most part members of the Calvinist Church, were buried according to custom in the graveyard of the city's parish church.

The centre picture in the epitaph panel commemorating Anna Kún, wife of István Tárkányi, depicts the family group which, on altarpieces where the central panel is decorated with biblical episodes, is often confined to the lower part of the structure. Anna Kún is seen kneeling in her widow's weeds under the cross, together with her two husbands and all the children of her two marriages. The detailed portrayal of the figures and meticulous representation of the contemporary costumes is very different from the sweeping style of painting employed for the crucified body of Christ and, in the background, the city of Jerusalem—the latter in sombre monochromes. The red crosses mark those members of the family who died before Anna Kún.

The fine open-work carving on the black frame is harmoniously coloured, sculptured in a lively design, and bears the characteristic gold, silver, white and black painted elements of the so-called pinna or cartilage style which spread from Silesia to Hungary by way of German pattern-books. The painters or sculptors of these epitaph panels can rarely be designated as "masters", but their work corresponded to the artistic level of contemporary church furnishings. The artist responsible for the carvings on Anna Kún's memorial may have helped to make the furniture of St. James's Church in Lőcse. Precedents of the heads on the pilasters flanking the frame and of the grotesque grimace distorting the sharp features of the sensitively carved cherub above the picture, can be found also on the figures adorning the pulpit steps of St. James's Church. At the very bottom, on an oval plate with carved edges, are inscribed some of the more important events of Anna Kún's life and the year of her death. The work comes from the fifteenth century church in Kisszekeres, Szatmár County, which was the burial place of the Rozsályi Kún family.

PAINTER AND SCULPTOR FROM UPPER HUNGARY first half of the seventeenth century

Epitaph tablet for Anna Kún, wife of István Tárkányi *c.* 1646

Oil on panel.
Size of the painting: 176 × 111 cm;
full size of the panel: 321.5 × 189 cm
Inv. No. 57.16 M.
Transferred in 1936 from the Historical Portrait Gallery
Bibliography: Garas 1953: 80, 117, Pl. XLII

We know mainly from literature that in the mid-seventeenth century family portraits were no longer confined to aristocratic homes but were also to be seen in the houses of the bourgeoisie. Of that period, however, little has survived and these remains include few portraits of the middle classes. Most of them are half-length portraits with neutral backgrounds, whereas in portraits of the aristocracy dignity and rank were indicated by the richness of the clothing and the elegant setting. In the picture illustrated here the artist has captured the individuality of the sitter, her rather hard features, the details and texture of her clothing—all testifying to the fact that aristocratic and bourgeois portraits were occasionally of equal quality. Indeed this portrait is the work of a talented painter who must surely have been a member of the painters' guild in Lőcse. Several members are known to us from the sources, among them Samuel Spillenberger, a member of the Kassa family of painters, active in Lőcse for a number of years at about that time. He was related to János Spillenberger, the painter who made a name for himself in southern Germany.

The painting also provides interesting information for students of the history of Hungarian national costume, for it shows a combination of European court fashion and the typically Hungarian style only then beginning to develop. The lace-hemmed rich colarette known as "the fraise", which came to Hungary from the Spanish court, was adopted both by the aristocracy and the middle classes. It is matched in an interesting way by a pearl-embroidered reticulated bonnet closed in front like a "párta" (a headdress worn by Hungarian girls), a bodice richly embroidered with gold thread and fastened with hooks, and a pleated green silk apron trimmed with gold lace. These profusely decorated pieces worn by Hungarian women provided the unique local character which foreign travellers visiting Hungary had so often admired. The subject of this portrait is seen holding a shawl embroidered with Turkish motifs, while round her waist is a superb enamel-painted, gilded belt.

PAINTER FROM THE SZEPES REGION
mid-seventeenth century

Portrait of a Woman from Lőcse
1641

Oil on canvas,
94.5 × 78.5 cm
In contemporary painted frame.
Inscribed in the upper right corner:
"Vier und dreissig Jahr war ich alt / Als ich lebt in der Gestalt /
O Herr Christe wolst mir gebn / Dass ich dier (?) mag Ewig lebn (?)" 1641
Inv. No. 75.1 M.
Purchased in 1975 from a private collection
Not previously published

132

Almost full-length, and above life-size, this portrait of Mária Toldalagi, is an interesting example of a style peculiar to the provincial art of Hungary. Its pleasing character comes from careful observation, keen characterization and an almost naïve sincerity of approach and solution. The artist's knowledge of portrait painting was limited and his work is based on conventions rooted in sixteenth and seventeenth century art. For instance, in full-length portraits details—a curtain drawn aside, a covered table with a Bible, a vase of flowers—were introduced in order to conceal the lack of perspective in the composition. The uncertain modelling of the figure is disguised by the bonnet, the rich, strongly stylized embroidery and the trimmings of the dress. The flat, decorative painting with linear designs suggests that the artist may have been gifted in the craft of making painted cabinets or as a painter of church ceilings and pews. Mária Toldalagi's portrait is characterized by a duality which rarely produces such harmony of manner. It is the result of a particular combination of folk art and traditional portrait painting, as required by members of the nobility.

TRANSYLVANIAN PAINTER
early eighteenth century

Mária Toldalagi, wife of Lajos Naláczi
1705

Oil on canvas,
188.5 × 124 cm
Inscribed top right corner:
N. Nalaczi Lajjos Úr:
m. Kedves házastársának
Toldalagi Marianak
igaz Képe mi-kor volt 30
Esztendős. ao. 1705.
[Lajjos N. Nalaczi: A true portrait of his dear spouse, Maria Toldalagi, made for her when she was 30. In the year 1705.]
Inv. No. 65.6 M.
Purchased in 1965 by the Museum of Fine Arts from Cecil Teleki
Not previously published

These figures kneeling in prayer form part of a larger group. The related statues of two men and two women—brown-stained, unpainted lime-wood—came to the museum from the Franciscan church in Pozsony. All the figures were commissioned for a family sepulchre with a niche and statues of the type developed in Italy in the sixteenth century and were quickly adopted beyond the Alps.

According to the custom of the age, the head of the family arranged for a memorial tomb to be built in his lifetime, usually decorated with carved likenesses of members of the family. One of these statues, now in the Gallery, shows the features of Count Pál Esterházy, preserved also in contemporary prints. Here he is shown wearing the Order of the Golden Fleece, received as Palatine of Hungary in 1681. He was an outstanding politician who also fought with Miklós Zrínyi against the Turks, and was an accomplished writer, poet and amateur artist. His work entitled *Harmonia Coelestis* was a valuable contribution to the literature of baroque music. The counterpart of his statue represents his second wife, Éva Thököly; the two other figures are his brother, Count Ferenc Esterházy and his wife, Katalin Thököly.

Statues for sepulchres were generally made of bronze or marble. The wooden statues in the Gallery were carved as models for bronze figures which were never completed. The Esterházy memorial was later erected in Kismarton in a different form. It is thought that the Palatine had wanted to have the wooden models cast in bronze by the leading brazier maker of Pozsony, Balthasar Herold, who came from Nuremberg, but the death of this master in 1683 prevented Esterházy from realizing his plan. The artist who carved the surviving wooden models has been conditionally identified, on the basis of stylistic analogies, as Pröbstl, also a native of Nuremberg. Similar statues now in Brno and carved by him, feature comparatively large heads, elongated bodies and somewhat awkward postures.

JOHANN CHRISTIAN PRÖBSTL (?) AND WORKSHOP OF BALTHASAR HEROLD (Nuremberg 1621–1683 Vienna)

Pál Esterházy and His Wife, Éva Thököly
After 1682

Lime-wood,
112 and 117 cm
respectively
Inv. No. 52.759, 52.762
Transferred
in 1950 from the Museum
of Applied Arts
to the Museum of Fine Arts
Bibliography:
Agghazy, Mária:
Les modèles
des statues monument
funéraire de la
famille Esterházy.
BMH (1958) 53 sqq.
with illustrations

134

This painting was commissioned by "Christophorus Georgius de Berge, at one time captain of Nagykanizsa Castle, Count of the Holy Roman Empire, lord of Herrendorf and Cladau [sic!], Colonel of His Imperial and Royal Majesty's cavalry, Governor and Ordinary Envoy of the Principality of Glogova", who may have met the painter at his seat in Bohemia or, even more likely, through his office in Silesia, whence the painter himself removed to Prague. The Count was an ardent votary of St. Joseph and also of his wife's patron saint, St. Barbara. This picture, destined above all to give solace to the sick, was probably part of his endowment to the Franciscan Order. The sick man is represented on his death-bed visited by St. Joseph and St. Barbara, the patron saints of "good death". The picture within a picture seen in the background, represents a parallel subject, Christ on the Mount of Olives with an angel comforting Him as He prepares Himself for death. The work is a baroque version of the earlier *ars moriendi*, didactic pictures demonstrating the art of making a good death, fashionable in the Middle Ages. The painter has endeavoured to devise a realistic, everyday setting and situation. This is, in fact, characteristic of his art, for his religious pictures are usually in the style of a genre painting. This work is one of his masterpieces. A middle-class orderliness is reflected in his accurate representation of the corner of the homely room, the eiderdown, embroidered bedclothes and the still life formed by the stool with a kerchief and a rosary. The sick man, holding a cross and a candle, prepares himself for death, composed even in the last minutes of his life, supported by pillows in a time-honoured pose. The vision marks his imminent arrival in heaven and is made to seem as natural as the orderly earthly existence he is leaving behind.

JOHANN GEORG HEINSCH
(Silesia
c. **1647–1712**
Prague)

Death of a Christian
1695

Oil on canvas, 198 × 139 cm.
Signed on the listel
of the stool,
bottom left corner:
"J. G. Heinsch fec. 1695"
On loan
from the Nagykanizsa
Downtown presbytery
Bibliography:
Mojzer MÉ 1981

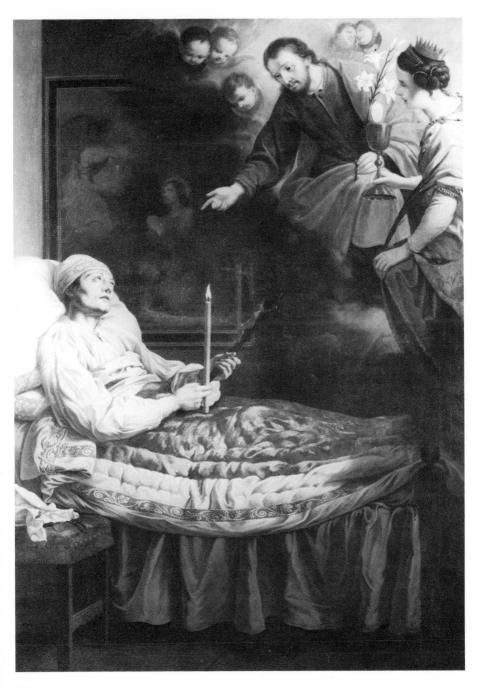

This is one of three huge statues, each representing an apostle, which stood for a long time in niches on the front of the Parish Church in Sződ, near Budapest, though it is thought that originally they were in the Lipótváros Chapel in Pest. Such a series of apostles—for there would have been several more figures—must have had a much earlier origin, perhaps part of some early remains acquired by this small provincial church. Quietly dignified, dramatic and severe, the group of figures, formerly coloured but now much worn, are indeed impressive. There is a vibrant tension between the static figures and their flowing robes, the closed faces and minutely elaborated hair and beard. The statue of Paul the Apostle is reminiscent of Roman sculpture bearing the later stamp of the mature baroque artist, Bernini. Yet the decorative treatment of the surface—whose stylized effect is reached by a special technique—and the studied, regular diagonal folds, undulating outlines and boldly undercut creases rolling one over the other (now broken off in some places), suggest distance in time and space. The working of wood in this manner is primarily characteristic of baroque sculpture as developed in regions (e.g. Silesia and certain Bohemian and alpine provinces) where, under the guidance of masters trained in other countries, the art of wood-carving had been continuously practised since the Gothic period. At present the nearest known analogies to the three statues from Sződ are to be found among the works of the Bohemian sculptors Hieronymus Kohl and Franz Preiss, active in the late seventeenth and early eighteenth centuries. Their joint work, the figures on the acanthus decorated altars (1701–1706) in St. Nicholas's Church in Louny, come closest to these figures, the link being especially discernible in the carving of the diagonally undulating drapery covering the figure of St. Paul the Apostle. The Hungarian counterparts of the apostle figures are the two king statues carved by Master János Strecius of Lőcse after 1700, and surviving from the ruined altar castle chapel in Sárospatak. St. Stephen's head is akin to that of St. Paul in almost every detail—the wrinkled brow, convex eyelids, and the curls of his hair and beard.

SCULPTOR ACTIVE IN THE POZSONY– NAGYSZOMBAT REGION
c. 1700

St. Paul from Sződ

Lime-wood, 200 cm
On loan
from the
Vác Uptown presbytery

Bibliography:
Aggházy, Mária:
Régi magyarországi faszobrok
[Old Hungarian wooden statues].
Budapest, 1958: 29;
cf. Neumann, Jaromir:
Das böhmische Barock.
Praha, 1970: 155;
and Mrs. B. Baranyai:
Mesterek és műhelyek az északkelet-magyarországi barokk szobrászatban.
Magyarországi reneszánsz és barokk
[Masters and workshops of baroque sculpture in north-eastern Hungary.
Hungarian Renaissance and baroque art].
Ed. Géza Galavics.
Budapest, 1975: 315–319

Jakab Bogdány, member of the Calvinist nobility, was born in Eperjes, Sáros County, around 1660. He left his native town while still a youth to continue his studies abroad, presumably in Vienna. Thence he travelled to the city of Amsterdam in Protestant Netherlands, and it was there, in the birth-place of still life and animal painting, that he developed his own art. The Netherlandish elements determinig his style have their roots in the art of Willem van Aelst, Abraham van Beyeren, Jacob van Walscapele and Jean-Baptiste Monnoyer.

The variegated bunch of flowers is not only the subject of his picture but also the means by which he could demonstrate his powers of expression and his ability to represent faithfully a variety of textured surfaces. The glass jug filled with water producing a dim reflection of light, and the hard and cold, finely veined marble, are deliberately brought into contrast with the flowers and with a velvety texture. The rose lying at the edge of the marble table represents the three phases of vegetal life, but is at the same time a symbolic reminder of the brevity of human life, frequently used in Dutch "vanitas" still lifes.

JAKAB BOGDÁNY
(Eperjes,
c. 1660–1724 London)

Still life with Flowers

Oil on canvas, 62 × 49 cm
Signed bottom right:
"J. Bogdani"
Inv. No. 3786
Donated
to the Museum of Fine Arts
by Marcell Nemes in 1908
Bibliography:
Pigler 1941: 18, Pl. XIII

Having completed his studies, Jakab Bogdány left the Netherlands in 1688 well-equipped to settle in England where before long he was deservedly recognized for his still lifes and animal pictures. He worked for the highest strata of the nobility and even members of the royal family. This patronage and the large number of paintings he produced, prove that the painter enjoyed the same degree of recognition and esteem as his British, Dutch and other foreign colleagues. His pictures show the influence of Melchior de Hondecoeter.

The blurred colours and misty atmosphere of the park surrounding the castle provides a unifying background for the motley flock of birds. The exotic birds from distant lands are selected from the rare species in private aviaries much admired by British aristocrats. The accuracy of the representation from the ornithological point of view suggests that Bogdány was able to visit aviaries and paint the birds from nature.

JAKAB BOGDÁNY

**Still life with Birds
(Fruits and Parrots)**

Oil on canvas,
98 × 88.5 cm
Signed bottom right,
on the ledge:
"J. Bogdani"
Inv. No. 3681
Acquired by the Museum
of Fine Arts
from a British
private collector in 1907
Bibliography:
Pigler 1941:
19, 22, Pl. XXIV;
Á. Mányoki
Commemorative
Exhibition 1957,
No. 19

137

138

Tóbiás Stranover, born in Nagyszeben, was the son-in-law and pupil of Jakab Bogdány. Unlike his master, however, he did not settle definitely, nor did he acquire any property in England. Apart from the fact that he was active in Western Europe, mainly Germany, over a period of several years, comparatively little information is available about his career. He probably returned to Transylvania where he continued to work for some time before his death.

In the main features of his art Stranover was a follower of Bogdány. He learned from his master not only how to group the birds and animals in his compositions, but also how to characterize this peculiar world by the use of bright colours, by highlighting details of the background and by portraying the nature and behaviour of a variety of domestic animals. In this painting Stranover invests the lord of the farm-yard, the swaggering cock, with almost human sentiments. He depicts the overbearing, vain creature showing off his fine quill-feathers in contrast to his companions modestly looking around and scratching for food. Here too, as in Bogdány's works, the background is closed by a misty, distant wooded landscape and the idyllic details of a farm.

Stranover's work includes some flower paintings and still lifes of fruit; the colouring is refined, showing the influence of Dutch still life painting. Some of his work can be seen in Schwerin and in Ahrensburg Castle, near Hamburg.

TÓBIÁS STRANOVER (Nagyszeben 1684–after 1724 Nagyszeben [?])

Poultry-yard with Cat and Pigeons (Landscape with Poultry)

Oil on canvas, 105 × 147 cm
Inv. No. 4633
Donated to the Museum of Fine Arts by Ferenc Kleinberger in 1913
Not previously published

139

Ádám Mányoki, the greatest Hungarian portrait painter of the baroque period, rightly occupies a prominent place an in the history of Hungarian art.

Mányoki was the son of a parson with a large family. While still a child, he was sent to foster-parents in North Germany where he soon found an opportunity to become a student of art. The first master to encourage and influence him was Andreas Scheitz of Hamburg, a portrait-painter trained in the Netherlands. From him Mányoki assimilated the contemporary French style imbued with a touch of the intimate spirit of Dutch portrait-painting in which the aim was to convey the character of the sitter. Later, through the works of Largillière, Mányoki came to know the finest portrait-painting in Europe at that time. After his years in Hamburg he became court painter at the Prussian court in Berlin. It was here that he met the consort of Ferenc Rákóczi II, at whose invitation he came to Hungary to act as court painter to the Prince. After two years Rákóczi sent Mányoki abroad to study Dutch painting and learn copper engraving. It must have been around this time that he painted his self-portrait.

In the pose commonly chosen by contemporary artists, Mányoki painted himself at work, a brush and palette in hand, his shirt open at the front, his sleeves rolled up. The painter's expression is serene and self-confident. In spite of the casual clothing and easy carriage, the portrait suggests a certain re-strained dignity—a characteristic found in all Mányoki's paintings. The softly modelled body painted with fine transitions of key, is covered by a white shirt hanging in loose folds, well adapted for the creation of painterly effects. The restrained colour-scheme, based on the harmony between gleaming white and brilliant warm colours, is also designed to give the natural simple atmosphere of the workaday occasion. The painter is shown wearing a soft velvet hat with upturned brim which leaves part of his face in shadow. The liveliness and gaiety of the eyes and the sensitive smiling mouth suggest the congenial personality of the successful, mature painter.

ÁDÁM MÁNYOKI
(Szokolya 1673–1757 Dresden)

Self-portrait

Oil on canvas, 87 × 61.5 cm
Inv. No. 6508
Permanent deposit by the Association of Friends of the Art Museums, 1929
Bibliography:
Lázár 1933: 13;
Garas 1955: 18, Pl. I;
Á. Mányoki Commemorative Exhibition, 1957, No. 15

This portrait of Ferenc Rákóczi II is not only the most beautiful example of Hungarian baroque portrait-painting but also one of Mányoki's most outstanding works. It is our finest memento of the Prince, splendidly conveying his distinction of mind and body, his pride, his dignity, his nobility.

Born into the Transylvanian nobility, Rákóczi received a modern education from the Jesuits under the watchful supervision of the Court in Vienna. His studies at the Jesuit schools in Neuhaus and Prague were complemented by travel in Italy where he spent lengthy periods in several large cities and developed a knowledge and appreciation of art. By employing the services of Ádám Mányoki, he hoped to establish a court art of his own, equal to that of other European courts, and to propagate at the same time his political endeavours through art. These considerations prompted him in 1709 to send his court painter to the Netherlands to study Dutch painting.

In his portrait of Rákóczi Mányoki made use of all that he had learned in the Netherlands. The picture dates from 1712 and was painted in Gdańsk, Poland, to which country the Prince had emigrated after the defeat of the War of Independence led by him. He is depicted in Hungarian costume adorned with embroidery on the front. The strong light on his face and the contrasting dark hair and fur-cap serve to emphasize the features, thus revealing the artist's sensitive understanding of the Prince's character. It is evident that Mányoki's study of Dutch portrait-painting had taught him how to produce consistent effect of light and tone and to create a pictorial balance whilst at the same time achieving a subtle degree of characterization in his portraits. In this painting of the exiled Prince the artist has merely hinted at the symbols of royalty. The scarlet dolman worn like a cloak and fastened at the front with a chain of Hungarian goldsmith's work, is lined with ermine, as befitted a royal personage. Round his neck the Prince is wearing the Order of the Golden Fleece, awarded in 1709.

ÁDÁM MÁNYOKI

Ferenc Rákóczi II
1712

Oil on canvas, 75.5 × 67.6 cm
Inv. No. 6001
Donated in 1925
to the Museum
of Fine Arts
by Marcell Nemes
Bibliography: Lázár 1933:
17, Plate III;
Garas 1953: 91, t. L;
Garas 1955: 18;
Á. Mányoki
Commemorative
Exhibition 1957,
No. 32;
Galavics 1980: 509–510

141

After a second longer stay in Hungary from 1724 to 1731, when he investigated the possibility of settling there, Mányoki returned to Germany where he lived for the rest of his life. He was active first in Dresden and Berlin; later he worked for a few years in Leipzig. Having no permanent employment or office—for he was not reinstated as court painter at the Saxon court until 1737—Mányoki painted half-length portraits of members of the nobility and the bourgeoisie, also officials of the Leipzig trade centre. His pictures dating from this period had an expansive and easy fluency about them. The portrait of G. W. Werthern is one of those dating from these years.

Many features of this portrait reveal the influence of French court painting in the style developed by Largillière and Rigaud. The element of formality and the details indicating the status of the sitter, had often been used successfully by Mányoki when he was court painter to Augustine the Strong in Warsaw and Dresden between 1714 and 1724. A sensitive treatment of light, a wide range of techniques and a strong sense of harmony distinguish all his portraits and indeed all his mature work. The colouring of this picture is dominated by the pinkish-white of the powerfully modelled, yet softly shaded face and heavy dense wig. The light but sober colouring, the distilled light cast over the body of the sitter, the soft fleshiness given to the face, are all means by which the painter demonstrates the character of the sitter. The glinting armour and the deep folds of the fur-trimmed red velvet cloak provide him with many different possibilities for a realistic and decorative representation of texture and plasticity.

Mányoki's paintings produced in the last decades of his activity were often reproduced as engravings, especially by his friend Bernigeroth, and later by Bernigeroth's son. It is only from these engravings that we know of numerous works by Mányoki which have not survived. These engravings and the paintings which have survived have ensured Mányoki's reputation as the most important Hungarian portraitist of the baroque period and indeed as one of the most distinguished painters in the history of Central European art.

ÁDÁM MÁNYOKI

**Portrait of
G. W. Werthern**

Oil on canvas, 82 × 69 cm
Inv. No. 54.327
Formerly
in the City Art Gallery
Bibliography:
Lázár 1933: 62,
Pl. LVIII; Garas 1955:
21, Pl. XV;
Á. Mányoki
Commemorative
Exhibition 1957, No. 35

Orient is the only landscape painter of Hungarian origin known to us by name from the late seventeenth and early eighteenth centuries. His career as an artist is, however, associated with Vienna where he participated in organizing and administering the Academy of Art.

Orient first studied under Anton Faistenberger, a landscape painter active in Vienna but trained in Rome and Venice. He is believed to have matriculated at the Vienna Academy after the death of his first master in 1708. In 1705, the school, originally a private academy, was transformed when it became an imperial institute. In 1726 it was reorganized along the lines of French art schools, under the direction of Jacob van Schuppen. Several departments were established, including one for the study of landscape painting. It must have been at about this time that Orient, already a mature artist, joined the teaching staff, for at his death in 1747 he was described as the assistant director.

In Orient's landscape, now in the Gallery, the interior of the forest is by no means true to nature. The entangled trees with long trunks end in a dark mass which does not suggest foliage, the featureless sky gives no hint of possible change. The peasant couple look as if they were characters in some unspecified legend. The woman riding a donkey indicates with a dramatic gesture the landslide bathed in a golden light. The sketchy figures, although introduced merely to enliven the picture, assume a curious importance in the stage-like landscape where no breeze stirs so much as a leaf.

The picture is one of two romantic paintings by Orient now in the Gallery, both of which must be regarded as early works. His later pictures are more akin to Dutch landscape painting. Around 1733–1735 he was active in Frankfurt am Main together with his pupil, Franz Christoph Janneck who, according to some sources, was responsible for the figures in Orient's pictures dating from that time.

JÓZSEF ORIENT
**(Feketeváros
1677–1747 Vienna)**

Landscape

Oil on canvas, 60 × 75.5 cm
Inv. No. 3926
Donated to the Museum
of Fine Arts
by Marcell Nemes in 1910
Bibliography:
Á. Mányoki
Commemorative
Exhibition 1957, No. 10

143

This outstanding master of Bohemian baroque art painted mainly altarpieces; he also painted historical and religious pictures, portraits and a very few genre paintings. An artist with a touch of genius, he was exceedingly temperamental, a spendthrift who led a hectic life which ended one night, perhaps suitably, in a tavern. He usually represented men or women in sad or sordid circumstances and in his genre paintings he hinted always at the cause— smoking for instance, or superstition, or frustrated love. This picture suggests the tragedy of old age. A toothless, poverty-stricken old woman holds up the pitcher as if begging; her obvious distress and apathetic expression shows us that this work is a vanitas type of the genre. Ever since Giorgione old women like this have been portrayed in vanitas pictures. Here the woman's attitude of patient resignation recalls the portraits of Rembrandt. This link was not intentional on the part of the artist but comes rather from a similarity of outlook, for Brandl had never visited the Netherlands; indeed he had never left his own country. The splendid impasto, the broken strong patches of deep reddish-browns and yellowish-whites imposed over the vibrant surfaces, the crumbling forms, all indicate that the painter must have created the picture probably in the 1720s. The work may have already found its way to Hungary some time in the eighteenth century.

PETER BRANDL
(Prague
1668–1735 Kutná Hora)

Old Woman with a Pitcher

Oil on canvas, 58.5 × 48.5 cm
Inv. No. 77.1
Purchased in 1977
from a private collection
Bibliography:
Mojzer MÉ 1981

Born in Prague, this artist was active first in Nuremberg, later in Frankfurt and Bamberg. He painted animal pictures, hunting scenes and battles; equestrian scenes are a feature of his work. This genre picture with Hungarian hussars is painted with great objectivity. It is unlikely that he painted these stocky, round-headed soldiers from hearsay: the Hungarian troops sent west at the time of the Austro-Prussian wars must have provided him with a topical subject. The composition suggests that it is one of a pair.

WENZEL IGNAZ PRASCH (BRASCH) (Prague [?]–1761 Schwabach)

Hungarian Hussars beside a Ruined Building

Oil on canvas, 66 × 82 cm
Signed bottom left:
W. I. BRASCH. F.
Inv. No. L. 5063
Bibliography:
Mojzer MÉ 1981

144

145

The work is a design in lead for the relief decorating the base of the Ark of the Covenant monument in Győr. This open-air monument executed in stone is one of the remarkable early relics of official monumental sculpture in Hungary. The scene shows two angels lifting the Ark of the Covenant. The monument was erected by Charles III as a propitiatory offering to the inhabitants of Győr because his soldiers had interfered with one of their religious processions. The idea underlying the composition, that is its intellectual content, came from Conrad Adolph von Albrecht, a theoretician of the Viennese court. The architectural design for the monument was the responsibility of Fischer von Erlach junior, and the statues were by Antonio Corradini, the court artist, a frequent collaborator. One of their best known works is the memorial sepulchre erected to St. John of Nepomuk in St. Vitus's Cathedral in Prague, for which Corradini also first made a small model. The Győr monument is a direct predecessor of the series of sarcophagus reliefs in Prague which are similar in style. The stone relief and its model in lead represent the Crucifixion with an animated crowd assembled in a confined space. A distant city forms the background to the scene. The main figures, the Captain on horseback, Christ on the Cross and Longinus holding a spear, form a regular triangle in the composition. The cast lead plate being rather thin, the design is in rather shallow relief. The large carved stone version was executed by a very different technique; in it the foreground lends depth to the scene which is made plastic by powerful light and shade effects.

ANTONIO CORRADINI
(Venice,
late seventeenth
century–1752
Vienna)

Crucifixion
1729–1730

Relief in lead,
66 × 46.5 cm
On loan from the Museum of Applied Arts
Bibliography: Voit, Pál: Ein unbekanntes Werk von Antonio Corradini. Arts Decorativa 3 (1975), 81 sq.

Donner was one of the most prominent sculptors in Europe in the first half of the eighteenth century. Austrian by birth, he created much of his work in Pozsony where he was resident sculptor of the Archbishop Imre Esterházy. These sculptures had a decisive influence on the development of the arts in the baroque style in Hungary. He also exercised a powerful influence on the large number of German and Austrian sculptors studying at the academy, even those whose art was originally inspired by other sources.

The high altar of the Cathedral in Pozsony was a work of art in which the master realized a highly effective combination of architectural and sculptural elements. The crowned canopy rested on huge free-standing columns. The central statue represented St. Martin, the titular saint of the church who, dressed in the Hungarian national style and bearing the features of Esterházy, was shown bending down from his horse to share his cloak with a beggar seated on the ground. Two large subsidiary figures represented kneeling angels who provided as it were an intermediate link between the faithful and the saint. The high altar was dismantled in the course of the neo-Gothic reconstruction of the church in the nineteenth century. The St. Martin group can now be seen in the side-aisle of the Cathedral, while the two lead angels are in the Hungarian National Gallery.

The angels are truly representative of Donner's life-work. They illustrate in a vivid manner the sculptor's development—his gradual alienation from the theological requirements of the age and his transition from the baroque tradition to his own version of the neo-Classical style. Their sweeping, emphatic gestures are essentially symmetric, differentiated only in subtle ways. The quiet, closed outlines lead the eye to the shaded surfaces of the powerful forms. Though massive, the bodies are not clumsy. They kneel on the volutes with a fine, momentary touch, and the bowed heads are coupled with an upward movement. All the statues on the high altar were cast in an alloy of tin and lead—a material often used by Donner. The dull surface sheen prompted the artist to exploit the potentialities inherent in plastic values, free of all painterly effects.

GEORG RAPHAEL DONNER (Esslingen 1693–1741 Vienna)

Adoring Angel from the chancel of the Cathedral in Pozsony
1733–1735

Lead, 200 cm
Inv. No. 76.4 M
Transferred in 1976
from the Hungarian
National Museum
Bibliography:
Pigler 1929: 46;
Schwarz, M.:
Georg Raphael Donner.
München, 1968: 21, 53, 87;
Kovács, Péter: Donner.
Budapest, 1979: 19–20

147

In 1738 Archbishop Imre Esterházy commissioned his resident sculptor, Donner, to make choir stalls with sculptural decorations for the Cathedral in Pozsony. It would seem from the surviving sections, and the design for the choir and furnishings, all still in the baroque style, that the master must have entrusted his workshop with the execution of the whole order on the basis of his own designs. At that time it was a general custom among leading artists heavily charged with commisions, to act virtually only as contractor and to hand over some of the work to be carried out by assistants. The high altar of the Paulines in Máriavölgy and the altar of the Blessed Virgin in the Holy Trinity Church in Pozsony, may have been produced by workshop assistants; in both cases there is documentary evidence that they were executed under the direction of "Tunner".

Donner borrowed the idea of decorating choir stalls with carved heads from his master, Giovanni Giuliani, who had produced similarly decorated church furnishings in Heiligenkreuz. When the Gothic cathedral was restored in 1867 the stalls were transferred to the Kinsky Palace in Vienna, while 24 pieces of the series of statues found their way to the Lanfranconi Collection in Pozsony, and thence to Budapest. These oak busts, impressive, grave and individualized to some degree, are difficult to identify; apart from the recognizable figure of Christ and St. Paul the Hermit, there are also monks, prophets, apostles and sibyls. The series was destined to recall the dignified and highly cultured occupants of the choir stalls; the theological connections lost in the mists of time. All the busts, including that of the sullen, bearded prophet, are formed of large, quiet surfaces; they have little in common with Donner's neo-Classical style, their rigid dignity being more closely related to the conservative, rather schematic pictorial language of their Heiligenkreuz archetype.

WORKSHOP OF GEORG RAPHAEL DONNER

Head of a Prophet from Pozsony
1738

Wood, 75 cm
Inv. No. 52.788
Transferred in 1952
from the Museum
of Applied Arts
to the Museum of Fine Arts
Bibliography:
Agghazy, Mária:
Neu entdeckte Werke
G. R. Donners
und seines Kreises
aus der Gegend von
Pressburg.
AHA 1954: 72–79;
Maliková, Maria:
Die Schule
Georg Raphael Donners
in der Slowakei.
Mitteilungen
der Österreichischen Galerie
1973: 77 sqq.

This gilded plaster relief is an exact copy of Donner's bronze-painted wax relief of the same subject now among the baroque works in the Belvedere Museum in Vienna. The counterpart of the latter is the relief showing the Consolation of the Blessed Virgin; both works are from a series of scenes showing the Passion as traditionally represented since the Middle Ages. Donner produced a series of reliefs on this subject for the chapel dedicated to St. John the Almsgiver, in the Pozsony Cathedral, when he first came to stay in Hungary. The chapel, built in the baroque style and adorned with unified monumental sculptural compositions, is the burial place of Archbishop Imre Esterházy. The altar containing the sarcophagus is flanked by two angels reminiscent of youths of classical Antiquity, while the kneeling figure at the side represents the Archbishop himself, deep in prayer. The elements of the composition all bear witness to the artist's knowledge of kindred works in the mature style of Roman baroque. Reliefs showing scenes from the life of Christ are arranged in a frieze on the predella of the altar. It is most probable that Donner designed the pair of wax reliefs now in Vienna as part of the same series, since from the iconographic point of view they complete the story represented on the altar. There is a belief, not altogether substantiated, that the plaster copy of the relief entitled *Christ before Pilate* was produced in Donner's workshop some time in the eighteenth century. Like the related pieces in Vienna and Pozsony, this too is an example of the revival of the classical relief which, while observing an imaginary frontal plane, suggest spatiality by fine transitions. The presentation of a biblical subject with historical implications is combined here with Donner's endeavour to archaize, while the emphasis on human relations and conflicts imbues the work with both emotional and sculptural values.

AFTER GEORG RAPHAEL DONNER

Christ before Pilate
After 1732

Plaster, 47 × 60 cm
On loan from the
Dobó István
Castle Museum
in Eger.
From the collection
of the archiepiscopal
Lyceum in Eger
Bibliography:
Pigler 1929: 55;
Schwarz, M.:
Reliéfy kaplnky
Sv. Jána Almužnika
od Juraja Rafaela Donnera–
štýl a ikonografia
[Georg Raphael Donner's
reliefs with scenes
from the life of St. John
the Almsgiver—Style
and iconography].
Ars 1969, 26–28

149

The figure of Archangel Michael who, in defence of Christianity, triumphed over the Devil, has been a popular subject among artists ever since the early Middle Ages. At the time of the Counter-Reformation the cult of St. Michael was given new impetus. His battle with Lucifer and the fallen angels was taken to represent the triumph of the Catholic Church over Protestant heresy. On this gilded wooden relief, now in the Gallery, the saint is seen in the moment of victory. He holds his sword ready to thrust it into the monster at his feet before the creature falls into the tongues of flame. The calculated arrangement of the two figures fills the whole surface, the upwards soaring angel forming an effective contrast to the downwards falling Devil. St. Michael's body is twisted: he holds the sword in his right hand ready to strike his enemy in the left side. This cunningly calculated movement had been a recurring feature in compositions of this subject since the advent of Mannerism. Occasionally it appeared also in works representing St. Martin helping the beggar.

This bas-relief, with its sharp breaks in the widely spread draperies, features which are regular but lacking in detail, and anatomical accuracy in the delineation of the archangel's graceful figure, is reminiscent of the art of Schletterer, a pupil of Donner, the well-known Viennese sculptor. Schletterer's early series of reliefs in the monastic church in Zwettl, Austria (after 1730), shows a certain affinity with the work illustrated here. His angels (1756) on the altar in Sonntagsberg are carved in the same posture as this —much smaller—figure of St. Michael, although they are given a quite different role. His academic statuette of Minerva (1756) is the artist's most mature composition depicting the struggle between good and evil.

Certain weaknesses in the relief shown here, for example in the composition of the figure of Satan, indicate that the work was executed by one of the master's pupils or followers.

FOLLOWER OF JACOB CHRISTOPH SCHLETTERER (1699–1774)

Archangel St. Michael Defeating Satan
c. 1750

Wood, 88 × 56 cm
Inv. No.: 54.1960
From the City Art Gallery
Bibliography:
not previously published.
cf. Windisch-Graetz,
Franz:
Jacob Christoph Schletterer;
die Plastiker
des Donner-Kreises
und die Wiener Akademie.
Paul Troger-Ausstellung,
Altenburg 1963:
27–36, illustrated;
Aggházy 1959 I: 89, 268;
G. Aggházy, Maria:
Die Immaculata-Statuen
des J. Ch. Schletterer.
Alte und Moderne Kunst 2
(1964), 24–25

Martino Altomonte, an artist well known for his altarpieces, historical paintings and frescoes, was commissioned by the Sopron Catholic Convent to paint a picture for the high altar in St. Michael's Church. Altomonte—who had already produced altarpieces for Győr and other Hungarian towns—passed this commission on to his son and collaborator. The Altomontes specialized in large church paintings, historical and triumphal compositions and frescoes in the Italian tradition. Martino, though of Tyrolean stock, was born in Naples and used an Italian version of his real name which was Hohenberg, believing this to have a greater appeal to contemporary ears. It was under his assumed name that he became known first at the Polish court, where he was invited to paint compositions about the hereditary rulers. Later he was active in Vienna. His son, Bartolommeo, was a pupil of Solimena in Naples for two years.

It is therefore not surprising to find that the composition for the vast altarpiece designed for Sopron is a pictorial echo of one of Solimena's particularly popular creations, the fresco he painted in San Domenico Maggiore in Naples in 1709. In a good many of his other works Altomonte the Younger continued to make use of details from this work which represented the Holy Trinity, St. Dominic with other saints, and the defeated heretics. In this picture, however, he adapted the subject to meet the wishes of his employers. The Virgin is represented as the patron saint of the country (indicated by the Hungarian coat of arms below her right hand), and the defeated are depicted as Turks wearing clothes and arms painted with pedantic accuracy. The impressive multi-coloured altarpiece, painted in the last years of the so-called Balkan campaign, illustrated for the faithful their release from Turkish rule which by then was gradually becoming a reality. This is suggested in the lower part of the picture by a battle scene, in the upper part by celestial rejoicing.

BARTOLOMMEO ALTOMONTE
(Warsaw 1702–1779 Linz)

Patrona Hungariae Sending St. Michael to Fight the Turks
1739

Oil on canvas, 435 × 226 cm
Signed bottom left:
"Barth Altomonte invenit et pinxit, 1739"
On loan
from St. Michael's Church, Sopron
Bibliography:
Csatkai, Endre: Magyarország Műemléki Topográfiája II. Sopron és környéke műemlékei
[A topography of Hungary's monuments, Vol. II. Monuments in and around Sopron].
2nd edition. Budapest, 1956, 404; Jávor, Anna: Bartolommeo Altomonte soproni főoltárképe
[Bartolommeo Altomonte's painting on the high altar of Sopron].
MÉ XXVI 288–291

These two statues made of gilded lime-wood, one and a half times life-size, were at one time in the Church of Our Lady in Körmöcbánya, now demolished. The interior decoration of the church was renewed in the 1760s: the decoration of the high altar and the painting of the ceiling was undertaken by Antal Schmidt, an artist trained in Vienna, while all sculptural work was commissioned from the local master, Dionysius Stanetti. There is evidence of Stanetti's activity in the mining towns from 1743 on. He first worked at Privigye and then, between 1755 and 1764, in Selmecbánya. Stanetti, though a citizen of Körmöcbánya, was undoubtedly of foreign origin. This is evident not only from his Italian name but also because his art is linked to that of other countries. Thus his two Holy Trinity monuments are constructed after an Austrian model: the one in Körmöcbánya is similar to the monument in Baden, near Vienna, created by the Viennese court sculptor, Giovanni Stanetti. Giovanni belonged to the "first generation" of the Italian artists who settled in Austria and was evidently the master, and probably also a relative of Dionysius of Körmöcbánya. Dionysius's style was closely connected with, and perhaps superior to, the closed, heavy, classically severe, formal idiom of the monumental sculptural decoration prevalent in Vienna in the first third of the century. St. Florianus and St. Donatus are saints from Roman times, venerated as guardians against elemental disasters. Florianus protected country dwellers and their crops against damage wrought by fire, Donatus against lightning and hailstorm. Accordingly, their statues were erected mainly in the open air, in town squares and along roads; they often appeared also on columns in honour of Our Lady and representations of the Holy Trinity. The two statues illustrated here did not therefore decorate the altar in the Körmöcbánya parish church but were placed somewhat apart from each other in the aisle of the church. The figures represent powerfully built men gesturing in a restrained manner; the heroic posture is borrowed from stone sculpture. The statues have been restored and some of the attributes are missing, for instance the flag held by Florianus and the wheat-sheaf held by Donatus.

DIONYSIUS STANETTI
(d. Körmöcbánya, 1767)

St. Donatus and St. Florianus from Körmöcbánya
1764

Lime-wood, gilded, 236 and 248 cm respectively
Inv. No. 52.799, 52.800
Transferred in 1951 from the Museum of Applied Arts to the Museum of Fine Arts
Bibliography:
Jávor, Anna: Dionysius Stanetti szobrai a MNG-ban [Statues by Dionysius Stanetti in the Hungarian National Gallery]. MÉ 1981/1, 50–54.

152

From about the middle of the eighteenth century it became customary to embellish pulpits with more and more sculptural work. This included relief compositions as well in which the subject was the preaching of the Gospel. This gilded wooden relief of St. Peter preaching, together with its counterpart known as St. Paul's Sermon in Athens, were two such reliefs which at one time decorated the front of a pulpit. Their place of origin is not known. They show some relationship to similar works by Lajos Gode, one of Donner's most prolific pupils, in particular to the reliefs in the Jesuit church in Pozsony which, in spite of rococo enrichments, follow in essentials Donner's classical style. The figures of apostles created by Gode may have served as models for the long-faced standing or recumbent provincial men and women in this relief. The way in which the artist tries to suggest space is, however, much more primitive than in Lajos Gode's works. Against a background closed by a window and a curtain, the figures are arranged in two planes in a relatively small space indicated by the illusory perspective produced by the flagstones and platform. St. Peter, a key hanging from his waist, arms outstretched as he preaches, is the central figure of the composition; the figures forming the congregation, worked as if they had been applied separately, fall into two groups. The rather simple technique of embossing, with ample use of curtains, clouds and steps to suggest space, is familiar from the works of sculptors active in the mining towns of Upper Hungary. The same means had been employed for example by Martin Vogerl for the execution of the reliefs on the base of the Immaculata monument in Nyitra, and also for the series of reliefs on the column of the Holy Trinity which he created jointly with Stanetti in Körmöcbánya. Many of Stanetti's sculptures in the round are directly analogous with the figures in the relief and since there is evidence that he undertook also the decoration of a pulpit in the Great Church in Körmöcbánya, it is possible that the two carvings found their way to the museum from there.

DIONYSIUS STANETTI (?)

St. Peter Preaching

c. 1760

Wood, gilded, 57 × 75 cm
Inv. No. 64.5 M
Transferred in 1951
from the Museum
of Applied Arts
to the Museum of Fine Arts
Bibliography: Jávor, Anna:
Dionysius Stanetti
szobrai a MNG-ban
[Statues
by Dionysius Stanetti
in the Hungarian
National Gallery].
MÉ 1981/1

153

The Palkos, a family of painters, settled temporarily in Pozsony in the 1740s. Franz Xaver Karl was taught by his brother, Franz Anton. Later he studied at the Viennese Academy where in 1745 he won a first prize with his composition entitled *Judith and Holofernes*. The success of the painting is demonstrated by the fact that it exists in several contemporary versions. The one in Budapest is thought to be the master's own work.

The romantic but cruel story of the biblical figures, Judith and Holofernes, was a popular subject, frequently represented in different forms in baroque art. In Karl Palko's painting the background is oppressive. The body of Holofernes lies on the ground in an embracing posture. In the dimly lit interior of the tent Judith, wrapping up the severed head with the aid of her servant, looks back upon her victim with both compassion and coquetry. The swirling contrast produced by heavy shadows, masses of drapery and patches of light, show the influence of Paul Troger who left a firm imprint on the work of every painter who came to the Viennese Academy in the 1740s.

**FRANZ XAVER KARL PALKO
(Breslau 1724–1767 Munich)**

Judith and Holofernes

Oil on canvas, 72 × 86.5 cm
Inv. No. 76.7 M
Purchased in 1976;
at the Art Auction No. 39
of BÁV Hungarian
Commission Shop;
No. 237
Bibliography:
Garas, Klára:
Zu einigen Problemen
der Malerei
des 18. Jahrhunderts.
Die Malerfamilie Palko.
AHA VII (1961), 247;
Mojzer MÉ 1981
After restoration)

In the 1740s Palko was resident painter to the Archbishop of Hungary, Imre Esterházy, in Pozsony, where he painted numerous portraits and altarpieces. The painting reproduced here shows a legendary scene set in a historic atmosphere. According to the legend, King Wenceslas IV tried to induce his wife's confessor to divulge a secret of the confessional for he wanted to find out whether his wife had been unfaithful to him or not. The painting evokes a theatrical atmosphere as if the painter wanted to represent a historic but theatrical event. The painting was at one time in the chapel of the manor house at Újfalu. Klára Garas and Maria Malikova were responsible for the attribution. Another work by the same artist, kindred in many respects, is in the archiepiscopal palace in Olomouc. It shows Bishop Count Maximilian Hamilton handing over a deed of foundation to a Piarist monk.

**FRANZ ANTON PALKO
(Breslau 1717–1766 Vienna)**

**St. John
of Nepomuk
before King Wenceslas**

Oil on canvas, 90 × 58 cm
Inv. No. 78.10 M
Purchased in 1978
at the Art Auction
No. 46 of BÁV Hungarian
Commission Shop;
No. 103
Bibliography:
Mojzer MÉ 1981

154   155

The cult of St. John of Nepomuk, the Prague priest canonized in 1729, spread throughout the Habsburg empire in the eighteenth century. Countless works of art, from open-air statues to small popular carvings, also prints of varying quality, were produced to honour him and help to revive Catholicism.

The small bust is one version of his representations: the Saint, absorbed in prayer, is supported by clouds as he looks down at a book resting on the head of a cherub. In other representations his attribute is most often a crucifix held in his hand. The meticulously carved, finely chiselled face, with decorative details similar to those seen on the work of craftsmen, are all reminiscent of South-German rococo sculpture. The original paint is worn and we know neither the provenance nor the original function of the bust.

GERMAN (?) SCULPTOR
first half of the eighteenth century

St. John of Nepomuk

Wood, 45.5 cm
Inv. No. 74.2 M.
Purchased in 1974
Not previously published

The Pietà usually adorns baroque altars but is also frequently found on a roadside Calvary. This lime-wood statue is simple in composition: the lifeless body of Christ lies in the Virgin's lap almost horizontally; the upper torso curves backwards, the right arm droops perpendicularly. The same posture is to be seen in the popular block-shaped stone Pietàs erected in the sixteenth and seventeenth centuries in the neighbourhood of Sopron and Felsőőr. The sculptor of this Pietà though talented, is not known to us by name; in this work he has combined the traditional composition with a type of Lamentation statue developed by leading Viennese artists.

The statue most closely related to the one illustrated here adorns the high altar of the Calvary Church consecrated in Pinkafő in 1748. There is a tradition, of uncertain foundation, that it is the work of Matthias Steinl. Certainly no one artist accounts for the link between the Pinkafő statue and the much finer Lamentation in the Capuchin crypt in Vienna; we must go back, therefore, to the work of the court artists, above all to that of the Strudel brothers. It is their style which, in addition to the local popular traditions, is most evident in the dramatic and beautiful carving now in the Gallery.

WESTERN–HUNGARIAN SCULPTOR
mid-eighteenth century

Pietà from the neighbourhood of Szombathely

Lime-wood, 101 cm
Inv. No. 8100
Purchased in 1941
by the Museum of Fine Arts
from the
Éva Almásy Teleki Institute
Bibliography: not previously published—cf.
Österreichische Kunsttopographie.
Oberwart–Wien, 1974,
Pl. 385 (Pinkafő);
L. Pühringer-Zwanowetz:
Die Meister des Altars
für die Kaiserliche Gruft
bei den Kapuzinern
in Wien. Wiener Jahrbuch
für Kunstgeschichte XXI
(1968), 39sqq.

156

157

The Society of Jesus and other Roman Catholic orders frequently supported a workshop of their own in which architects, painters, goldsmiths and other artists produced the furnishings needed for the church or monastery. Their work was in a class of its own and, in the baroque period much of it was of a high standard. In contemporary records the master joiners who made finely carved painted and gilded furnishings, are referred to as "arcularius". These zealous artists even created small statues as additional decoration for the woodwork in vestries or dining halls. The most eminent, for instance the Jesuit Bernát Baumgartner, created quite large sculptural works. The small carved Crucifixion from Selmecbánya, now in the Gallery, is the work of just such a craftsman-monk. According to Mária Aggházy, it must have belonged to a special revolving tabernacle. A kindred relic, a crucifixion group carved with even greater virtuosity if possible, is now in the Liszt Ferenc Museum in Sopron.

The group in the Gallery is made of two different kinds of wood: lime-wood for the cross and box-wood for the figures. To carve fine details, as on figures, it is necessary to have a hard bone-like wood such as box-wood. Beside the very expressive figures of the mourners wrapped in undulating cloaks, the sensuously shaped quiet, slender body of Christ crucified may appear slightly stylized. In the middle of the base divided by spiralled columns, a shell-decorated niche contains a small statue of St. John of Nepomuk.

SCULPTOR OF THE JESUIT ORDER
first half of the eighteenth century

Crucifixion from Selmecbánya

Wood, 50 cm
Inv. No. 62.9 M.
Purchased in 1962
by the Museum of Fine Arts
Not previously published

158

This is one of a group of paintings intimate in atmosphere and intended to inspire humility and piety; it is a religious genre picture, somewhat flattering and sentimental, created specifically to encourage the cult of the child Mary. The heads and hands are inclined towards one another to give an encircling effect. On Anne's face we see a lighter shade of the intense rust used for Joachim's flesh, and this is further reduced to a faint glow on the cheeks of the child Mary. This type of scene was particularly popular in the first half of the century. Paul Troger's paintings—among them St. Joseph with the Infant Jesus—are similar in spirit and atmosphere. The painter of this picture followed Troger very closely both in spirit and in the use of colour. He, too, must have come from the Tyrol, as did both Joseph Ignaz Mildorfer, who settled in Vienna, and Michelangelo Unterberger. Both artists were colleagues of Troger at the Vienna Academy of Fine Arts and painted several works commissioned by Hungarians. Not only their altarpieces but also some of their smaller paintings found their way to Hungary. According to Klára Garas Michelangelo Unterberger was most likely the master of this painting.

MICHELANGELO UNTERBERGER (?)
**(Cavalese
1695–1758 Vienna)**

**The
Child Mary Taught
by Joachim
and Anne**

Oil on canvas, 39 × 36 cm
Inv. No.: 78.6
Purchased in 1978
from a private collection
Bibliography:
Mojzer MÉ 1981

159

This statue, of unknown provenance, was acquired recently for the Gallery from a private collection in Vác. Its ecclesiastical role is, however, beyond doubt. It must have stood on a high altar dedicated to the Holy Family, the counterpart to a Joachim statue. The carving is of the high standard characteristic of sculpture originating from the Austrian Alps. The itinerant life of artists has ensured that in the ecclesiastical art of the baroque period and originating in western Hungary, numerous statues of the same trend and quality can be found. The slightly forward movement of the feet, firm static carriage, logically emphasized anatomy of the body, the robes sculpted to follow the lines of the body; St. Anne's strong features, are somewhat out of keeping with the animated, loosely fluttering, convoluted wing of the cloak on the left side of the statue.

The special feature of the piece is the unusual appearance of the figures. St. Anne is shown carrying her daughter, Mary, but the child, her hair fastened in a knot, is more like a young adult. In the Middle Ages Mary was often represented as a young woman lying in her mother's arms and holding on her own knee the Infant Jesus. Another subject which recurs in baroque art is the rearing of Mary, usually represented as a little girl learning to read at the feet of St. Anne.

HUNGARIAN SCULPTOR of the mid-eighteenth century

St. Anne with the Child Mary

Wood, 118.5 cm
Inv. No. 76.6 M.
Purchased in 1976
Not previously published

Living in Pozsony, Archbishop Imre Esterházy naturally patronized the local charitable institutions and religious orders, as for instance the nursing members of the Elizabethan Sisterhood and the ransomer Trinitarians. He also commissioned numerous works of art to honour the saints who give aid to men in earthly troubles. The baroque furniture made for the chapel of St. John the Almsgiver in the Cathedral of Pozsony—where the relics of the saint have been preserved since 1632—is the work of Donner and his associates; the sculptural decoration on the façade of the church of the Elizabethan Sisterhood was created by Lajos Gode; St. Martin who, according to legend, helped a beggar was similarly regarded as one of the "welfare" saints and his statue on the high altar of the cathedral, Donner's finest work, was also commissioned by Esterházy. The two small statues illustrated here represent two of these charitable saints: St. John the Almsgiver with a small beggar and St. Elizabeth of Hungary, who was canonized in 1235 after performing miracles on German soil; she is shown distributing bread and is similarly accompanied by the small figure of a poor man. Judging by the similarities in style, the figures must have been created by one of the lesser, more conservative masters who worked with Donner. The two small groups, showing little movement and forming closed blocks of quiet surfaces, are carefully elaborated; the faces, hair and body were originally in the natural colour of the wood, only the clothes being embellished with gilding. Similar perfectly finished small coloured wooden statues are known to have served as models for larger works. Many such *bozzettos* have survived on Czech territory. The small statues in the Gallery may of course have been part of the furnishings or even of the altar of a private chapel.

SCULPTOR OF POZSONY
first half of the eighteenth century

St. John the Almsgiver and St. Elizabeth of Hungary

Wood, 51 cm
Inv. No. 7598/1–2
Purchased in 1939
by the Museum of Fine Arts
at the auction
of Lajos Ernst's collection
Bibliography:
Agghazy 1959. II. 52

Paul Troger, born in the Tyrol, was unquestionably the painter who, from an early age and throughout a lengthy career, exerted the strongest influence on his pupils and colleagues in Austria, Moravia and Hungary, that is in the countries under Habsburg rule. In Hungary he was active in Győr and Pozsony. Many of his works created elsewhere came to this country and Maulbertsch was one of his pupils in Vienna. It was mainly due to Troger that, up to the time of Joseph II, the classicist academic style fostered by the Viennese Academy was suppressed in favour of a dissolved painterly approach permitting free play to the imagination and at the same time preserving its popular appeal. Troger was an excellent fresco painter (according to his own statement, this was his true means of expression) but he also painted numerous canvases. They were almost exclusively of religious subjects, commissioned for the most part for devotional purposes. Many of his compositions became so popular that he repeated them in several versions, and sometimes they were copied by members of his workshop and his pupils. The painting illustrated here is a version of the composition made for the altarpiece of the Vranov Liechtenstein votive church. (Other variants dating from 1738 to 1752 are to be found in Austrian private collections and the museum of Troppau, Loosdorf, Mauer bei Wien and Dommelstadt in Bayern.) This manner of representing the Holy Trinity had been traditional both in painting and sculpture since the Middle Ages. Here the artist conveys the mystery of the Trinity by a scene rich in draperies and mysterious light and shade effects. It shows the Father, creator and guide of the world, the Saviour with the crucifix, and the all-pervading Holy Ghost, the latter in the shape of a dove seen only faintly against the glowing atmosphere. Angels encircle a globe symbolizing the universe.

VIENNESE WORKSHOP OF PAUL TROGER (Zell im Pustertal 1698–1762 Vienna)

The Holy Trinity

Oil on canvas,
95 × 75.5 cm
Inv. No. 79 L.
Formerly in the chapel of the
Miskolc-Tapolca resthouse of the Sisters of Mercy (the Daughters of St. Vincent) of Szatmár
Purchased in 1979
Bibliography:
Mojzer MÉ 1981

The painter represented Count Ferenc Károlyi in the customary pose of a military leader, one hand on his hip, the other grasping a sword. However, the rigidity often seen in this conventional type of portrait is dissolved here by the lively, somewhat defiant glance, jaunty carriage and strength of character of the corpulent, middle aged man represented here. Using a wide range of artistic devices, the painter has endeavoured to impose on this ruddy, round-faced Hungarian aristocrat with waxed moustache and thick eyebrows an appearance befitting his rank. This finds expression in the lavishly decorated clothing, the delicate realistic details enriching the closely knit composition, particularly the texture of the fur trimming, and the fine feathers and goldsmith's work of the aigrette. The unfaltering, steady modelling, sweeping brushwork and high degree of technical skill are indications of the painter's considerable talent. These qualities are further enhanced by the effective presentation of the model's individual character.

Ferenc Károlyi—depicted in the uniform of a cavalry general—gave his name to a cavalry regiment but it was not only for this that he became widely known. The activities of this aristocrat who showed himself responsive to French learning and the French spirit while still a young man, prove that the ideals of French enlightenment reached Hungary with little delay. Ferenc Károlyi established a printing shop in Nagykároly, the centre of his estates, his chief aim being to issue textbooks and geographic works. Perhaps it was not only the close proximity of Calvinist Debrecen, but also the ideal of religious tolerance that caused him, although a Catholic, to maintain a lively intellectual relationship with theologians of the Calvinist Church.

In this portrait the Count's features and figure are immortalized by a painter active in Vienna or Pozsony some time between 1748–1750.

HUNGARIAN PAINTER
c. **1750**

Portrait of Count Ferenc Károlyi

Oil on canvas, 88.5 × 74 cm
Inv. No. 60.4 M.
Bibliography:
Not previously published.—cf. Vörös, I.:
A Károlyi család és a korai felvilágosodás [The Károlyi family and the early age of Enlightenment].
Irodalomtudományi Közlemények 1977/2, 197–198

163

The career of Antal Grassalkovich was much influenced by the fact that he was highly regarded by the monarch. He owed his schooling to the Franciscans but in later life, besides being entrusted with various important and confidential duties, he was made first a baron and then a count. He had a great deal of building done on his extensive estates. His residence with a *cour d'honneur* at Gödöllő became known as the "Grassalkovich-type residence" and served as an example of characteristically Hungarian baroque architecture. This portrait comes from Gödöllő where it may have been hung in his mansion. In 1767 the Count was awarded the Grand Cross of the Order of St. Stephen, founded by Maria Theresa a few years earlier. As the portrait had been completed by then, the decoration is a later addition and does not serve to date the picture; from indications of Grassalkovich's age it would seem to have been painted between 1750–1755.

With one hand resting on a table and the other held akimbo, the count is presented in the conventional pose characteristic of mid-eighteenth century portrait painting; it was, at the same time, the simplest pose to provide a variegated outline of the figure. The sophisticated treatment of light in the picture is inconsistent with the harshly drawn, elaborately detailed ornamentations on the uniform intended by the painter to form the principal decorative motifs of his work. The over-emphasized features render the facial expression stiff and cold, diminishing the characterization. Although the painting shows some of the stylistic marks of Dutch "fine painting" and has some of the refined elegance of French portrait painting, these qualities are expressed in merely superficial solutions.

The painted surface of the canvas recalls the stylized shape of a lute, emphasized by a contemporary carved frame ornamented with a laurel-leaf and bow. The setting of the figure on the heraldic left —which indicates that it had no female counterpart —permits the assumption that the painting formed part of a series.

HUNGARIAN PAINTER
c. **1750–1755**

Portrait of Count Antal Grassalkovich

Oil on canvas,
93 × 73.5 cm
In contemporary carved frame
Inv. No. 75.2 M.
Purchased in 1975
Not previously published

164

The Counter-Reformation in the second half of the seventeenth century turned the concept of Regnum Marianum into an effective political programme. Devout Catholics entertained the hope that conditions in Hungary, divided for so long by political and religious strife, would be improved by the protective power of the Madonna. This partly emblematic, partly allegorical composition depicts her in the role of Hungary's patroness. The Hungarian crown is held by two angels above two oval pictures of the Virgin and Child. The painting is a mixture of medieval and baroque iconographic motifs. In the Middle Ages, the Virgin alone was entitled to the celestial crown carried by angels, but following the appearance of the illustrated Augsburg edition of *Thuróczi's Chronicle* in 1488, the Hungarian holy crown was also represented in Hungarian iconography held aloft by angels above the head of St. Stephen. In this painting the Hungarian crown appears in association with the representation of the Virgin.

The landscape background has a heraldic significance. The three hills are identical with those representing the country in the Hungarian coat of arms. In the painting they are completed with fortresses symbolizing and showing traces of the country's devastation. The liturgical objects thrown into a heap in the foreground symbolize the offences of the Calvinists against the Catholic Church and liturgy; the fiercely anti-Protestant spirit of the painting expresses the belief that the Protestants were responsible for the destruction of the country. Of the two male figures in Hungarian costume the younger represents Hungary, the elder Transylvania. This is indicated also by the heraldic shields. The seven towers refer to Transylvania's German name, Siebenbürgen. Each figure holds in his hand a white kerchief symbolizing grief at the ruined state of the country. They lift up their eyes to the Virgin imploring her to assist them in the restoration of the country to its former glory and the reinstatement of the Catholic Church.

The concise composition in which the message is conveyed can be traced back to earlier prints but the definitely anti-Protestant mid-eighteenth century mood could not be accounted for so far.

HUNGARIAN PAINTER mid-eighteenth century

The Allegory of Regnum Marianum with the Hungarian and Transylvanian Coats of Arms

Oil on canvas, 43.2 × 31.3 cm
On loan from the Esztergom bishopric, to which it was bequeathed
Bibliography: Not previously published—cf. Galavics 1973: 112–118

In 1756 Imre Esterházy, Bishop of Nyitra, commissioned a new altar for the church in Máriatölgyes (Dubnica). This was embellished, like the high altar in Pozsony Cathedral, by a canopy supported by columns and surmounted by a huge crown. The Bishop transferred this devotional statue of the Virgin from the chapel in the Illésházy's castle in Trencsén, and had it placed in the new altar to give the effect of a celestial crown. The richly embroidered clothes of the Virgin adorned with beads are similar to those of the devotional statue of Jesus in Prague. She is shown supporting the Child in her left arm. Both figures wear baroque crowns. The Virgin, standing on a narrow crescent-shaped ledge, holds a sceptre in her right hand; round her head is a wreath of stars and she is seen against a background of radiant light. This statue, much revered, was faithfully copied by the painter so that it is easy to recognize in his work the sculptural model provided by the altarpiece. He was even gone so far as to include the suggestion of a slightly concave niche in the background of the painting and to emphasize the curved base bearing the Hungarian coat of arms, which symbolizes the offering of the crown to the Virgin. The date of consecration of the altar and the statue adorning it is concealed in the chronostichon of the banderole surrounding the base and bearing the inscription: "CLara Mater DVbnICzae". The painting was probably done by a local master in the second half of the eighteenth century. He has adorned the robe of the Virgin with Turkish flower motifs embroidered by a special Hungarian technique. The same figure cut in copper at the end of the century was shown clad in similarly ornate clothes and its reproduction in this form became very popular.

HUNGARIAN PAINTER, second half of the eighteenth century

The Virgin and Child from Dubnica
After 1756

Oil on canvas, 157x98 cm
Inv. No. 50.1
Purchased in 1950
by the Museum of Fine Arts
Bibliography:
Radocsay, Dénes:
A Rudnicza-i Madonna
[The Madonna
of Rudnicza].
1952: 75

St. Notburga was rarely represented in Hungarian baroque art; the cult of this saint arose first in the western regions of Austria and the southern Tyrol. The legend of the pious village maiden served as an example to religious servant girls and she was widely venerated in the seventeenth century. She was the patron saint of domestic animals and maid-servants but women in childbirth also invoked her help. To indicate her charity, she was usually represented as a Tyrolese peasant girl with a jug of milk or—as here —with bread in her gathered apron. Her most common attribute was, however, the scythe, not found in the statue illustrated here. The coloured, half-length wooden statue of the Tyrolese servant girl stands on a voluted base of imitation marble within the hollow of which relics were preserved. This simple female figure, youthful and charming, with multi-coloured glittering surfaces faithfully imitating various fabrics, has survived to this day as an ornate reminder of simple piety.

HUNGARIAN SCULPTOR, first half of the eighteenth century

St. Notburga

Wood, 81 cm
Inv. No. 64.7 M.
Transferred in 1964
from the Museum
of Applied Arts
to the Museum of Fine Arts
Not previously published

As a representation of the Virgin this small wooden statue may be grouped with other outdoor monuments. The long-established tradition of wayside crucifixes and columns with sacred images was revived in the early eighteenth century. The figure of the Virgin was central to the sculptural groups commemorating those who died in the plague: often she seems to hover beside the Holy Trinity, apparently among the clouds, and above the patron saints adorning the base of the column. Single statues of the Virgin were also erected to commemorate certain battles. These "victorious" Virgins were later replaced by the Immaculata represented poised, one foot on a snake, on a globe surmounted by a crescent. The *Immaculata* statue from Kassa is the work of Simon Griming and dates from 1722. Another similar S-shaped figure with closed outlines is the Virgin from Nyitra, the work of Martin Vogerl dating from 1750. The small—scarcely more than 60 cm—*Immaculata* illustrated here, is painted ivory, the clothes gilded at the hems; it may have served as a model for a larger statue of the type mentioned above.

SCULPTOR OF KASSA (?), mid–eighteenth century

Immaculata

Wood, 67 cm
Inv. No. 55.940
Transferred in 1939
from the Hungarian
National Museum
to the Museum of Fine Arts
Not previously published

167

168

Comparatively rare in other countries, representations of souls burning in Purgatory were not uncommon in Hungary; most of them are known to come from altars of the Holy Cross in Franciscan churches. In style they show a fusion of two different types of altar statues, both dating from the Middle Ages: the first depicting purgatory—not traditionally related to the idea of the crucifixion; the second showing Christ passing through the limbo of hell. These two themes united during the baroque period to give a form free of every active detail, a form first seen in the Netherlands, and later in Silesia. It probably came to Hungary through the supposedly Silesian relations of József Hartmann, a sculptor in Kassa, who followed the extremely characteristic plastic style of Thomas Weissfeld of Wrocław. Hartmann was the most sought after sculptor in Kassa in the middle of the century. His work is mentioned in numerous documents now in the archives, but his qualities as an artist can be judged only on the basis of the few statues which have survived: the Florian, an open-air monument in Kassa, and the altars in Lelesz, Varannó, Svedlér and elsewhere. The agonized figures now in the Gallery, all originating from a demolished predella of an altar of the Holy Cross, are typical of his work. The eight different half-length figures, tortured by flames, depicted in a variety of movements and with realistic individual facial expressions, provide a moral lesson and also a terrifying example to bring home to the congregation the mystery of the redemption.

THE CIRCLE OF JÓZSEF HARTMANN (active between 1740 and 1764)

Souls Tormented by Fire in Purgatory from Kassa

Wood, 42 × 65 cm
Inv. No. 55.740, 55.741
Acquired from the National Centre of Monuments and Museums, Budapest
Bibliography:
Aggh ázy, Mária:
Les représentations du purgatoire au XVIII\e siècle
BMH 1957; 53, 102

This carved and coloured group of wooden figures representing the Holy Trinity is a provincial relic of Transdanubian urban sculpture, one of a series of statues based on this theme created by the Veszprém sculptor, József Ferenc Schmidt. He was born in Pest, but worked as a journeyman and obtained his master's certificate in Székesfehérvár in 1741; from the second half of the forties he was active in Veszprém.

The Veszprém Bishop Márton Bíró de Padányi attached great importance to the veneration of the Holy Trinity which he regarded as a way to generate spiritual support for the Counter-Reformation revived in the mid-eighteenth century. He ordered special processions in his diocese, disseminated Holy Trinity songs of his own composition and made it compulsory for every parish to procure a portable group of wooden statues representing the Father, the Son and the Holy Ghost. He commissioned Schmidt to produce such carvings, and the sculptor delivered his first work of this type to Zalaegerszeg, but it is known from contemporary accounts that he made similar carvings for parish churches in Nova, Lenti and Császár, and for the cathedral in Veszprém, for each of which he received three gold coins.

JÓZSEF FERENC SCHMIDT
(active between 1739 and 1760)

The Holy Trinity

Wood, 105 × 80 cm
Inv. No. 74.7 M.
Purchased in 1974
from the BÁV Hungarian
Commission Shop
Bibliography:
Aggházy 1959: I 269

170

One of the guest artists who came to Hungary from Austria in the eighteenth century, Cimbal was always welcome, especially in the Transdanubian region. He was employed to paint altarpieces as well as frescoes and, influenced first by Troger and later by Maulbertsch, he endeavoured to complete his varied tasks to the satisfaction of his patrons. The composition he devised for the violin-shaped canvas of this altarpiece tends to inspire laughter rather than religious fervour. The Saint is depicted in the baroque period costume favoured by the Hungarian nobility—the style Hungarian nobles appreciated in pictures of medieval saints and kings. He wears a sword but his eyes are turned heavenwards, the lily in his hand being the symbol of his virginity. Standing with his belly thrust forward, he tramples on blind Cupid—symbol of love. The powerful God of love is embracing the globe. This exemplary stance is witnessed by two Hungarian noblemen in high "kuruc" fur-caps who stand in the background. St. Emeric was traditionally referred to as "dux" (duke), and could not therefore be depicted wearing a Hungarian or any other royal crown. With guileless anachronism the painter has placed an Austrian archducal hat on the saint's head.

The painting is believed to originate from Nagyszombat where it adorned the altar of a chapel. A counterpart shows the Baptism of Christ.

JOHANN IGNAZ CIMBAL
(Bílovec
[Wagstadt]
1722–1795 Vienna)

St. Emeric

Oil on canvas,
Violin-shaped;
232 × 147 cm.
In original frame
On loan
from the
archiepiscopal seminary
in Esztergom
Bibliography:
L. Slaviček:
Poznámky k Zivotu
a dílu Johanna Cimbala
[Remarks
on Johann Cimbal's life
and work].
Uměni (1979), 159 sqq.

The figures of St. John of Nepomuk and St. Venance, at one time decorating the wall of a late eighteenth century church, must earlier have formed part of a larger sculptural work, perhaps including other figures and intended for an altar. St. John of Nepomuk is represented in an unusual manner: lost in thought, kneeling with a cross on a bridge over the river Moldavia, thus evoking his martyr's death. The water flowing between the piers is also represented in an unusually naturalistic way. In Hungarian baroque sculpture the legend of the saint praying on a bridge has been known from the side-altar dedicated to St. John of Nepomuk in Ercsi and it was also depicted in a niche of the high altar in Perlak (Veit Königer, 1767). The archetype, to which both are related in style, is the monument by Philipp Jakob Straub in Graz. The closest analogue to the statue in Lövő, the standing figure of St. John of Nepomuk originally made for the chapel of Nove Celje Castle (now in the Ljubljana National Gallery), may be seen in the same environment. The delicately stooping figure, with regular features, thin hands and of graceful carriage, is clad in minutely represented clerical robes with lightly gathered folds; the lower part, stylized with rocaille ornamentation, confirms the supposition that the statue represents the trend of Transdanubian sculpture which was determined by Styrian rococo. By removing a layer of paint added in the nineteenth century, restorers revealed a lustrous surface of gold foil combined with flesh colour.

SCULPTOR FROM THE SOPRON AREA
c. **1760**

St. John of Nepomuk

Wood, 113 cm
On loan
from the parish church
in Lövő
Bibliography:
Not previously
published—cf.
Aggházy 1967:
337, 341,
with illustrations;
Vrišer, Sergej:
Werke Veit Königers
in Slowenien
und Kroatien.
Alte und Moderne Kunst
1969 (103), 13–19,
with illustrations

Angels supporting devotional pictures are a customary feature of baroque altars; they serve to support long preserved and venerated paintings or copies of relics from places of pilgrimage, generally representing the Virgin and mounted in ornate frames. Such are these two angels, hovering with arms outstretched and palms propped against the original framework. This type of angel supporting a devotional picture was made popular in Hungary by Donner and his workshop. The figures originating from Fejér County should be classed rather among the Styrian rococo statues whose style asserted itself in the western Transdanubian region in the second half of the eighteenth century. Similar hovering angels, with adult features but serving different purposes (created by Veit Königer in 1767) can be seen on the high altar in Perlak of the Muraköz region; and there is also a Slovenian analogue, namely the angel on the Leibnitz altar by Caspar Puchheim.

TRANSDANUBIAN SCULPTOR
c. 1760

Two angels supporting a devotional picture from Fejér County
c. 1760

Wood, 100 × 80 cm
Inv. No. 66.1 M, 66.2 M.
Purchased in 1966 by the Museum of Fine Arts
Bibliography:
Kampis, Antal:
Magyar faszobrok
[Hungarian wood-carvings].
Budapest, 1939 19, ill. 18;
cf. Kohlbach, R.:
Steirische Bildhauer
von Römerstein zum Rokoko.
Graz, 1956: 360–362

The reclining figure of St. Rosalia is thought to have come to the Museum from Rózsaszentmárton. For more than a century, from 1730 on, this community in Heves County was part of the Grassalkovich family estate at Hatvan. The exact place of origin of this statue is not known; however, it was most probably commissioned by Antal Grassalkovich. The Master should therefore be sought among the sculptors Grassalkovich liked to employ.

The cult of St. Rosalia was connected with successive epidemics of the plague. The Saint was most frequently represented in the form of a statue erected in the open air, but wood-carvings of the Saint are known to have had a place in church interiors.

These representations were always based on the legend. In representing this young and beautiful female figure lying on a bed of rock, the artist scarcely deviated from tradition. It is a work pervaded by tranquillity; Rosalia appears to be sleeping, her robes slightly crumpled. The "natural" colours—only recently uncovered during restoration—the glow on her cheeks, the brown of her hair and the deep green of the mossy rock form a harmonious and decorative unit.

SCULPTOR FROM THE VICINITY OF PEST
c. 1770

St. Rosalia from Rózsaszentmárton

Wood, 153.5 cm
Inv. No. 7153
Donated in 1937 by a group of patrons to the Museum of Fine Arts
Bibliography:
A Szépművészeti Múzeum 1937, 1938, 1939-ben
[The Museum of Fine Arts in 1937–1938–1939].
OSZMÉ 1940 (IX), 271;
Heves Megye Műemlékei
[The monuments of County Heves] III.
Ed. by Pál Voit. Budapest. 1978

173

174

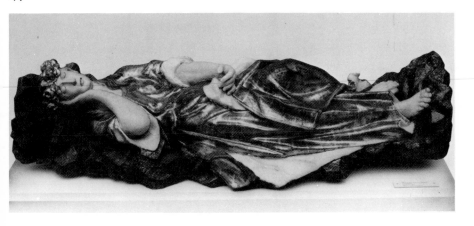

These two splendid statues came to the Museum from the huge high altar of the parish church in Egervár, Zala county. They have been replaced in the church by faithful copies. The altar, richly decorated with statues, represents two periods and is the work of at least two masters or workshops. The reredos with its large, somewhat heavy, yet superbly carved statues is directly linked in style with the Alpine plastic art of the period and was completed under the patronage of György Széchényi around 1730. Other statues related to them can be found in several Transdanubian churches with baroque decoration, most of them belonging to the Franciscan Order. More than twenty years later Ignác Széchényi commissioned a separate tabernacle with niches and statues to stand in them. The statues of St. Roch and St. Sebastian, protectors from the scourge of plague, are notable for a sensitive expression of pain and suffering; marked by a bold balance between plastic and pictorial values, they represent the peak of sculptural art in Hungary in the second half of the eighteenth century. St. Roch, the pilgrim, is represented with matted hair and fluttering clothes; his posture summarizes his legend: with his right hand he points expressively at his plague-sores, while the dog at his feet brings him bread to eat. The saint's face reveals the intensity of his pain; his eyes are turned to heaven; his lips are open as if to let forth his moans. The broken outlines and surface of the fluttering garments create contrasts of light and shade, increasing both the decorative and the dramatic effect of the colouring.

There is a calmness about the young figure of Sebastian. Bound to a tree and wounded by arrows, the young martyr saint is shown as a resigned figure, his head resting against his shoulder. The fine slender body seems to tolerate pain with languid movements. The statue is an excellent example of naturalistic rococo art and demonstrates also the vast possibilities of enhancing the overall effect by independent motions of the extrinsic parts—in this case the single piece of garment serving as loin-cloth. Quite apart from their religious significance, the statues inspire imaginative insight, horror and reverence.

These two masterpieces are directly related to the

PHILIPP JAKOB STRAUB
(Württemberg 1706–1774 Graz)

St. Roch and St. Sebastian from Egervár
1757

Wood, 121 and 119 cm respectively
Inv. No. 4963, 4964
Purchased in 1916 by the Museum of Fine Arts
Bibliography:
Aggházy 1967: 340–344

175 a

finest examples of Styrian rococo sculpture—the products of Straub's workshop in Graz: Plastic art in the Alpine regions remained for a long time unaffected by the classicist endeavours of the Viennese Academy, but the activities of the German-born Straub brothers who, trained in Munich, settled in Graz in the mid-eighteenth century, greatly enriched its development. The more impressive of the brothers was Philipp Jakob whose works in Graz and its neighbourhood greatly resemble not only the figural decoration of the tabernacle of the Egervár high altar—including the cherub heads concealed in the ornamental design—but also many other particularly fine works surviving in the Transdanubian region; among these are the side-altars in the churches of Ercsi and Szécsisziget, similarly within the gift of the Széchényis and Szapárys, families with active trading interests with the centre of neighbouring Styria and who are recorded as having engaged artists from Graz to work for them. Philipp Jakob Straub's brother, Joseph, worked at the Franciscan church in Nagykanizsa and the work of two other leading sculptors from Graz, Joseph Thaddeus Stammel and Veit Königer the Younger, can also be seen in the south-western border area of Hungary. Their work, together with the widespread activities of their pupils and followers, established a sculptural trend in the Transdanubian region, avoiding the broad range of influence of Donner's Classicist Baroque style. It was more extreme and in a certain sense more conservative, but enriched our eighteenth century sculptural art with a number of statues evoking a ready emotional response and being more easily understandable for the people of the time.

175 b

Although the Scriptures make no mention of Joseph's death, in both legends and pictorial representations, the Virgin and her Son are found to be present when he died. In this interior a brownish mist, playing cherubs and mysterious light suggest the Divine presence. The eternal Father looks down upon the lined old face of Joseph, Christ's earthly father. The figure of Christ belongs equally to the earthly Holy Family group and that of the celestial Holy Trinity, representing, as it were, an intermediary between the two in the composition. Lost in thought, the Virgin looks gently downwards at the little angels in the foreground as they play with the old carpenter's tools and a spray of lilies. Although the spiral composition rises in sweeping curves to a height, the figures are represented in the foreground. Reality and vision pervade each other: neither the figures nor the objects are given a definite surface; there are only indistinct coloured forms and shadows. A certain visionary manner of painting still dominates the work of the artist, then around thirty, but the soft brown mist and mysterious lights grow clearer in his later paintings.

The painting is thought to have been commissioned by the Trinitarians of Buda for their church. Maulbertsch painted a number of larger but in many respects similar altarpieces and frescoes depicting the death of St. Joseph for the Carmelites in Székesfehérvár at about the same time. The painting in Buda was left in its original place for scarcely fifteen years. When Joseph II dissolved the Order, the structure of the altar was removed to an unknown destination, while the painting found its way to Nagytétény. However, Maulbertsch, the greatest master of baroque painting in Central Europe, continued to work in Hungary where his later large frescoes and altarpieces were for the most part commissioned by local bishops.

FRANZ ANTON MAULBERTSCH
(Langenargen 1724–1796 Vienna)

Death of St. Joseph
c. 1767

Oil on canvas; with arched termination above; 324 × 159 cm
Inv. No. L. 5121
Bibliography:
Garas 1955: 234;
Garas, Klára:
Œuvres inconnues de Maulbertsch au Musée des Beaux-Arts.
BMH 8 (1956), 54–55;
Garas 1960: 82, No. 222;
Garas 1974: 16

Leicher was Maulbertsch's friend and follower, an artist who also often collaborated with him. He created mainly altarpieces, much of his work being commissioned by Hungarians. The picture illustrated here was painted for the Piarist college in Tata on the occasion of the canonization in 1767 of the founder of the Order, Joseph of Calasanz. The artist had been educated by the Piarist fathers who taught mainly the children of the bourgeoisie, the lesser nobility, the landed gentry and craftsmen. The Hungarian inscription on the picture indicates the practical methods of teaching adopted in the school. Few altarpieces are known bearing such commemorative references. The saint, kneeling among pupils wearing the customary dress of young noblemen, is shown beseeching the protection of the Virgin who appears with the Child in a celestial vision. Leicher's work—though the figures may seem heavier than those created by his paragon—reflects much of Maulbertsch's brilliance of colour, playful light effects and deep piety. As it was destined not for a church but for the corridor of the monastery, the painting evokes a happier and more intimate atmosphere than the artist's large altarpieces.

FELIX IVO LEICHER (Wagstadt 1727–1812 Vienna)

St. Joseph of Calasanz with Hungarian Youths before the Virgin
1767

Oil on canvas, 182 × 115 cm.
Inscribed below:
"Calasanctius Szent Ios'ef kegyes oskolák szerzője; született 1556 Aragóniának Petralta nevű Várossában, meghalt 1648. Szentek Számába vétetett 1767 Eszten"
[St. Joseph of Calasanz, the founder of pious schools; born in the town of Petralta in Aragonia in 1556; died in 1648. Canonized in 1767].
Original frame.
On loan from the Kuny Domokos Museum in Tata
Bibliography:
Garas, Klára:
Felix Ivo Leicher 1727–1812.
BMH 13 (1958), 97–98

CALASANCTIVS.SZENT IOSEF
KEGYES OSKOLAK SZERZOIE SZVLETETT 1556 ARAGONIANAK
Petrana nevü Varosseban megholt 1048 Szentek Szamaba veletett 1707 Hzien

Johann Karl Philipp Count Cobenzl, and Maria Theresa's Minister Plenipotentiary in the Netherlands—whose wife was of Hungarian origin—was decorated with the Grand Cross of the Order of St. Stephen in 1769. As a generous patron of the fine arts, he commissioned Verhaghen, a rising Flemish painter of historic events, to create a work representing St. Stephen receiving his crown from the hands of the Pope's envoy. After the death of the Count, the Empress and Queen—who was also the Grand Master of the Order—purchased the painting and had it sent to Pozsony to be hung in the castle there. The painter himself saw his work once again when, in 1773, he visited Pozsony while staying in Vienna. It was at about this time that he was appointed court painter. Ten years later his painting was exhibited in the Belvedere in Vienna. The honour proved justified: the picture, which revived effectively the traditions epitomized in the work of Rubens, was one of the artist's masterpieces. The composition and painterly qualities of the work provide for the birth of the kingdom of Hungary a providential setting. The foundation of the country was at that time put at 1003 and the ceremony was believed to have taken place in the former Cathedral in Székesfehérvár. The holy crown is strongly baroque in form but, together with the sceptre, it is basically an accurate copy of a print. The abbot Astric, the principal envoy is seen handing the king a large apostolic cross. There is a reference to the cross in the legend of St. Stephen. The painter was clearly aware of these details as also of the kind of clothes worn by the Hungarian gentry which he tried to archaize on the basis of eighteenth century fashion. In the centre, behind the new crown, we see an imaginary "old" fur and pearl ornamented princely crown; while the angel pointing to the two crowns indicates that the ruler who, although Christian in faith, had until then been recognized only as a prince (or leader), now became a king at the moment of receiving the crown.

PIERRE–JOSEPH VERHAGHEN (Aerschot 1728–1811 Leuven)

St. Stephen Receives the Pope's Envoys Who Bring the Crown
1770

Oil on canvas,
284 × 342 cm.
Marked at bottom right:
"P. J. Verhaghen
Aerschotonus F.1770."
On loan from
the Museum of Fine Arts.
It is one of the works
of art which,
by virtue
of the Venice convention
of 1932, were allotted
to Hungary
from the collections
of the Viennese Court.

Bibliography:
Munter, Victor de:
Pierre-Joseph Verhaghen.
Bruxelles, 1932, 53–54;
Pigler, Andor:
Katalog
der Galerie Alter Meister.
Budapest, 1967, 741;
Galavics 1971: 20

178

Shortly after the withdrawal of the Turks the reconstruction of the parish church of Buda Castle was begun, and in the course of the eighteenth century the noble families, military leaders and members of the middle-classes made significant donations for the baroque furnishings and the setting up of side-altars. As yet it is only the high altar about which we have verifiable information: this huge structure was mounted in 1758 and Caspar Franz Sambach of Vienna was commissioned to make the altarpiece representing the Assumption of the Virgin. The red copper tabernacle was the work of the Pozsony master locksmith, Antal Tober; the gilded wooden statues which once flanked the altar, namely the kneeling figures of St. Aloysius and St. Stanislaus, are now in the National Gallery. The baroque interior is known to us only from a few surviving drawings, since no photographs were taken prior to the reconstruction directed by Schulek. Thus the small hovering angel now in the Gallery can only be identified conditionally as the figure decorating the pulpit depicted in a nineteenth century drawing. The baroque pulpit had already been donated elsewhere by Countess Zichy in 1769. She commissioned the sculptural decoration which was executed by her marshal and resident sculptor, Károly Bebo. The Putto in the Gallery shows many similarities with the chubby child figures characteristic of Bebo's work; thus there is little evidence—apart from the exceptional size of the statue—with which to dispute the fact that the statue was intended for the altar. The soft, roundish forms of the white and gold wooden statue are reminiscent of hand-moulded gypsum stucco work: though massive, the figure appears to hover effortlessly.

Bebo was an extremely prolific sculptor, active in Buda in the second half of the century. Most of his works, including the high altar of St. Anne's Church, the banisters in the Zichy residence in Óbuda and the pulpit of the former Cistercian church in Székesfehérvár, can still be seen in their original setting and bear witness to the genius for decoration with which the Master and members of his workshop were endowed.

KÁROLY BEBO (?)
(*c*. 1712–1779
Buda)

Angel from the Budavár Church of Our Lady
1769

Wood, 119 cm
Inv. No. 6573
Purchased in 1933 by the Museum of Fine Arts from György Zala
Bibliography:
A Szépművészeti Múzeum 1931–1934-ben
[The Museum of Fine Arts in 1931–1934.]
OSZMÉ VII (1935), 188;
cf. Schoen, Arnold:
A budai Szent Anna-templom
[St. Anne's Church in Buda].
Budapest, 1930:
22, 153–154;
AgghAzy 1959: I, 79, 169

179

József Lénárd Weber was born in Buda where he was granted civic rights in 1757. He was presumably related to the Silesian sculptor family, one of whom was a citizen of Nagyszombat in 1749. The master active in Buda first worked on the sculptural decoration of St. Anne's Church, and later on that of the Florian Chapel; in 1766 he also undertook to make the high altar for the Florian Chapel. This is a columned structure with two large statues of male saints, painted white, on either side of a picture of St. Florian by Franz Xaver Wagenschön, above it a group of figures representing the Holy Trinity surrounded by kneeling angels. In the 1920s the chapel was twice reconstructed with the result that the sculptures from this baroque altar were dispersed. The two figures representing God the Father and God the Son, the one slightly turned towards the other, were acquired by the Gallery in comparatively good condition, though the painting was badly worn. Richly gathered garments characterize the carvings: the smooth surfaces of the drapery clinging to the bodies are cut by sharp creases into angular shapes. The same network of crinkles can be observed on the work of practically every sculptor of the period in Pest-Buda. In the surface treatment—sometimes in other ways too—the work of Antal Lipót Conti, József Hebenstreit, József Lénárd Weber and others is related to the rococo plastic art of South Germany.

JÓZSEF LÉNÁRD WÉBER
(Buda 1702–1773 Buda)

God the Father and God the Son from the Florian Chapel in Buda
1766

Wood, 103 and 107 cm respectively
Inv. No. 79.1 M., 79.2 M.
Purchased in 1979
Bibliography:
Aggházy 1959: 296;
Budapest műemlékei
[The monuments of Budapest]. II.
Budapest, 1962:
200–206, illustrated

The dramatic and intensely emotional qualities of this figure are achieved entirely by means of the posture. The Mother of Sorrows was at one time a calvary group but nothing is known of its place of origin. It shows, however, some similarity with a number of figures executed by one particular outstanding baroque sculptor who, though unknown to us by name, influenced his contemporaries. The Crucifixion altar of the Inner City Parish Church of Pest, set up in 1762, provides a starting point for its identification. The artist would seem to have been far more gifted as a sculptor than most of his contemporaries in Pest-Buda—for instance Antal Lipót Conti and József Hebenstreit, whose works have been authenticated on the basis of documentary evidence. The crucifixion group comprised four stucco figures, that of the Virgin being balanced by that of John the Evangelist; the heavy draperies of these sorrowful figures seem to float away, as if independent of the wearers. The postures of the two figures were used as models for a whole series of calvaries in the neighbourhood. These may be seen for instance in Gödöllő and Esztergom where they constitute open-air monuments, while in Buda, Gyöngyös, Jászberény and Kecskemét similar figures are found on the Holy Cross altars in churches.

The painted and gilded Virgin in the National Gallery shows certain simplifications when compared with its predecessor in the Inner City Parish Church of Pest. It has lost some of the heaviness of that work; here the emphasis is on the contour lines of the folds rather than on the fullness of the draperies, and the primary means of expression employed by the sculptor is the near spiral twist of the body.

MASTER OF THE CRUCIFIXIONS OF PEST

c. 1770

Mother of Sorrows

Wood, 102 cm.
Marked on back:"BJ" (?)
Inv. No. 55.964
Transferred in 1936 from the Hungarian National Museum to the Museum of Fine Arts
Bibliography: Aggházy 1959: II, 52; Eszláry, Éva: A pesti belvárosi templom kálváriája és köre [The Crucifixion of the Inner City Parish Church of Pest and its circle]. MÉ (1956), 145 sqq.

As indicated by the arch painted on the canvas to enclose the composition, this small, unusually fresh colour sketch was probably made for an altarpiece. There is no doubt that it was commissioned by a Hungarian but there is as yet no evidence to indicate the place for which it was destined. The artist employed Maulbertsch's unmistakable spirited, clear manner of painting. The choice of posture for Our Lady, the Infant and the angel, has given rise to the belief that the artist was Vinzenz Fischer, who at a later date, worked in the neo-Classic style (Klára Garas). If this is correct, he could hardly have preserved on a large altarpiece the clear colours of the sketch. It is, however, possible that the altarpiece was never executed. In the sketch an angel appears above the king, offering the crown and the sceptre to the Virgin; at the King's feet a cherub holds an elaborately framed Hungarian coat of arms. The king is in national costume. The picture is a version of a medieval legend transformed, to meet national requirements, into one of the most popular subjects among Hungarian baroque artists. The sibyl of Tibur was said to have shown the Emperor Augustus a heavenly vision of the Virgin and Child, before whom the Emperor fell on his knees. In representing this legend it was but a small alteration for the artist to show the King offering his crown. Thus the picture acquired a content of national significance. From the last third of the seventeenth century Hungarian representations of the offering of the crown by the first Hungarian king, that is the commending of the country to the care of Our Lady, have been modelled after this composition.

FOLLOWER OF MAULBERTSCH (Langerangen 1724–1796 Vienna) St. Stephen Commending Hungary to the Patronage of Our Lady

Oil on canvas,
31 × 19.5 cm
Inv. No. 6332
Donated in 1929
to the Museum
of Fine Arts
by Gusztáv Schatz
Bibliography:
Hoffmann, Edith:
A felajánlás
a Szent István
ábrázolásokon
[The commendation
in representations
of St. Stephen].
Lyka Károly Emlékkönyv
[Károly Lyka
Commemorative Volume].
Budapest 1944, 181;
Garas 1974: 17

St. Stephen offering the crown was the favourite and perhaps the most frequently chosen subject for Hungarian late baroque altarpieces. The nucleus of this idea—associated with the *Regnum Marianum* doctrine—was a sentence from the medieval Hartvik legend of the life of St. Stephen.

The legend served to link in the commendation a veneration for the first holy king and for Our Lady. Thus in the religious conflicts of the Counter-Reformation, in the second half of the seventeenth century, this representation on the newly erected altars of parish churches in towns and villages provided effective propaganda for the Catholic Church. By the end of the eighteenth century the subject lost its topical political value; as a spectacular expression of the gradually growing cult of St. Stephen, it became a mere symbolic artistic summary of the direct relationship that existed between the monarch in power and Our Lady.

The setting for the offering of the crown is generally the interior of a church, a background intended to evoke the festive atmosphere of the occasion. Additional figures were included to suit the purpose of the work—to decorate an altar for private prayer or to provide an impressive work for a church. In the picture the Virgin appears vision-like, hovering among the clouds above the altar; the Infant on her lap blesses the king as he kneels on the steps. An angel holds out the crown and sceptre for the attention of the celestial beings. Nationalist feeling, as strong in the people as in the nobility, is reflected in the Hungarian costumes worn by the king, and the noble gentlemen, the objective spectators of this mystic scene, in the background. The motif is emphasized by the display of the Hungarian coat of arms indicating the special significance of the Hungarian crown in the history of the nobility and indeed of the country as a whole.

In the *sfumato* of the outlines and the important role given to the slightly hazy light effects, the painting shows a certain relationship with the art of the Sopron painter, István Schaller.

TRANSDANUBIAN PAINTER
second half of the eighteenth century

St. Stephen Offering His Crown to Our Lady

Oil on canvas, 172 × 124.5 cm
On loan from the Xantus János Museum in Győr
Bibliography: not previously published—cf.: Galavics 1971: 16–17; Galavics 1973: 112–118

The Nagyvárad see was founded by St. Ladislas. This is accepted as a fact in many legends and representations. Only in the baroque period did the idea of a miracle arise. The Virgin herself was therefore now depicted pointing out to the king the site where the cathedral was to be built. The king was hunting (see the running stag on the left and the escort of noblemen on the right) when he heard a celestial voice. The plans for the building were also supposed to be of celestial origin: two angels are seen unfolding the ground-plans before the astonished king. The new cathedral had just been completed when this picture was painted, while in 1778 the same scene had already been represented on one of the large side-altars by Vinzenz Fischer, Professor of the Viennese Academy. Bachman's work was painted after either Fischer's large composition or his earlier sketch for it. Baroque sketches were a special form of art: they were not always preliminaries to a final larger and more detailed version but were often intended to be works of art in their own right. They were usually modelled after some popular work. Bachman was not as brilliant a painter as Vinzenz Fischer but he shows a certain gift for extending the composition: he has included a larger number of attendants behind the King, also an additional tree and angel in front of him. He has popularized the Baroque style bordering on the neo-Classic in a cabinet picture with a somewhat provincial flavour.

GÁSPÁR J. BACHMAN (active in the last third of the eighteenth century)

The Virgin and Child Indicate to St. Ladislas the Site for the New Cathedral to Be Built in Nagyvárad
1782

Oil on canvas, 63 × 47 cm
Marked bottom right:
"J. Caspar Bachman Pinxit
11. Dec. 1782"
Inv. No. 3136
Acquired
from the Miklós Jankovich
Collection
Bibliography:
Széll, Kálmán:
Nagyvárad, Szent László
városa
[Nagyvárad, the city
of St. Ladislas].
Budapest, 1940, Pl. 15

During the late baroque period there were already a great many gifted sculptors in Hungary in whose work there were signs of the rococo trend. The Transdanubian and Styrian styles can be sharply distinguished from the formal idiom which developed east of the Danube and in the north and north-eastern regions of Hungary. Johann Anton Krauss's powerful stucco figures in Jászó and Eger, their fluttering clothes and violent gestures, are reminiscent of the works of the most prominent south-German rococo sculptors. During a career of which little is known, Krauss introduced into Hungary the style of Joseph Anton Feuchtmayer, Johann Joseph Christian and the Silesian Joseph Winterhalter. It is also possible to associate—though there is not enough evidence for authentication—the statues of two side-altars in the church in Tarcal, Zemplén County, to a typically south-German sculptor in the rococo style. Figures, more sedate than those of Krauss, are directly related to the models for plastic figures produced by the Würzburg court sculptor, Johann Peter Wagner. Because of identical stylistic features and the fact that their work is based on the same model, Mária Aggházy has classified the pair of statues originating from Gyöngyös together with the Würzburg sculptures. The S-shaped posture resulting from finical exaggerations in the contraposition, and the surfaces formed by densely gathered folds, have their counterpart in the St. Anthony and St. Wendelin figures decorating one of Wagner's early side-altars (Grafenrheinfeld, 1764–1767). The figures of St. Francis of Assisi and his first follower and biographer, the monk later known as Cardinal Bonaventura, were some of those often seen in churches of the Franciscan Order. The curve of the body lends grace to the block-like closed figure of St. Bonaventura. Especially decorative elements of the statue are the broad brim of the cardinal's hat and the lace-hemmed, delicately carved loose surplice falling in narrow folds.

FOLLOWER OF JOHANN PETER WAGNER (Obertheres 1730–1809 Würzburg)

St. Bonaventura From Gyöngyös
*c.*1770

Wood, 108 cm
Inv. No. 55.946
Transferred in 1939 from the Hungarian National Museum to the Museum of Fine Arts
Bibliography: Elek, Artur: A Nemzeti Múzeum újra elrendezett régiségtára [New arrangements of the Archaeological Department of the Hungarian National Museum] MM 1925: 252–253; cf. Aggházy 1959: I. 138 (Tarcal); Trenschel, Hans Peter: Die kirchlichen Werke des Würzburger Hofbildhauers Johann Peter Wagner. Würzburg, 1968, 161,275, Pl. 40

Just as the statues of the side-altars in Tarcal are directly related to Johann Peter Wagner's models, so this pair of small figures reveal the artist's knowledge of the *bozzetti* produced by the Würzburg master. The prototype for the Tarcal figure of a father of the church was the carved figure of St. Nicholas of Bari, now in the Pfaff Collection; this served also as model for the episcopal figure of St. Nicholas illustrated here. Both Hungarian versions preserve the stylistic elements of the Wagner *bozzetto* more truly than does the "official" enlarged version by Johann Sebastian Pfaff on the façade of a church in Mainz. The Wagner heritage also provides the model for the emphatic but at the same time fragile figure of St. Florian—a clay statuette (1773), Würzburg Museum—identified as the plastic model for an Estenfeld statue of St. Maurice.

These two finely carved small lime-wood figures form a harmoniously united pair. The curve of the finical, yet appealing S-line posture is coupled with perfect anatomical composition; the movement of the leg is as free as that of a dancer. The rhythm of the movement is intensified by the corresponding fluttering of the draperies and the wind-blown, floating, lace-hemmed surplice—often seen on clerical figures and very characteristic of south-Bavarian Rococo. The refined features of both figures are worthy of special attention; the meticulous elaboration suggests that the statues are finished works. The minor damage—the loss of Bishop Nicholas's hand holding the attributes and St. Florian's water pail—is insignificant compared to the quality gained by the successful uncovering of the original white-gold surfaces long hidden by the coat of paint applied in the nineteenth century.

CIRCLE OF JOHANN PETER WAGNER

St. Florian and St. Nicholas
c. 1770

Wood, 52.5 and 57 cm respectively
Inv. No. 74.4 M. 74.5 M.
Purchased in 1974
Bibliography:
not previously published—cf.
Aggházy 1959:
I, 138 (Tarcal);
Trenschel, Hans Peter:
Aus der Bozzetti-Sammlung des Mainfränkischen Museums
Würzburg.
Mainfränkisches Jahrbuch für Geschichte der Kunst 1971; 31–40

186

The angel is seen in a burst of flame revealing a dimly lit rocky and shrub-covered landscape in which the prophet awakes from sleep, starting up from his multi-coloured blanket. The romantic Baroque style might well deceive us, for it is a style employed by North Italian masters of the first third of the century and also by the Venetians. This picture, as well as a counterpart, Daniel in the Lion's Den which is also in the Hungarian National Gallery, prove that biblical scenes set in romantic landscapes were still very popular in the third quarter of the century; artists were therefore encouraged to keep this attractive form of pictorial art alive by creating ingenious and effective new compositions in which to represent traditional stories. Braun had a special gift for accomodating his art to historic developments: he soon adapted his style and painted a wide range of pictures in the manner of the Dutch artists whose work had become popular in the seventeenth century; he even assimilated the manner of individual masters. He signed his pictures using various characters in his signature according to the style of a particular work. The baroque period had of course already seen the rise of other gifted artists of a chameleon-like disposition, but Braun excelled among late-baroque artists. Joseph II, who encouraged all attempts to provide education for the people and to raise the standard of public taste, paid 100 ducats for one of his paintings exhibited in the Belvedere. The subject of the work, Two Seamstresses, would have delighted even the French encyclopaedists. Braun was a versatile person: as a painter of the Academy and a restorer of repute, he bought pictures on behalf of Prince Nicholas Esterházy and was engaged to restore pictures in the Prince's collection. He was also a connoisseur who used his knowledge to acquire a collection of about eighty old masters' works, while his wife collected about fifty modern paintings. He was one of Ferenc Kazinczy's Viennese acquaintances who have recorded that Braun also received commissions from Hungarians. A number of his pictures which came to Hungary provide evidence that he sold his work in that country. The picture illustrated here is the earliest so far known to us.

ADAM JOHANN BRAUN (1748–after 1827)

The Angel Waking the Prophet Elijah from His Sleep in the Desert
1771

Oil on canvas, 66.5 × 86.5 cm
Marked bottom right:
"Adam Braun 771"
Inv. No. 74.6 M.
Formerly in the
Dezső Rexa Collection.
Purchased
from Nándor Kapos in 1974
Bibliography:
Mojzer MÉ 1981
(with reproduction of the counterpart)

187

The colouring and brushwork of this small painting, as well as the posture of the model, are somewhat late Renaissance in character. It may have been inspired by Padovanino's (Alessandro Varotari's) picture of the same subject, which Fogel probably saw in the Viennese Imperial Collection. In Fogel's portrait Judith is a provincial model—or an "extra" in a walk-on part. Her sword and the severed head of Holofernes are her attributes only, not the means by which she has slain her lover. The romantic-historical style fashionable in the last third of the century was here reduced to Italian Mannerism and an evocative atmosphere, and even these characteristics are provincial in flavour. However, we now know enough of Fogel to say that the picture of Judith is by no means typical of his work. Fogel owed his popularity to the altarpieces and frescoes. From the mid-1740s he performed various duties as resident painter in the service of the Zichy family in Óbuda. In 1752 he went to study at the Viennese Academy, probably supported by his rich patron.

GERGELY FOGEL
(Vác
1717–1782 Buda)

Judith
1771

Oil on panel,
21.8 × 14.8 cm
Marked top left:
"G. Fogel pinxit 1771"
Inv. No. 78.3 M.
Acquired from the
City Art Gallery
Bibliography:
Garas 1955:
65, 259, Pl. LVII; cf.
Ehrenstein, T.:
Das Alte Testament
im Bilde. 1923, 859

Ferenc Antal Bergmann was one of the most popular portrait painters in Transylvania in the second half of the eighteenth century. It appears from his still largely unresearched œuvre that he was usually commissioned by members of the bourgeoisie and some of the more important Transylvanian noble families.

We have no information regarding his training or artistic orientation. The basic characteristics of his art are: firmly drawn sharp outlines, a kind of dry and acrid manner of presentation in a colour scheme scarcely to be described as painterly, and a lustreless background of antique green. The weak drawing and striking anatomical inaccuracies are compensated for by a talent for modelling and the pronounced plasticity and good characterization of the faces. His works represent the Transylvanian version of rococo portrait painting, restrained and subdued both in colour and formal solution. In this female portrait the features of the rather plain young woman and her fashionable costume are represented with equal accuracy in the traditional pictorial style.

FERENC ANTAL
BERGMANN
(active
in Nagyszeben
around
1762–1807)

Portrait
of a Woman

Oil on canvas,
89 × 68.5 cm
Inv. No. 62.3 M.
Purchased
in 1962 by the Museum
of Fine Arts
Not previously published

188

189

Only a few decades ago the walls of Réde Castle, owned by the Esterházy family, were decorated with a series of eight panels depicting social life in the country, views of the sea and idyllic scenes of life in Mediterranean countries. These large canvases were intended to serve the purpose of frescoes. The choice of subject, also the internal spatial arrangement, was often influenced by the requirements of late rococo fresco painting. In addition to their decorative role, the pictures, painted mostly after a pattern, served to give an illusion of spaciousness to the interior. For this reason the artist who painted these canvases from Réde created pale, airy landscapes of a pale bluish basic tone, in which the horizon was lost in the distance.

In this panel the landscape not only provides a background for a happy, informal social occasion but also serves to complement it, being the manifestation of a nostalgic rapture over nature.

HUNGARIAN PAINTER second half of the eighteenth century

Landscapes from the decoration of the Esterházy Castle in Réde

Oil on canvas,
345 × 255 cm
Inv. No. L. 5. 112
Not previously published

The fascination of this amateur painting lies in the informal presentation of a refined environment in a naïve pictorial language and a thorough knowledge of the subject-matter and its setting. The painter's family is depicted with a meticulous accuracy extending to every detail. The intimate music enhances the authenticity of the atmosphere. The mistress of the house and her daughter are dressed according to the latest European fashion; her two sons wear Hungarian costume. The group is depicted in a neo-Classic colonnaded interior, complete with an archaic statue in one of the niches in the background.

Amateur painting was by no means rare in aristocratic circles at the end of the eighteenth century. Noblemen interested in art took up painting after travelling to see the great works abroad and were also stimulated by the pictures in their own collections. The amateur aristocrats favoured, above all, bourgeois subjects and forms of art, such as portrait painting, conversation pieces, animal and still-life painting, which form the greater part of their œuvre.

HUNGARIAN AMATEUR PAINTER around 1780

Woman Playing the Lute, with Children

Oil on zinc-plate,
24 × 32 cm
Inv. No. 77.23 M.
Bibliography:
Joseph Haydn
in seiner Zeit –
catalogue of the exhibition.
Eisenstadt, 1982, No. 29.

191   190

Ferenc Esterházy, young, wealthy and of noble birth, was known in fashionable circles in Vienna by the nickname Quinquin. He was a favourite of Maria Theresa and her husband Francis of Lorraine, and was appointed Chancellor of Hungary in 1763. The Order of St. Stephen was founded in the following year on Esterházy's initiative and he was among those who were granted this decoration. Learned in the fields of literature and the sciences, he was also well known in intellectual circles. He had a valuable library in his castle at Cseklész, an entail secured by himself. He was an effective supporter of the reforms devised during the age of Enlightenment, the reforms relating to socage and educational affairs were carried into effect under his government. He sponsored a school for the sons of the nobility and an orphanage, the expense being met almost entirely out of his own pocket. The freemasons of Vienna also claimed him as a member.

Esterházy's portrait may have been painted by an artist from either Vienna or Rome. He is shown as a man just beginning to develop the heaviness but his eyes are alert and humorous. The artist emphasized his aristocratic rank only by depicting him in a braided and fur-trimmed coat.

VIENNESE OR ROMAN PAINTER

Portrait of Count Ferenc Esterházy
c. 1770

Oil on canvas, 70 × 54 cm
Inv. No. L.5059 (deposit)
Not previously published

Vendel Bacsák, member of the Hungarian Royal Guards, was sent to Rome and Naples as the courier of Joseph II in 1784. His diary of the journey has survived. Like other foreign tourists visiting Italy at that time, he did not fail to have his portrait painted there. For this he turned to Maron, a pupil, fellow-worker and brother-in-law of the Viennese artist, Anton Raphael Mengs. In style, his neo-Classic portraits followed his master's example so closely that scholars are only now finding it possible to distinguish their works. In the Bacsák portrait, for instance, we find the pose characteristic of a number of similar self-portraits by Mengs. The finely chiselled surface and dull diffused light are also similar. These highlighted details, seldom found in neo-Classic pictures, represent the only heritage from baroque portrait painting.

ANTON VON MARON (Vienna 1731–1808 Rome)

Portrait of Guardsman Vendel Bacsák
1784

Oil on canvas, 67 × 54 cm
Inv. No. 74.11 M.
Purchased in 1974 at Auction No. 35, BÁV Hungarian Commission Shop, No. 201
Bibliography: D. Buzási, E.: Bacsák Vendel testőrgárdista arcképe Anton von Marontól [Portrait of Vendel Bacsák, Officer of the Guards, by Anton von Maron]. MÉ XXIX (1981) /1, 55–59

192

193

The life of the Pozsony sculptor, Antal Marschal, is known to us in more detail than is his activity as an artist, for little of his work has survived. We know that Marschal was born at Stomfa, near Pozsony, that he attended the Viennese Academy of Fine Arts from 1778, and that he later settled in Pozsony. The bust, for which he provided an unusually long signature: *Anton Marschal natus 1740 se ipsum fecit. A. 1781,* represents the artist wearing a fashionable wig and the style of clothes worn by the well-to-do in the 1780s; the expression suggests considerable self-assurance. The stylistic relationship between his works and some of those by Franz Xaver Messerschmidt, the prominent sculptor of busts active first in Vienna, then in Pozsony can be ascribed to Marschal's academic training. In private collections there are two more busts of bronze-coated wood similar to the self-portrait, both marked with his initials. These, representing Vergil and Aristotle, also the head of Cicero in Betler which probably belonged to the same series, demonstrate the cult of antiquity associated with the erudition and enlightenment which characterized the age of Joseph II.

ANTAL MARSCHAL (Stomfa 1740–1794 Pozsony)

Self-portrait
1781

Wood, 61 cm. Signed: "Anton Marschal natus 1740 se ipsum fecit A. 1781".
Inv. No. 4593
Acquired in 1912 by the Museum of Fine Arts
Bibliography:
Aggházy, Mária: Deux sculpteurs inconnus, Antoine Marschal et Jean Kutschera BMH 1959: 55, 95;
Luxová, Viera: Sochári A. Marschal a K. G. Mervill v Bratislava [The sculptors A. Marschal and K. G. Mervill in Bratislava].
Uměni 18 (1970), 540–542

There are several contemporary portraits of Antal Károlyi by prominent Viennese artists (J. M. Militz, G. Weickert, J. Hickel). Weickert painted him twice: in 1786 when he painted the portrait illustrated here; and later when he made a three-quarter length portrait showing the Count in the gala uniform of a captain in the Hungarian Royal Guards, and wearing the Order of the Golden Fleece.

Georg Weickert studied at the Vienna Academy under Meytens. By the last third of the eighteenth century he had become a popular Viennese painter. The thick layers of paint, a technique hardly suggesting the characteristic texture of the clothing, is far removed from Weickert's smooth and elegant manner of painting. At the same time the portrait of Antal Károlyi reveals the painter as a keen observer of human character who concentrated on essentials.

The portrait illustrated here shows the aged Károlyi wearing the uniform of a lieutenant-general decorated with the military cross of Maria Theresa's Order of Knighthood. Antal Károlyi carried on the family tradition and was greatly revered as the wealthy benefactor who sponsored schools, individual scientists, students, and the foundation of the Royal Academy in Nagyvárad; another major contribution he made was for the building of villages and the installation of water-systems.

GEORG WEICKERT
(Vienna
c. **1745–1799 Vienna)**

Portrait of Count Antal Károlyi
1786

Oil on canvas, 69 × 54.5 cm
Signed right centre:
"Weickert p. 1786"
Inv. No. L.5.062
Not previously published

This self-portrait is Antal Taferner's only known work. By arranging the light to come from the side, and to fall full on his face, he accentuated his plain features, making no attempt to improve them; so too he mocked his receding hair by wearing his fur cap as high as possible. Apart from this mildly ironic self-mockery, the painter depicts himself with the unaffected sincerity of a craftsman. Taferner's portrait is related to the self-portrait by Anton Graff. However, where Graff's brushwork is pastose, Taferner's fine transitions in tonality and his smooth treatment of surfaces are characteristic of Viennese painting. Taferner became a student of the Vienna Academy in 1744. He was born in Buda, where he was probably active to the end of his life.

ANTAL TAFERNER
(Buda 1730–
after 1789 Buda)

Self-portrait
1789

Oil on canvas,
54.5 × 40.7 cm
Signed bottom right:
"A. Taferner pinx. anno 789"
Inv. No. 57.10 M.
Acquired from the Collection of the City Art Gallery
Not previously published

195

196

Zirckler was a pupil and follower of Kracker in Eger. After the death of his master it was he who continued running the workshop, creating frescoes and altarpieces. When he received commissions from the Eger bishopric, he gradually departed from Kracker's style, painting his altarpieces in the neo-Classic manner. In his larger works the drawing is dry and colder than in his lighter and more colourful sketches.

Although there is no reference in the Scriptures to the rearing of the child Mary, the subject was often represented in baroque art. In the foreground on the right, we see Joachim; his aged wife, Anne, pointing to the stone slabs bearing the laws of Moses, is instructing her daughter. The subject had already been represented in a similar composition by Johann Samuel Hötzendorfer on the high altar of the Servite Church in Pest around 1740. To this picture Károly Esterházy, Bishop of Eger, took a liking and in the 1780s commisioned János Zirckler to paint a picture modelled after it for the side-altar in the church at Pápa. The Bishop instructed Zirckler to make a preliminary drawing before starting on the colour sketch illustrated here; this sketch was the basis for the altarpiece in which, however, he used cooler colours and forms.

JÁNOS ZIRCKLER
(c. 1750–1797 Eger)
The Rearing of Mary

Oil on canvas, 49 × 26.5 cm
On loan
from the parish church
in Kápolna
Bibliography:
Garas 1941: 43;
Garas 1955: 176;
Voit I. 1969: 422–423;
Jávor 1979: No. 17;
Művészet Magyarországon
1780–1783

This painting was the preliminary sketch for an altarpiece in the chapel of the archbishop's palace in Pozsony. The chapel constitutes the last remaining example of the finest late baroque art associated with the cult of St. Ladislas in Hungary. The fresco decorating the dome was painted in the same year by Maulbertsch and represents the king striking water out of a rock. The painter's intention was to revive the memory of the ruler who alleviated the thirst of his people by performing a miracle. The fresco shows the king on horseback as he performs the miracle, while in the altarpiece he is seen ascending to heaven. According to one legend current at the time the king arranged for a portrait of Our Lady of Hungary to be painted on his battler flags. Thus the white flag unfurled above his head bears the inscription "S. Maria Mater Patrona Regni" and shows the Virgin and the Infant Jesus—as if the flag was intended as a substitute for a more traditional celestial appearance. In other parts of the painting St. Ladislas is seen offering his crown, together with the coronation regalia and the battle axe, the latter being the king's usual attribute.

The painter worked in Pozsony from the 1770s; he was a pupil and follower of Maulbertsch, sometimes assisting him in the execution of his work. The sketch illustrated here shows the influence of the Master's late style, his clear colours, silvery lights and realistic representation of historic costumes and objects which gradually dominated his work as his earlier passion and artistic inspiration began to leave him.

ANDRÁS ZALLINGER
(Vienna
1738–1805
Pozsony)

The Apotheosis of King St. Ladislas
1781

Oil on copper-plate, 62.5 × 43.3 cm
Inv. No. 74.10 M.
Purchased at Auction No. 35 of BÁV Hungarian Commission Shop in 1974. No. 200
Bibliography:
Mojzer MÉ, 1981;
Művészet Magyarországon 1780–1830,
(About the painter);
Petrová-Pleskotová, Anna: Prispevok
k problematike maliarskej rodiny Zallingerovcov
[Contribution to the problems of the painter family Zallinger].
Ars 1 (1969). 31–51

The art of sculpture, emerging during the late Renaissance period, continued to flourish steadily in western Hungary, and it was Kismarton, where the Esterházys had their estates, that gave Pest-Buda the first sculptors such as Antal Hörger and Fülöp Ungleich, with the ability to undertake monumental projects in the baroque style. The Vienna-born Jakab Ham belonged to the succeeding generation. He became a citizen of Kismarton in 1744, and in 1747 he started work on the sculptural decoration of the parish church there. He first made the side-altars, and the organ-loft which he embellished with reliefs and rococo ornamentation. After completing several other commissions in and around the same town in 1779, he worked again in the parish church. The high altar of the church was decorated with a painting of St. Martin by the Sopron master, István Dorfmeister; the marble pillars were supplied by the stone carver Joseph Gottschall of Wiener Neustadt. Although originally Jakab Ham only agreed to make the standing statues of the apostles James and Philip, it is most probable that the two adoring angels kneeling on the cornice of the altar, one on either side of the Eye of God, are also his work. The high altar was dismantled when the church was restored in semi-Gothic style in 1904 and of the statues then acquired by art dealers only one of the large angels is now in the Museum.

The figure of the young angel, calm and dignified, his head bowed in prayer, is modelled in unbroken surfaces except for the dense parallel folds of the robes. It exemplifies the restrained style of this master of unexceptional talent—a white-gold coloured statue representing the Classicist trend of late baroque sculpture.

JAKAB HAM
(Vienna
1721–1780 Kismarton)

Adoring Angel
from Kismarton
1777

Wood, 151.2 cm
Inv. No. 6857
Purchased in 1935
by the Museum of Fine Arts
Bibliography:
Csatkai, Endre:
Ham Jakab
kismartoni rokokó szobrai
[Jakab Ham's
rococo statues
in Kismarton].
MM XIV (1938), 150 sqq.

199

Local and national historic events were represented side by side on the panels of the former reception hall of the monastery; the antique ruins of Pannonia and examples of baroque architecture were linked by self-assertive artists who once again aspired to the monumental. Legends and myths were banished from art. Although this painting of a historic scene does not disclaim precedents on existing altars, it definitely differs from the earlier type. It is an earthly scene and, as such, rather realistic. The legendary trimmings are replaced by historic scenes of minor significance; behind the archaized heroic triumphal arch and the figure of the king depicted in the garb of a nobleman, there is a view of Pest and the castle of Buda (which, in the painter's time, looked like a university with an observatory tower). This view of the city reveals long destroyed, non-existent medieval buildings such as the Stephen tower. In this picture there are no kneeling figures, no hovering angels; heaven is closed and the piety of the figures concerns them alone; it is not fostered by celestial apparitions. Behind the monks the imaginary buildings of the Szentgotthárd monastery are represented in baroque style. The patriotic fervour prevalent in the age of Enlightenment induced the artist to set the scene in the new capital of the country, thus enabling him to associate the reigning monarch with this historic event. The painting represents an administrative occasion in bright and light colours; it is a work devoid of any heroic pose or nostalgia, thereby expressing more vividly a feeling of optimism.

ISTVÁN DORFMEISTER THE ELDER (Vienna 1729–1797 Sopron)

Béla III Founding the Cistercian Monastery at Szentgotthárd in 1183
1794–1795

Oil on canvas, 344 × 254 cm
Inv. No. 53.389
From the reception hall of the
Szentgotthárd Monastery
Bibliography:
Garas 1955: 214;
Galavics 1971: 13–14;
Zlinszky-Sternegg,
Mária 1980

After the dissolution of the monastic orders and their partial reestablishment on the death of Joseph II, very few monasteries were decorated or provided with large paintings, one of them being the Cistercian monastery in Szentgotthárd. The topical pictorial content supplies references to the classical age of Roman Pannonia, decisive changes in the country's history and the agricultural, building and scientific work of the order—that is, only true historic facts and details of historic events. These the artists were required to represent with historic fidelity, as demanded in the age of Enlightenment. István Dorfmeister the Elder was very experienced in the representation of important moments in the history of Hungary. In painting this picture he had to pay particular attention to historic details as described in literature. In depicting the king's armour he went to the trouble of copying a surviving suit identified by contemporary scientists as having actually belonged to the monarch. The painter represented the death of Louis II as described by Miklós Istvánffy in the first edition of the . . . *Historiarum de rebus Ungaricis* . . . (1622): ". . . on pulling at the reins of his horse the beast fell on its back and while it was struggling in the bottomless mire, the king himself—a man of excellent character and outstanding talents, blessed with all good physical and spiritual qualities—was weighed down by his heavy arms and found an undeservedly miserable death . . ." In fact, however, the national catastrophe of Mohács was represented in Hungarian painting—also in earlier pictures by Dorfmeister—before it was ever described in literature.

ISTVÁN DORFMEISTER THE ELDER

The Battle of Mohács in 1526
1794–1795

Oil on canvas,
344 × 227 cm
Inv. No. 53.387
From the reception hall of the monastery in Szentgotthárd
Bibliography:
Garas 1955: 214;
Galavics 1971: 13;
Zlinszky Sternegg,
Mária 1980

The busts representing Greek and Roman poets may once have been part of the furnishings of a library. In the age of Enlightenment when new cultural ideals were emerging, the library and study became ever more important to the way of life followed by the Hungarian aristocracy. Regarded as a sort of "intellectual ancestral gallery" these busts played an important role in the design of these rooms. They indicated the particular interests of the owner. Religious Orders and schools usually embellished their libraries with reliefs or a series of busts representing famous theologians. In secular circles, where a classical education was taken for granted at that time, busts of the ancients were in vogue. There is a series of six busts of this type in the Gallery. The sculptor may have copied the sharply defined, somewhat exaggerated, even caricatured profiles from reliefs on medals or plaquettes. He was a highly skilled master with a unique experience in wood-carving and may have made, single-handed, the complete set of book-cases together with the group of statues.

HUNGARIAN SCULPTOR
last third of the eighteenth century

Bust of a Poet of Antiquity

Wood, 32 cm
Inv. No. 52.765
Transferred in 1950
from the Museum
of Applied Arts
to the Museum
of Fine Arts
Not previously published

202

The work of János Márton Stock—born in Nagyszeben—occupied an outstanding and special place in Transylvanian painting of the late eighteenth century. His popularity was equally due to the fact that he was a talented artist with an ability to express himself in simple and moderate pictorial language free of irrelevant devices and to the fact that he enjoyed the patronage of Samuel Brukenthal, then Governor of Transylvania. The portrait of Sámuel Teleki with that of Samuel Brukenthal in the background was known as the "friendship picture"—a type of painting rare in Hungarian art.

Spiritual and intellectual relationship and an identity of aims and interests are the conditions and characteristics of such portraits. The two men portrayed here were prominent both in official and cultural life, anxious to improve the common lot and to bring culture and scientific knowledge to Transylvania. The means by which these aims were to be achieved was a subject of great concern to the freemasons whose activities extended to Transylvania. As members of the masonic movement, Teleki and Brukenthal helped to encourage and supervise the methodical preparation of an encyclopaedia undertaken by the Nagyszeben masonic lodge, a project intended to cover the history and contemporary conditions of all three nations inhabiting the region.

Stock portrayed both Teleki and Brukenthal at their desks, Teleki in Hungarian national costume in the pose commonly adopted by scientists, and placed him against a background suggesting a workroom. In the background the portrait showing Brukenthal dressed in lighter garments and in a pose appropriate to a French encyclopaedist-philosopher, provides a fitting detail for the interior. In addition to the figures, the picture includes a motif relating to freemasonry: on the desk, among other objects suggesting scientific work, there is a map of Transylvania with the names of the cities where freemasons were particularly active. The bust of Joseph II, also on the desk, is similarly significant in that the Edict of Tolerance issued by the Emperor in 1781 made Sámuel Teleki's public career possible, permitting, amongst other things, his appointment as Vice Chancellor of Transylvania in 1787.

JÁNOS MÁRTON STOCK
(Nagyszeben 1742–1800 Nagyszeben)

Portrait of Sámuel Teleki, with half-length portrait of Samuel Brukenthal
1787

Oil on copper-plate, 41.5 × 33 cm
Signed lower right edge of frame: "Joh. Mart. Stock p. Cibini. 1787"
Inv. No. 55.1606
Formerly in the City Art Gallery
Bibliography: Garas 1955: 151, 254 (Portrait of a Man)

Stock made a good start to his career by remaining in Vienna in the service of Samuel Brukenthal, former Governor of Transylvania and the owner of the finest art collection in the imperial capital. As curator of this collection, the painter carried out restorations and copied some important works; he also represented and advised Brukenthal on the purchase of works of art.

Stock painted Brukenthal's nephew, Mihály Brukenthal. The pose showing the sitter full face, with one arm akimbo and holding in the other hand a letter, recalls the baroque traditions of Hungarian portrait painting. The group of statues in grisaille seen in the background, has a significance beyond that associated with family portraits. The base of laurel-wreathed head of Joseph II. bears a slogan-like, somewhat tendentious inscription glorifying the Emperor—or perhaps the tenets of freemasonry—"One who renders the most people happy". The picture is completed by apparently inappropriate details: an allegorical female figure at her feet is a chain and a hat, symbols of the freemasons. By the inscription Mihály Brukenthal wished to portray Joseph II. as the patron of the Society of Freemasons, although the reference had by then lost topicality. Brukenthal joined the Nagyszeben St. Andrew's lodge in 1789, the year his portrait was painted.

JÁNOS MÁRTON STOCK

Portrait of Mihály Brukenthal
1789

Oil on canvas,
93.5 × 74.8 cm
With inscription under the medallion:
"DER WELCHER DIE MEISTEN GLÜCKLICH MACHT"
Inv. No. 57.2 M.
Acquired in 1929
by the Museum
of Fine Arts
by way of exchange
Bibliography:
Garas 1955:
151, 254, Pl. CXX;
Bielz, J.:
Johann Martin Stock,
Siebenbürgischer Bildnismaler
des 18. Jahrhunderts.
Muzeul Brukenthal,
Studii
și comunicari, Sibiu, 1956

The patronage practised by the Teleki family was characterized by sober considerations and almost puritanic scruples. Their castles were designed by local masters; their portraits were painted or engraved by talented, but not outstanding, artists. The more illustrious members of the family were interested in the exact sciences, history, education and, Sámuel in particular, bibliography. He built up a vast library at Marosvásárhely which he made accessible to the public. To him we owe the publication in 1784 of the works of Janus Pannonius. During the reign of Joseph II, he furthered the cause of a centralized system of public education—for which he made contributions out of his own pocket. At the time his portrait was painted, he held supreme office as Chancellor of Transylvania. The painter represented him as a noble and witty man.

JOHANN TUSCH
(Tyrol 1735–1817 Vienna)

Portrait of Count Sámuel Teleki
1798

Oil on canvas,
71.5 × 56.5 cm
Original Louis XVI frame.
On loan
from the Bakony Museum
in Veszprém
Not previously published

204

205

In his day the wealthiest and most distinguished of his peers, Prince Miklós Esterházy, grandson of Prince Miklós Esterházy the Magnificent, is portrayed here as Lieutenant of the Hungarian Guards. His outdoor ermine-trimmed cloak and shako are seen on the chair he faces. It is in fact a small version of a larger painting, made in 1793, which is in the Esterházy Palace in Kismarton. The prince is shown leaning against a statue of Minerva, the goddess of the sciences and the arts, a pose first seen in Batoni's portrait of Joseph II, now in Schönbrunn, and intended to emphasize that the Prince was a patron of these branches of learning. The Prince fully deserved to be honoured by his contemporaries and by posterity, for in addition to his scientific collection, he had made a collection of pictures and drawings which was already famous and which now constitutes the basis of the collection in the Budapest Museum of Fine Arts. He travelled extensively and was a knowledgeable patron of the arts. The sums expended on his collections were so vast that his property was eventually sequestrated and the Prince had to be content with an annuity—which, however, was by no means insignificant. The portrait may have been intended to commemorate a friendship (possibly political) as there exists a counterpart, formerly in Pápa, now in Austrian private ownership, representing Archduke Charles Louis Habsburg. In 1796 Parliament sent Esterházy to greet the Archduke—the only Habsburg with a talent for leadership on the battlefield—after a successful campaign against the French. The Prince was known to favour the imperial and royal policy.

MARTIN KNOLLER
(Steinach am Brenner 1725–1804 Milan)

Portrait of Prince Miklós Esterházy
1792–1793

Oil on canvas, 39 × 37 cm
Inv. No. 74.3 M.
Formerly in the Esterházy Residence in Pápa
Purchased at Auction No. 33 of BÁV Hungarian Commission Shop in 1974, No. 192
Bibliography: Reproduced in the catalogue of BÁV Auction No. 33, p. 192;
Joseph Haydn in seiner Zeit—catalogue of the exhibition. Eisenstadt, 1982, No. 736

206

The painter, Károly Fülöp Schallhas, was born in Pozsony. Of his life we know little beyond the fact that he studied at the Vienna Academy and was active in that city. He was admitted to the school probably between 1783–1786; he had a stimulating master in Johann Christian Brand, a teacher of landscape painting who at one time had been active in Hungary. In January 1787 Schallhas shared with Anton Troger an Art School Prize, his own painting being based on a theme from Gessner's idylls. In 1790 he became a member of the Academy and in 1795 was appointed teacher in the Faculty of Landscape Painting. He died an early death in 1797 by which time he was an assistant professor under Friedrich August Brand.

The five oil paintings and about one hundred drawings surviving from an œuvre still not fully researched, show Schallhas to have been an artist sensitive to nuances of colour, capable of delicate brushwork and interested in the relationship between man and nature, he was fascinated by the beauty of the Austrian countryside and the drawings he made on his journeys reflect personal experiences. In his oil paintings he tried to give a more general representation of airy landscapes, hazy light and local atmosphere. His choice of subject suggests a slightly romantic outlook and, especially in his sketches, a leaning towards historicism. His landscapes with wide horizons, the details merging hazily with the sky, are often charged with tension but the view itself is always composed of quietly arranged harmonious structural elements. In this picture the approaching storm is indicated by changes in the light, dark shadows of the accumulating clouds and a rising wind that stirs up the dust raised by the homeward bound cattle. And this is represented by the painter in hazy colours and with a touch of nostalgia.

KÁROLY FÜLÖP SCHALLHAS
(Pozsony 1769–1797 Vienna)

Landscape in Approaching Storm

Oil on canvas, 56.5 × 74 cm
Inv. No. 2152
Purchased in 1902
by the Museum
of Fine Arts
at the Wawra auction
in Vienna
Bibliography: Sz. Lajta, E.: Schallhas Károly művészetéről [Károly Schallhas's art]. MMMÉ 1954: 500; Garas 1955: 138, 247, Pl. XV

207

Köpp studied at the Vienna Academy. He was a versatile artist, perhaps even excessively so, if we consider his many innovations. Some of his excellent religious works and sketches were modelled after Maulbertsch. He painted frescoes and altarpieces commissioned by Hungarians but his finest achievements were the plaster mosaics *(scagliolas)* created by a technique of his own devising, also his copies of works by great Italian masters, executed by a variety of techniques. He also made mosaics from bark, moss, leaves, glass, straw, feathers, and wax.

At the close of the eighteenth century philanthropists anxious to improve the conditions of the people and cultural standards generally, regarded him as an original creative artist engaged in the noble task of popularizing the arts. His works were well received in the European courts and even found their way to museums.

The picture illustrated here is an example of one of his innovations. It is painted in ink and watercolour on a panel of particularly hard limestone-like stucco giving the effect of artificial marbling. The composition includes every element necessary for a neo-Classic landscape painting: an antique round church, ruins and Arcadian details. Köpp's more sketchily drawn smaller works are rather like *coulisses* rich in Italian motifs. Few of them have to our knowledge survived.

**FARKAS KÖPP
(Kismarton
1738–1807 Vienna)**

**Water-side
Landscape
with Anglers**

Ink and water-colour
on stucco,
57 × 83 cm
Inv. No. 3161
Donated in 1863
to the Hungarian
National Museum
by Mihály Keszt
Bibliography:
Művészet Magyarországon
1780–1830;
Garas, 1955: 140, 178

208

The painter was Füger's pupil in Vienna and his faithful follower as a painter of historic pictures in the neo-Classic style. He lived in Poland for a short time and spent a longer period in Rome. His copper engravings made his name especially widely known but he also painted portraits and undertook a variety of tasks commissioned by Hungarians. For instance he painted the curtain of the former Theatre of Pest. The painting now in the Gallery shows a young woman in Empire style dress, embracing her son with a noble gesture; the picture gives, in a way, the impression of a painted memorial. The flesh and the clothing are painted in broken transparent colours that have the effect of pastel but the composition recalls the cool formality of an antique relief. Even the type of art is indefinite: one may take the picture for a portrait, although it is in fact a conversation-piece.

JOSEF ABEL
(Asdach,
Upper Austria
1764–1818 Vienna)

Young Woman and Child
1799

Oil on canvas,
95 × 72.5 cm
Signature incised
on rim of the plate:
"Josef Abel pinx 799"
Inv. No. 78.2 M.
Purchased in 1978
from BÁV Hungarian
Commission Shop
Bibliography:
Mojzer MÉ 1981

209

In the eighteenth century there were few foreign painters who did not limit their stay in Hungary to the time required for the execution of a particular commission. Their only connection with Hungarian art was to be seen through their influence on other artists. By the end of the century there was increasing public demand for a higher standard in Hungarian painting, particularly that most important form of bourgeois art—portrait painting. The most enthusiastic of those who patronized the arts, was Ferenc Kazinczy and a circle of friends.

One of the foreign artists who came to Hungary was the Danish-born Jakab Stunder. He settled in Besztercebánya in 1793.

The Portrait of a Man painted at the turn of the century is characterized by an unprejudiced, formal, restrained manner of painting, corresponding to the aesthetic endeavours of the age; the painter use few colours and the picture is free from pretentious painterly effect. In spite of this, it is made attractive by the engaging personality of the sharp-featured sitter whose character is most felicitously indicated.

JÁNOS JAKAB STUNDER (Copenhagen 1759–1811 Besztercebánya)

Portrait of a Man
1800

Oil on canvas,
75 × 56.5 cm
Signed left centre:
"J. Stunder"
(date illegible)
Inv. No. 60.22 T.
Not previously published.
Cf.: Petrová-Pleskotová,
A.: K životu
a dielu maliara
Jána Jakuba Stundera
[Life and œuvre
of the painter
Jan Jakub Stunder].
Ars 2 (1967), 35–67

After four decades of successful activity in Vienna, the portrait painter János Donát settled in Pest at the invitation of Kazinczy.

Among the family portraits, now in the Gallery, Donát's painting of Ürményi is representative of his officially commissioned pictures. József Ürményi was one of the creators of the *Ratio Educationis,* intended to integrate the practical modern educational endeavours of the age of Enlightenment. He held a number of other high public offices and was Lord Chief Justice when the portrait was painted; from 1782 he also acted as Lord Lieutenant of Bihar County, and was depicted as the holder of this office in Donát's portrait. He is seen holding the county's Statutes of 1784, standing at a desk covered with papers. In the background a glass filing cabinet indicates his official status.

JÁNOS DONÁT (Kloster-Venzell 1744–1830 Pest)

Portrait of József Ürményi
After 1808

Oil on canvas,
129 × 93.5 cm
Inv. No. L. 5.109
Not previously published

210

211

LIST OF ILLUSTRATIONS

Printed in Hungary, 1984
Kossuth Printing House, Budapest